NOEL TYL'S GUIDE TO
ASTROLOGICAL
CONSULTATION

ABOUT THE AUTHOR

Noel Tyl is one of the foremost astrologers of the world. His thirty-three textbooks have led the teaching of astrologers for two generations. His master work *Synthesis & Counseling in Astrology* securely places astrology in company with the most sophisticated disciplines of humanistic studies extant today.

Tyl is a graduate of Harvard University in Social Relations (triumvirate study: psychology, sociology, and anthropology). He lectures in twenty-six countries, traveling from sixty to eighty thousand miles annually, and maintains a client list of individuals and corporations all around the world. His office and home are in the Phoenix, Arizona area of the United States.

NOEL TYL'S GUIDE TO
ASTROLOGICAL CONSULTATION

NOEL TYL

Llewellyn Publications
Woodbury, Minnesota

First Edition
First Printing, 2007

Book design by Donna Burch
Cover design by Gavin Dayton Duffy
Cover images © Images.com, Inc.
Editing by Connie Hill
Llewellyn is a registered trademark of Llewellyn Worldwide, Ltd.

Chart Wheels were produced with Win*Star Software, by permission of Matrix Software.

Library of Congress Cataloging-in-Publication Dataa

Tyl, Noel, 1936–
  Noel Tyl's guide to astrological consultation / Noel Tyl. — 1st ed.
      p. cm.
  Includes bibliographical references and index.
  ISBN 13: 978-0-7387-1049-5
  1. Horoscopes. 2. Horoscopes—Case studies. I. Title.
  BF1728.A2T95   2007
  133.5—dc22
                                                                          2007005715

Llewellyn Publications
A Division of Llewellyn Worldwide, Ltd.
2143 Wooddale Drive, Dept. 978-0-7387-1049-5
Woodbury, Minnesota 55125-2989, U.S.A.
www.llewellyn.com

Printed in the United States of America

To prepare the Horoscope
You prepare your Mind

CURRENT BOOKS BY NOEL TYL

Synthesis & Counseling in Astrology—The Professional Manual

The Creative Astrologer

Astrology of Intimacy, Sexuality & Relationship

Solar Arcs

CONTENTS

INTRODUCTION

Please know that this book about preparing the horoscope and its analysis, and creating the discourse of the consultation is not simply a compendium of techniques and passive trait descriptions. It is much more. It vividly addresses how measurements are brought literally and figuratively *to* life, the life of your client, all within the process of becoming. It appreciates the portrait of a human being in his or her development within time.

This is a book with a premium on creativity, your creativity: how you interpret the symbolisms of astrology in terms of the interaction of human needs and behaviors. The entire process ideally leads to personal fulfillment: the client's and the astrologer's.

It is important to know that this book is "a first" in presenting verbatim transcripts of consultations, with no editing whatsoever. There are five of them, with commentary on the flow of conversation and the turns of understanding as well. We must be most appreciative of the clients who gave their permission to share their consultations so that we may all learn more together.

Noel Tyl
Fountain Hills, Arizona
April 2006

opment, that often accompany conspicuous change...and that's what most of us want within the progress of life! [What works *against* this view is the human being's anxiety about transient insecurity; giving up the predictable reliability of the *status quo* while en route to a changed position...even if that *status quo* is steeped in uncomfortable values!] Trines and sextiles are stabilizers; they keep things as they are.

So within this mindset—that we are guided most strongly in our work by the *stronger* aspects—I recommend that you ask your computer to present you with these aspects: *conjunction, semisquare, sextile, quintile* (72°), *square, trine, sesquiquadrate, quindecile* (165°), and *opposition* among all planets (including the Sun and Moon) and the angles.

Orb

We can appreciate the measurement of orb two ways.

First, measurement of orb is an *organizing tool* among many numbers. It works to help the astrologer organize measurements. Arbitrarily and with some empirical back-up over perhaps three centuries—and not without a good dose of numerological nuance—orbs have been set quite liberally, focused most often upon 7 degrees, and ranging up to 14 degrees.

On the one hand, we benefit from organizational help in our work, but on the other hand, we do not want that organization to introduce more problems: untenable relationships between symbols, so many aspects cluttering our analytical insights, overlapping measurement considerations, etc. When we are talking about the degree relationship between two planets, we must remember that we are not measuring distance as much as we are measuring *affinity*. And this brings us to the second way of appreciating orb: *as a span of consciousness.*

There are people whose consciousness, for one reason or another, can/does reach out beyond conventional orb measurement and establish an affinity, a relationship between behavioral faculties (the planetary symbols). For example, Pablo Picasso [October 25, 1881 at 11:15 PM LMT in Malaga, Spain] has his Moon in Sagittarius 9 degrees away from square with his Uranus. That is a wide orb by conventional measurement; but Picasso was anything but a conventional personage. His consciousness did include the highly individualizing and self-intensifying square between Uranus and the Moon. His arch opinions about the world motivated enormous political commentary through his art; his mother was an extreme influence in his female-dominated upbringing. The shoe would fit. We would learn this from our client's reality; we would anticipate and then know this; we would incorporate that square for this special person…but to have such a wide orb for *every* portrait would simply clutter our work with a multiplicity of aspects, divergences, and tangents. The vast majority of people will not be reaching that far, so to speak, to link behavioral faculties within our symbolic procedures.

Because of the Picasso "fit," we are not saying that the guidelines of tighter, conventional orbs are wrong or impractical. It means that the portrait artist, the astrologer, must be aware of exceptions.

Another example: self-styled "King of All Media" Howard Stern [January 12, 1954 at 1:10 PM EST in New York City] has Mars 12 degrees away from opposition with his Moon, ruler of his communications 3rd. With Stern's full-time job being amplification and broadcasting of his persona, his emotionally excitable, disruptive, and hyperactive personality, this opposition *is* valid! We would simply see and sense that this shoe would fit, that those colors of Mars and the Moon would go together in the portrait. There is surely an affinity here between the two behavioral faculties.

The thesis I espouse with regard to orb is to keep the measurement of orb reasonably tight: the tighter the orb, the fewer the aspects shown in the aspect grid, *the more reliable those aspects are.* And we keep an eye out for the occasional special-case exception.

I recommend orbs of 7 degrees for the conjunction, opposition, and the square, for the Sun, the Moon, and the planets. I recommend 6 degrees orb for the trine; 4 for the sextile; 2.5 for the semisquare and the quintile; and 2 degrees for the quindecile. These values organize measurements extremely well. Any rare, outstanding exceptions can easily be noted visually during analysis. The aspect grid is kept uncluttered and readily helpful.[2]

As will be developed strongly in chapter 2, "Humanizing the Data," we must recognize now, at the outset of our preparation for analysis and consultation, that our portrait, the horoscope, is not created to capture our subject in tightest detail. This is relating our client to the horoscope, actually *confining* the personality's development and bloom to what we know about astrology! Rather, the horoscope is created to relate *to* the life of our client, to reflect it; the horoscope is brought to life *within the reality experience of the individual.* The measurements and the colors of potential meanings are animated, verified, and given significance by the life reality being lived by the client.

---

2. Many software manufacturers weigh the astrologer down with default aspects like the novile, bi-quintile, septile, etc., which have no ready significance in the mainstream of astrology. The artist-analyst must have aspects at hand that are efficient for portraiture, kept keen by a meaningful grasp of orb.

Our techniques guide us to that reality information, and our measurements are given ultimate meaning by the client's life experience. Stockpiling myriad measurements in hopes of capturing some magical nuance is a manifestation of the astrologer's insecurity. How many measurements do we need to begin a meaningful discussion with our client? The stronger measurements are the strongest guidelines. And then the interpretive art begins.

Peregrination

Classically, a planet is peregrine when it makes no Ptolemaic aspect in the horoscope (conjunction, sextile, square, trine, or opposition) and has no essential dignity (being in the sign it rules, in the sign of its exaltation, detriment, or fall). Etymologically, "peregrine" means "beyond the border"; we get our word "pilgrim" from the Latin *pelegrinus* or *peregrinus*. The peregrine planet is not tied down by any sense of belonging; it is free and easy in its presence; it goes where it wants; it easily runs away with influence within the horoscope. It is like a dominating splotch of color that commands the eye, and its tone spills throughout the picture.[3]

In faster moving times, more intensely developing life-experiences, for me, the absence of Ptolemaic aspect *is enough* to qualify a planet as being *peregrine*. There is no doubt about this in my work over years and years. It is an extremely reliable working guideline seen in a flash in the aspect grid, and the cumbersome evaluations of dignities, etc. are avoided. Modern times need the symbolism of peregrination, the intensive resource of particular behaviors, not an academic distillation and delay for the sake of over-refined purist measurement achievement.

Naturally, how we ask our computer to help us organize measurements—the concept of orb—is extremely important in the determination of peregrination (being unaspected in Ptolemaic terms, as I use the concept). The orb allowances recommended on page 4 have, in my experience, been extremely successful in showing peregrine planets dramatically and reliably.

As an example: highly controversial broadcaster Howard Stern has Jupiter in Gemini. Jupiter makes no Ptolemaic aspect in his horoscope portrait, yet it is semisquare with the Moon, ruler of his communications 3rd.

---

3. Please see full development of the peregrination concept in Tyl, *Synthesis & Counseling in Astrology*, pages 155–190.

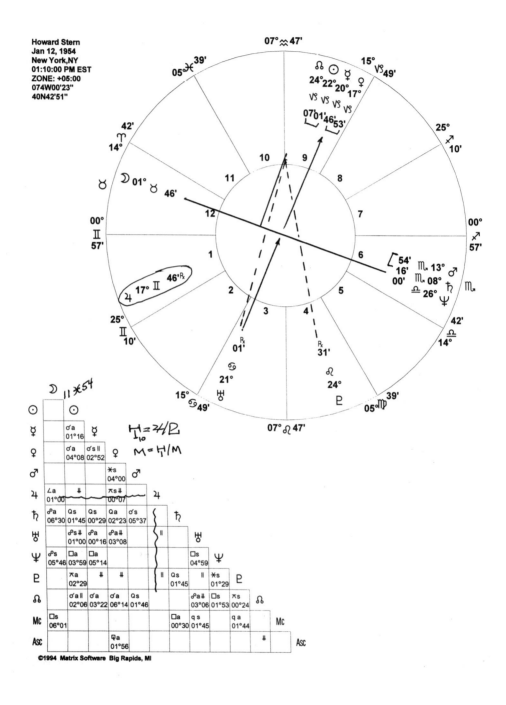

Howard Stern
Jan 12, 1954
New York,NY
01:10:00 PM EST
ZONE: +05:00
074W00'23"
40N42'51"

©1994 Matrix Software Big Rapids, MI

Case Example: Howard Stern

Jupiter in Gemini suggests reward needs that involve social acceptance for one's views; an insatiable appetite for new ideas, a perpetual motion whirlwind searching for intriguing tidbits of information. The mind easily becomes inflated with edgy self-awareness and may stimulate continuous nervous activity. Being talkative and agitated, trying to place everything into some scheme of significance…these are dramatic manifestations of Jupiter in Gemini, and we feel this strongly in Stern's persona; he exhibits this behavior as a badge attesting to his self-importance, i.e., the "King of all Media."

There is no doubt that Jupiter in Gemini "runs away" with the portrait, with Stern's horoscope. It *is* peregrine—even though Jupiter in Gemini is "in its detriment." And the semisquare (non-Ptolemaic aspect) with the Moon simply pipes the Jupiterian trumpets developmentally into the core of his being, and through the Moon into the communications 3rd, ruled by the Moon. With Jupiter ruling the public 7th, how Stern communicates to the public and the rewards he wants out of the process are vividly clear.

THE LUNAR NODAL AXIS

We know that the Nodal axis describes the two opposing points on the ecliptic (the apparent path of the Sun) where the Moon crosses in its orbit around the Earth. These two orbital paths incline to each other at a plane of a little over 5 degrees. The axis proceeds irregularly from day to day because of a "wobble" reflecting the gyroscopic relationship of the Sun and the Moon. The so-called "true node" takes this tiny wobble into account; therefore, there are periods of direct motion and retrograde motion when using the true node. The "mean node" position, on the other hand, averages the wobble out and is always retrograde.

In Stern's horoscope shown on page 6, the nodal axis shows the mean node at 24 Capricorn 07. Stern's true node is 24 Capricorn 00 and is retrograde. That 07' of arc is totally insignificant, and even the retrogradation means nothing as any kind of supplement or divergence within our portrait. The point for our analysis of Howard Stern's horoscope is that *the Sun and node are in conjunction* (and Neptune is square the axis), suggesting a very, very strong maternal influence, echoed by the fact that the Sun rules Stern's 4th.[4]

Although this wobble—the difference between the true and the mean Node positions—can approach 1.50°, I do not consider it at all. I work with the mean node exclusively.

---

4. I recommend using a very tight orb for the nodal axis: 2.5°. Please see the full presentation for the lunar nodal axis developed in Tyl, *Synthesis & Counseling in Astrology,* pages 49–64.

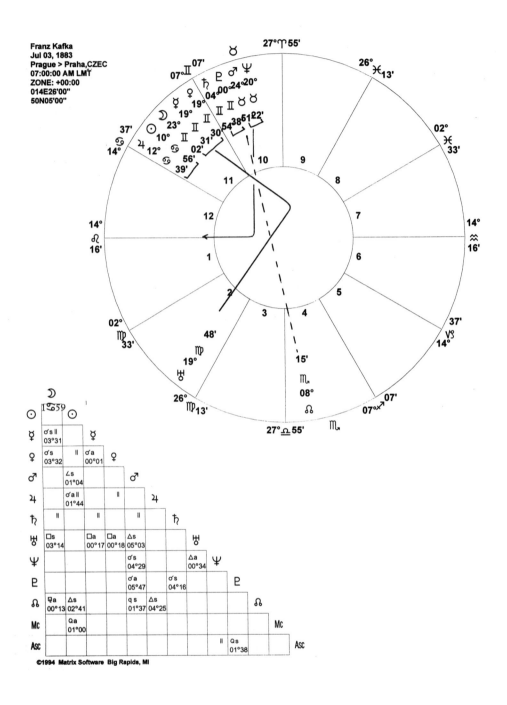

Franz Kafka
Jul 03, 1883
Prague > Praha,CZEC
07:00:00 AM LMT
ZONE: +00:00
014E26'00"
50N05'00"

©1994 Matrix Software Big Rapids, MI

Case Example: Franz Kafka

This is the horoscope of Franz Kafka, one of the leading writers of his *fin-de siècle* era. Kafka suffered an enormous identity anxiety, lifelong depression, haunted by self-deprecating images communicated in bizarre metaphors. Kafka commented, "My talent for portraying my dreamlike inner life has thrust all other matters into the background; my life has dwindled dreadfully, nor will it cease to dwindle." He observed that he represented all "the negative elements," referring to his life predicament as a German Jew in Czechoslovakia, within horrid class and religious struggles and a dreadful family situation. He felt estrangement in all forms.

The suppression Kafka absorbed in his reality and in his mind was focused on a tyrannical father who had no understanding for him whatsoever. Additionally, Kafka felt that his mother also failed completely to understand him. He had no sense of love whatsoever in his family life, and the family was hated in its society; they were religious, political, and economic scapegoats.

We can see the potential of such suppression in this horoscope portrait ever so clearly through *the Neptune square to the Ascendant* [any strong natal aspect, arc, or transit contact between Neptune and an angle may guide us to considerations of suppression and Ego wipe-out to one degree or another]. This aspect is beyond the regular orb discipline we are using, but Kafka is an exceptional case indeed, and the Neptune dimension screams out of the portrait; it is easily recognized in Kafka's reality and incorporated into analysis.

Going further, we see Mars quindecile (obsession) with the nodal axis: Kafka's estrangement from his father, the focus of his hate (Mars ruling the 10th; and note that Neptune conjoins Mars); and also his problematic obsession with his mother (the nodal axis), which theorists cite as the base for Kafka's angel-whore complex within his loathing for things sexual.

So much has been awakened here by just two measurements brought to life in their occurrence within Kafka's reality.

Lean but circumspect aspect measurement leads us to reliably incisive analysis.

MIDPOINT SYNTHESIS

The developmental pressure within astrological portraiture is to bring more and more symbols together into more and more telling units. It can be discussed that, in the end, all planets are in aspect to all other planets, that there is a *primal force to cohesion* within the personality and that we work to portray that. It is more practical to say that the more we know about the parts, the clearer focus we have upon the whole. Midpoint synthesis helps us recognize that pressure; midpoint synthesis brings behaviors together helpfully.

X=Y/Z says that planet X is conjunct, square, or opposed the midpoint of planets Y and Z (when using a 90^0 sort). Please note that the slash "/" connotes midpoint and should be used only in that reference.[5]

To obtain a midpoint table of a particular horoscope that will be most productive, we want to work again only with the strong aspects (the fourth harmonic). We ask our computer to give us what is most commonly called a "90^0 midpoint sort," displaying all midpoint locations in relation to natal planets and points within the 4th harmonic. All midpoint pictures within a 2^0 orb can be relevant, excluding pictures with the same planet or point positioned on *both* sides of the equals sign.[6]

Howard Stem				Jan 12, 1954 01:10:00 PM EST 074W00'23" 40N42'51"							
Midpoint Sort: 90° Dial											
♄/♇	001°24'	♀/☊	021°00'	☊/Mc	030°57'	♇/Mc	046°09'	♆/☊	070°04'	♂/☊	079°00'
♀/♃	002°50'	♅	021°01'	☽	031°46'	☽/Asc	046°22'	☽/☿	071°16'	☽/Mc	079°46'
♂/♇	004°12'	♃/♇	021°09'	♄/♆	032°08'	♄/Asc	049°37'	☽/♅	071°24'	♄/Mc	083°02'
☿/♃	004°16'	☉/☿	021°24'	♂/♆	034°57'	♃/♆	051°53'	☽/☉	071°54'	♀/Asc	084°25'
Mc/Asc	004°22'	☉/♅	021°31'	☽/♄	035°01'	♂/Asc	052°25'	☽/☊	072°57'	♆/♇	085°16'
♃/♅	004°24'	☉	022°01'	♀/♇	036°12'	♇	054°31'	♀/♄	073°05'	♂/Mc	085°50'
☉/♃	004°54'	☿/☊	022°27'	☿/♇	037°38'	☽/♃	054°46'	☿/♄	074°31'	☿/Asc	085°51'
♃/☊	005°57'	♅/☊	022°34'	♅/♇	037°46'	♃/♄	058°01'	♄/♅	074°39'	♅/Asc	085°59'
♇/Asc	012°44'	☉/☊	023°04'	Mc	037°47'	♂/♃	060°50'	☉/♄	075°09'	☉/Asc	086°29'
♃/Mc	012°46'	☊	024°07'	☽/♂	037°50'	Asc	060°57'	♀/♂	075°53'	☊/Asc	087°32'
♀	017°53'	♆	026°00'	☉/♇	038°16'	♀/♆	066°57'	♄/☊	076°12'	☽/♇	088°09'
☿/♀	019°20'	♀/Mc	027°50'	♄	038°16'	☿/♆	068°23'	♆/Mc	076°53'		
♀/♅	019°27'	☽/♆	028°53'	♇/☊	039°19'	♅/♆	068°31'	☿/♂	077°20'		
☉/♀	019°57'	☿/Mc	029°16'	♂/♄	041°05'	☉/♆	069°01'	♂/♅	077°27'		
☿	020°46'	♅/Mc	029°24'	♆/Asc	043°29'	♃/Asc	069°22'	♃	077°46'		
☿/♅	020°53'	☉/Mc	029°54'	♂	043°54'	☽/♀	069°50'	☉/♂	077°58'		

5. The hyphen is used to link planets in textual reference, i.e., the Sun-Moon conjunction; but the Sun/Moon midpoint.

6. 00-29°59', Cardinal degrees; 30°00'–59°59', Fixed; 60°00'–89°59', Mutable.

Again, our objective is not to note *all* contact pictures; instead, we want the *strongest* pictures; they will add important substance to our analysis and to our conversation with the client. These pictures are obvious to the eye.

AP=Saturn/Pluto—The Aries Point (AP)[7] suggests that there are some skeletons in Stern's closet [Saturn/Pluto, things tough to live with], usually from early home life development, that could be problematic, but, with the Aries Point involved, we can expect that he has openly come to grips with the situation—the problems have been brought out to the light—and converted it all into externalized energies for ambition. Finding out what the situation was would be helpful in anchoring understanding of strong behaviors in adult life.

Astrologer Don McBroom has written a masterful work on midpoints.[8] One of his inspired innovations is to translate the equals sign within any midpoint picture with the words *"is accomplished through"*!

For example, Stern has Uranus=Jupiter/Pluto (together, very often an index of affluence): we read this as individuality (career status, since Uranus rules Stern's Midheaven) *is accomplished through* public (Jupiter rules the 7th) power presence (Pluto), acclaim from the public. In other words, this is a picture that pushes for influence, and very often suggests the strong motivation to make much money.

Stern shows Mc=Uranus/Pluto (this pair always shows rebelliousness for change): professional status is accomplished through rebellious activity (individuation bucking the social power structure). In other words, an obvious synthesis of behaviors is a dedication to and talent for changing the big picture.

Additionally, we see the strong picture Jupiter=Mars/Uranus: reward is accomplished through making things happen in an individualistic way, probably through cantankerous or rebellious activity.

Although there is no midpoint picture here in Stern's horoscope involving the Sun/Moon in the fourth harmonic, it is to be noted firmly that *that Sun/Moon midpoint is of highest importance and sensitivity in the horoscope.* A planet configured strongly (i.e., fourth harmonic) with Sun/Moon can easily dominate the portrait. This midpoint must be noted appropriately for every horoscope; it will be vitally telling in relation to arcs and transit development as well.

---

7. Any position between 29 Mutable and 1.5 Cardinal connotes the *Aries Point*. There are four of them, of course, and each of them "brings forward" (shows, exposes) the substance on the right side of the equation.

8. *Midpoints* by Don McBroom; Llewellyn Publications, 2007.

THE DIRECTED "SOLAR ARC" HOROSCOPE

We need to be ready for the future within our portrait for our client's development.[9]

Our well-known system of Secondary Progressions is important for the principle of symbolic time development within the beautiful day-for-a-year equation developed by astrologers over some fifteen centuries from the time of Claudius Ptolemy. An extension of this principle is the fundamental premise of "Solar Arcs," the most effective prediction system I know of in astrology. Using Solar Arcs in combination with the Secondary Progressed Moon and Transits presents state-of-the-art delineation of developmental time; this sophisticated measurement system is the best we have in astrology today.[10]

The time increment of solar arc development is based upon the symbolism of secondary progressed Sun development; the SA Sun and the SP Sun are the same. In solar arcs, that symbolically vital increment of time and distance (the measurement of the SP-SA Sun advanced from the natal Sun position) is applied *uniformly in counter-clockwise motion to every planet and point in the horoscope.* The solar arc positions are placed in the outer ring of a double-ringed horoscope drawing, and we note the new aspect relationships made with the natal base.

It is an easy matter to ask our computer program to provide us with this double-ringed horoscope for every portrait we work with. Let's look at Howard Stern's future projection to early January 2006.[11] Of course, this picture could have been studied one year ago, two, five, with the same anticipation of a grand new start in his career: his move into "satellite radio," for complete freedom of expression. The announcement of this plan was accompanied by enormous publicity.

Four key measurements show this new-start event-potential dramatically:

• See SA Saturn at 00 Capricorn. The symbol of ambition has come to the Aries Point. This is extremely important as an indication of Stern's career development since his natal Saturn is conjoined with Mars [I can do *anything,* and you better believe it!] and both are square the Midheaven! The Aries Point brings all of this forward.[12]

• Similarly, we see SA Midheaven coming to another Aries Point, at 00 Aries!

---

9. Detailed analysis outline for past development is accomplished directly from the natal horoscope, using arcs and transits. Preparation will be covered at great length in chapter 2 and thereafter.

10. This discussion is explored fully and the system of Solar Arcs is presented completely, with full annotation of all possible measurements—some 1,600 of them—in Tyl, *Solar Arcs.*

11. This manuscript was being written in December 2005.

12. Two years' research has conclusively corroborated that the arc or transit of a planet to an Aries Point has high potential of manifesting in public exposure, in terms of the planet *and its natal House of tenancy,* even if the Aries Point is not occupied or aspected natally.

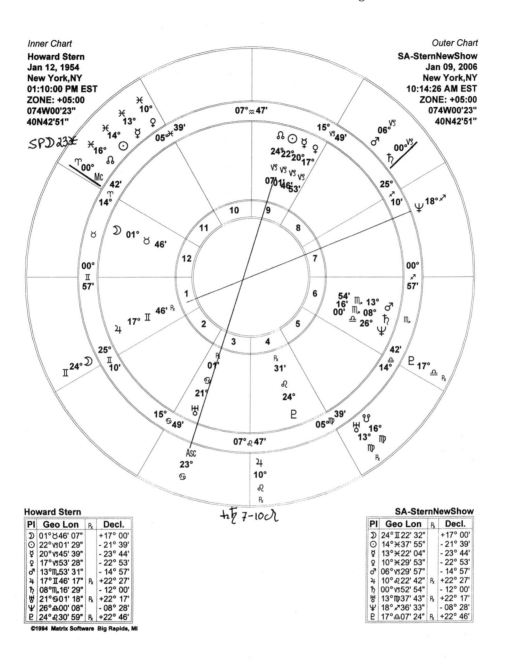

Inner Chart
Howard Stern
Jan 12, 1954
New York,NY
01:10:00 PM EST
ZONE: +05:00
074W00'23"
40N42'51"

Outer Chart
SA-SternNewShow
Jan 09, 2006
New York,NY
10:14:26 AM EST
ZONE: +05:00
074W00'23"
40N42'51"

Howard Stern

Pl	Geo Lon	Rx	Decl.
☽	01°♉46' 07"		+17° 00'
☉	22°♑01' 29"		- 21° 39'
☿	20°♑45' 39"		- 23° 44'
♀	17°♑53' 28"		- 22° 53'
♂	13°♏53' 31"		- 14° 57'
♃	17°♊46' 17"	Rx	+22° 27'
♄	08°♏16' 29"		- 12° 00'
♅	21°♋01' 18"	Rx	+22° 17'
♆	26°♎00' 08"		- 08° 28'
♇	24°♌30' 59"	Rx	+22° 46'

©1994 Matrix Software Big Rapids, MI

SA-SternNewShow

Pl	Geo Lon	Rx	Decl.
☽	24°♊22' 32"		+17° 00'
☉	14°♓37' 55"		- 21° 39'
☿	13°♓22' 04"		- 23° 44'
♀	10°♓29' 53"		- 22° 53'
♂	06°♑29' 57"		- 14° 57'
♃	10°♌22' 42"	Rx	+22° 27'
♄	00°♑52' 54"		- 12° 00'
♅	13°♍37' 43"	Rx	+22° 17'
♆	18°♐36' 33"		- 08° 28'
♇	17°♎07' 24"	Rx	+22° 46'

- SA Ascendant has just finished opposition (awareness) with the natal Sun (personality clarification through the reactions from others) and is now on the nodal axis (tremendous public projection).

- SA Venus is about to conjoin Sun/Moon at 11 Pisces, promising much initial success in his new relationship with the public (and in his personal life).

- Transiting Saturn, in December 2005–January 2006, is at 7–10 Leo exactly conjunct the fourth cusp of *new beginnings*, opposite the Midheaven! And square natal Saturn!!

- And we can anticipate quite an uproar about Stern's rebellious activity as we see tr Uranus, ruler of his Midheaven, coming to the Sun/Moon midpoint throughout 2006!

What an astounding projection of potentials within Stern's career.

The SP Moon in January 2006 at 23 Pisces is not directly involved with the picture for Stern's debut on satellite radio, but note that *six months earlier* [the SP Moon moves reliably, forward or backward, 1 degree per month of real time] the SP Moon was square Stern's Jupiter at 17 Gemini (ruler of the public 7th, discussed on page 7). This was the time of early announcements and final contract talks, etc., for the new start in his career. Again, we must make astrology's biggest point: all of this was viewable *much ahead of time*.

The computer can help us mightily in organizing all the solar arcs, SP Moon contacts, and major transits for any given time period, to be read "at a glance"! Your software should supply you with a "combination search," a time period overview… some organizational format and printout that displays what you ask it to display, integrating all the measurements within a time continuum.[13] I strongly recommend dealing only with arcs in the fourth harmonic, indirect arcs (arcs involving midpoint pictures) in the fourth harmonic, the SP Moon in fourth harmonic relationship with natal positions, and major transits in the fourth harmonic (the planets Mars, Jupiter, Saturn, Uranus, Neptune, and Pluto).[14]

This search follows my recommendations made above. What is really important here are the first two columns, left to right, the astrological picture and the date of occurrence.

---

13. The format presented here (page 15) is the Combo-Search from Matrix WinStar 2+ software.

14. It is extremely important that only square, conjunction, opposition, semisquare, and sesquiquadrate aspects be programmed. These are the strong aspects that correspond to strong activities in life. Involving the softer aspects makes the presentation excessive, bewildering, and basically meaningless. Some software will allow the programming request for quindecile contacts as well, and I strongly recommend that.

Search From Sep 30, 2005 to Jan 31, 2006 GMT Howard Stern

Aspect	Date	Time	Event	Type	P1 Pos.	P2 Pos	E/X/L
♂ -- S℞	10-01-2005	10:16 pm	♂ S℞	Tr-Na	23°♉22'℞		
♃ -- ☌ ♆	10-07-2005	04:43 pm	♃ ☌ ♆	Tr-Na	26°♎00'	26°♎00'	Exact
♀ - q ♆/♇	10-14-2005	01:49 pm	♀ q ♆/♇	Ar-Na	10°♓16'	25°♍16'	Exact
☉ - ∠ ♅/Mc	10-17-2005	03:27 am	☉ ∠ ♅/Mc	Ar-Na	14°♓24'	29°♈24'	Exact
♆ ---- SD	10-26-2005	06:01 pm	♆ SD	Tr-Na	14°♒49'		
♃ -- ☍ ☽	11-03-2005	06:10 am	♃ ☍ ☽	Tr-Na	01°♏46'	01°♉46'	Exact
Asc --- ⚼ ☿/♆	11-05-2005	03:47 am	Asc ⚼ ☿/♆	Ar-Na	23°♋23'	08°♐23'	Exact
♂ -- ☍ ♂	11-10-2005	01:11 pm	♂ ☍ ♂	Tr-Na	13°♉54'℞	13°♏54'	Exact
♅ ---- SD	11-15-2005	10:15 pm	♅ SD	Tr-Na	06°♓51'		
♄ -- S℞	11-22-2005	07:07 am	♄ S℞	Tr-Na	11°♌19'℞		
♃ -- ∠ ♆/♇	11-27-2005	05:01 am	♃ ∠ ♆/♇	Ar-Na	10°♌16'	25°♍16'	Exact
☉ - □ ☿/♄	11-29-2005	00:14 am	☉ □ ☿/♄	Ar-Na	14°♓31'	14°♐31'	Exact
♃ -- □ Mc	12-01-2005	08:04 pm	♃ □ Mc	Tr-Na	07°♏47'	07°♒47'	Exact
♃ -- ☌ ♄	12-04-2005	07:44 am	♃ ☌ ♄	Tr-Na	08°♏16'	08°♏16'	Exact
♂ -- ☍ ♄	12-07-2005	06:45 pm	♂ ☍ ♄	Tr-Na	08°♉16'℞	08°♏16'	Exact
♂ -- SD	12-10-2005	04:00 am	♂ SD	Tr-Na	08°♉14'		
♂ -- ☍ ♄	12-12-2005	02:52 pm	♂ ☍ ♄	Tr-Na	08°♉16'	08°♏16'	Exact
☽ ⚼ ♇/☊	12-20-2005	12:35 pm	☽ ⚼ ♇/☊	Ar-Na	24°♊19'	09°♏19'	Exact
Asc --- ∠ ♅/♆	12-22-2005	05:23 pm	Asc ∠ ♅/♆	Ar-Na	23°♋31'	08°♍31'	Exact
♃ -- ☌ ♂	01-04-2006	05:41 pm	♃ ☌ ♂	Tr-Na	13°♏54'	13°♏54'	Exact
♂ -- ☍ ♂	01-10-2006	08:36 pm	♂ ☍ ♂	Tr-Na	13°♉54'	13°♏54'	Exact
♄ -- □ ♄	01-22-2006	10:22 pm	♄ □ ♄	Tr-Na	08°♌16'℞	08°♏16'	Exact
☊ --- ∠ ☽	01-23-2006	02:54 am	☊ ∠ ☽	Ar-Na	16°♓46'	01°♉46'	Exact
☽ □ ♀/Asc	01-26-2006	05:38 pm	☽ □ ♀/Asc	Ar-Na	24°♊25'	24°♓25'	Exact
♄ -- ☍ Mc	01-28-2006	11:45 pm	♄ ☍ Mc	Tr-Na	07°♌47'℞	07°♒47'	Exact

The time references in the third column are for the computer; the "Type" column labels the measurement, and the other columns are not vital.

Note the indirect arc for October 17, basically for the whole month of October. We see SA Sun=Uranus/MC:[15] "Strong illumination of individuality; getting what one deserves; eagerness for achievement; nervous drive." This certainly fits Stern's reality at that time; very appropriately since Uranus rules his Midheaven.[16]

We can see the concentration of ambition in January 2006, the month of Stern's debut, his new start. Central is the arc Node=Moon: "Contact with others brings assistance and comfort (fulfillment)." All measurements are keyed to the transit of Saturn over the fourth cusp of new beginnings.

15. The equals sign in solar arcs connotes "hard aspect," the aspects we are working with.

16. Picture delineations used through this book and presented in quotation marks are verbatim extracts from the Solar Arc-Transit Appendices of Tyl, *Synthesis & Counseling in Astrology* and Tyl, *Solar Arcs.*

REVIEW

For our preparation for client consultation, we have the natal horoscope—prepared as clearly as possible by our computer, preferably with the MC-IC axis straight up and down for every horoscope in order to eliminate any tilting in our brain's scanning of data. The wheel should have a well-manicured aspect grid, which we understand fully for its orb sensitivity and aspect inventory. Then, we have the 90° midpoint sort. We have the double-ringed solar arc picture, and we have a "combination search" presentation for a specified period of time into the future (I suggest no more than two years from the time of consultation), showing direct and indirect arcs, the SP Moon, and major transits, all in terms of hard-aspect contact to the natal.

This is a miraculously powerful compendium of data: five or six pieces of paper that capture the portrait of any living soul, as he or she was born, as they develop, and as they aim to be.

2 HUMANIZING THE DATA
—BRINGING MEASUREMENTS TO LIFE

Measurements are beguiling. There is the natural hope that one measurement or another will "tell the tale," will open the Sesame portal to illumination; therefore so many astrologers add measurement after measurement after measurement to their preparation, constantly hunting and hoping for the golden insight!

That futile process betrays the inexperienced and insecure astrologer; it always brings confusion and ineffectiveness.

Illumination is not in a single measurement but in an artful synthesis of several or many, with the focus of them all framed humanistically *within the astrologer*. That's where the magic measurements are: they are within.

Much of the insecurity we feel is a carry-over from the past, from conspicuously fatalistic astrology, where one dramatic measurement would supposedly foretell a cataclysmic change of life or an enormous change of fortunes, the difference between life and death. In modern, viable astrology, we serve our client best *not* with a catalogue of descriptions intended to prove astrology and reflect back favorably upon the individual astrologer, but with meaningful, insightful conversation toward a goal of further life development, behavioral improvement (modification), goal realization, change. That's what a consultation is all about, and we should ask ourselves often, "How many measurements do we need in order to begin a meaningful conversation with our client?"

PSYCHOLOGICAL NEED THEORY

The astrological portrait comes to life literally and figuratively in terms of *the process of becoming*, our development in *the fulfillment of needs* through behaviors that are progressively exercised and refined throughout life.

The overlay of Psychological Need Theory upon traditional astrology was startling to the astrology world when I introduced the concepts in the early '70s: *it is behavior to fulfill needs that makes things happen in life;* the planets do nothing.

Astrology shows us with utmost clarity and insight what our individual needs are. Astrology guides us to appreciation of the human condition and our behaviors working toward fulfillment. Life and our development comprise a humanistic spectrum of formative events in time. Within this dynamic collaboration between psychology and astrology, "need" became a spectacularly helpful four-letter word.

Our next steps in horoscope preparation for the consultation will be to bring the data literally and figuratively *to* life. As we gain an orientation to the natal horoscope, it is extremely helpful to see the Sun in its sign not as an abject label, but as a signal of *the kind of energy we instinctively use to live our best.* Every astrology student learns these twelve archetypes of energy well. We must see them as active potentials rather than passive description.

Synthesis begins when we realize that that Sun energy viewed solely in itself is without outlet, without application, without actualized potential. Studying the Sun alone, focusing on it exclusively, burns our retina. We see the energy of the Sun better, its light directed meaningfully, *through reflections upon the Moon*…and eventually throughout the solar system, touching every planet to one degree or another (the aspect connections).

A most important key to the thought revolution in the '70s was that the Moon in its sign is the symbol of the **"reigning need" of the personality**. Using the Sun's energy, the Moon leads the entire personality—*all* of its dreams and behaviors—forward to fulfillment. For example, Howard Stern has the Sun in Capricorn and the Moon in Taurus. The Sun's Capricorn energy is administratively forthright, determined to be effective, and the "reigning need" focus of the Moon is to achieve a solid organization of values in life to fit some ideal or a format he thinks best, to establish and settle a new order around him in the world. That's the Sun-Moon blend for Stern, and we can know that it courses throughout his public persona. In short, we can think/feel the synthesis this way: the energy to organize, strategize, and deploy resources dominates his persona…it fuels his need to focus ambition…to establish security, to keep things as they are or make them as they should be, often working toward a new order.[1]

Naturally, the Sun-Moon blend is tempered, modified, enhanced, jarred, etc., through aspects from the other symbols within the horoscope. In our orientation to Stern's horoscope, we see/feel a strong intensification of the Capricorn energy through the opposition of Uranus to the Sun (high individualization, independence, emphasis). We see/feel a possible neurotic compulsion through the Saturn-Neptune oppositions to the Moon.[2]

The planets symbolize *subsidiary needs*: Mercury in its sign suggests our need to think a certain way in order to be maximally efficient (Mercury in Capricorn, for example, needs to hear the grass grow, needs to analyze everything strategically!); Venus in its sign suggests the need to relate socially to the world in a certain way in order to feel fulfilled (Venus in Capricorn needs more time than usual to grow up and mature with regard to relational values; people are held at bay until that is established; a loner position is preferred when it comes to intimacy); Mars suggests the need to apply a certain kind of energy in order to be efficient (Mars in Scorpio needs deeply to control all issues; and in conjunction with Saturn, the combination can be residually overpowering, indomitable); Jupiter is the need for a particular kind of reward (Jupiter in Gemini, see page 7, needs reward through societal feedback and enthusiasm for one's values and programs); Saturn in its sign focuses ambition on how one needs to be seen with regard to the drive and energy to succeed (in Scorpio, a deep drive to prove oneself through the control of others).

Uranus, Neptune, and Pluto add intensity, chiaroscuro (the shadings of light and dark), and perspective, respectively.

We can see how Stern's Uranus stirs up and intensifies his ego energy, the way he thinks, and the way he relates: the Uranus oppositions to Sun, Mercury, and Venus. We see an aesthetic—be it bright or shady—through Neptune square Sun, Mercury, and Uranus…perhaps alternatively inciting creativity galore (echoing the five quintiles in the horoscope) or clouding issues to the point of self-detriment. Through the Pluto quindecile to the Midheaven, we see the projection of enormous professional perspective for optimum achievement.

---

1. All 144 Sun-Moon blend possibilities are thoroughly discussed in Tyl, *Synthesis & Counseling in Astrology*, pages 65–102.

2. "If you are not like me, I hate you" is the title of chapter 8 in Stern's autobiography, *Private Parts*.

HEMISPHERE EMPHASIS

We have learned that Nature tells us much about the life through hemisphere emphasis (planet tenancy makes a clear statement by hemisphere; groupings of retrograde planets in one hemisphere call attention to the *opposite* hemisphere). To the north, below the horizon, there is an emphatic statement about *unfinished business in the early home* that will flow through life development—we must ask, "What was it?" To the east, centered around the Ascendant, we anticipate much *defensiveness* in the personality—we must ask, "Why?" To the south, centered around the Midheaven, there is the very real life-situation of being swept away by life's winds, *being victimized*—"Why? What is the vulnerability?" And to the west (as with Stern), we see the hemisphere focus centered around the seventh cusp; we anticipate perhaps being taken advantage of, exploited, *giving one's self away*—"What is the person trying to accomplish in terms of such a pressing need to be accepted?"[3]

We appreciate already what drives this portrait into focus. With experience, these initial synthesized deductions—which are, in the main, quite simple, yet deep when the concept of "need" is foremost in the mind—can be made very, very quickly as we begin to manage the data, to humanize it in our next steps of preparation.

TENSION NETWORKS AMONG HOUSES

This organizational step is surely the most vital step in synthesis as we prepare the horoscope for consultation. It brings the planets "down to earth." We link planetary developmental tension—the behaviors to fulfill needs—*to House issues of experience*. It can be accomplished very smoothly.

The magical process of relating planetary aspects to life experience puts the inner environment together with the outer environment: *our responses to what is happening around us define the development of our personality*. Our individualized efforts to fulfill needs through our behaviors fit themselves into *social patterns*. We are rewarded toward fulfillment or we are forced to alter the behaviors and to change.

We learn to see those social patterns of development in a flash; personalizing them becomes the stuff of the astrological consultation toward which we are working.

---

3. Full development of the significances of hemisphere emphasis is presented in Tyl, *Synthesis & Counseling in Astrology*, pages 5–34.

We must carry in our diagnostic awareness the three following incontrovertible organizational guidelines, based upon the three Grand Crosses of houses…angular, succedent, and cadent:

1. *Angular.* The Ascendant is always square the experiential zones of the 4th and 10th, the parental axis. Aspect tensions *to the rulers* of these houses (or major planet tenants) alert us *to problems of identity development related to problems with parental interaction and influence.* When there is similarly indicated tension involving the 7th House, *the formative early-life anxieties are so very often carried over into adult relationship experience.* They repeat.

2. *Succedent.* The 2nd House is always square the experiential zones of the 5th and 11th, the axis of giving and receiving love. Aspect tensions to the rulers of these Houses (or major planet tenants) alert us to problems in the self-worth profile (2nd); they are linked to difficulty with feeling lovable (11th) and, in turn, giving love easily (5th). These are developmental tensions that go very deep and are related all too easily to tensions shown with the angles (parental issues) as the source and into the 7th as an extension of influence. When there is tension similarly indicated involving the 8th House, the undermining of self-worth and love-exchange profiles threatens our relationships with others, and very often this involves the sexual component as well (the 8th joining the 5th to comprise the sexual profile).

3. *Cadent.* The 3rd House is always square the experiential zones of the 6th and the 12th. Aspect tensions to the rulers of these houses (or major planet tenants) alert us to problems in the mindset (3rd): how we think, how we interact (communicate) with the world. When there is tension similarly indicated involving the 9th House, the probability of the education being interrupted is high (in the North American culture especially); how we view the world and how the world views us…the determination of level…are strongly affected. Differences in learning, information, opinions easily upset the cooperation dynamic focused in the 6th House.[4]

Now we put pencil to paper for the first time! We identify the Houses with major tensions related to them as seen through *hard aspects to the ruler of any particular House.* These aspects

---

4. Full presentation of the psychodynamic interaction of the houses is presented in Tyl, *Synthesis & Counseling in Astrology*, pages 225–270.

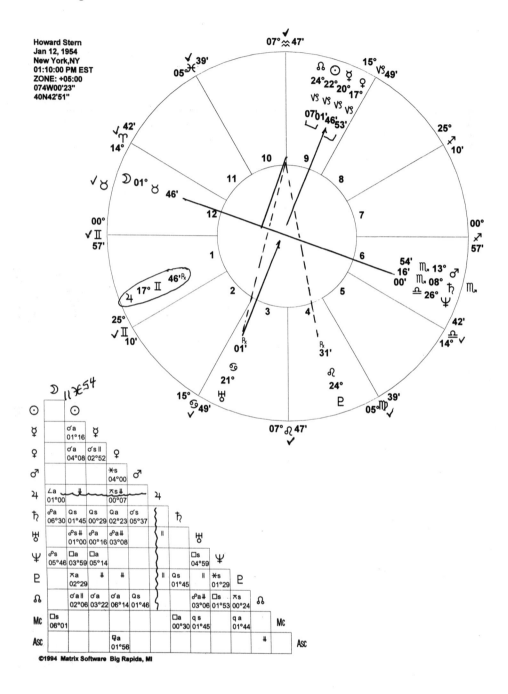

Howard Stern
Jan 12, 1954
New York,NY
01:10:00 PM EST
ZONE: +05:00
074W00'23"
40N42'51"

©1994 Matrix Software Big Rapids, MI

are immediately observable in the aspect grid. I recommend putting a discreet check mark on the cusp of each house whose ruler is under high developmental tension.

Normally, not *every* house is going to be affected. Stern is a complicated and driven individual, so maximum developmental tension roars through his horoscope, and every House ruler except Jupiter (ruling the 7th and the 8th) is under high tension. [But very often, peregrination can be viewed as a high-tension state, running away with the horoscope in terms of the peregrine planet's house rulership(s). Here, public thrust and sexuality concerns run rampant in Stern's life, with the reinforcing echo of 5th House ruler Mercury's strongly intensified aspect condition.]

The multiplicity of checkmarks does not diminish the helpfulness of making these notations; *the process of applying the checkmarks puts into the astrologer's mind that there is an experiential focus within development that is highly charged in terms of particular life experiences.* And it is key to analysis to know that these House tensions fit the patterns outlined above; the idea of societal structures is activated.

For example: Mercury here rules the Ascendant, the 2nd House, and the 5th. Mercury is under high developmental tension (the opposition from Uranus—intensification—and the square from Neptune…suppression, molding in the unconscious). This tells us immediately—in a flash—that there are identity development problems to discuss with Stern, especially with regard to self-worth anxiety, and how those problems have made difficult the giving and receiving of love, the slowed maturation (Venus in Capricorn, remember, itself opposed by Uranus) of love-exchange sensibility. With Uranus in square with Neptune, the ruler of the 11th, we know that this identity development and self-worth anxiety have at their source a tremendous feeling of not being lovable. We suspect enormous anxiety within these specific developmental networks; there is little doubt about it, and they require clear, objective, supportive discussion in consultation.

We see the pattern involving the rulers of the 4th and 10th, the parents. This is not at all unusual. The consultation will reveal the details, the level of intensity, and the extent of retaining the problem and concomitant behaviors into adult life.

While the ruler of the 9th is under high developmental tension (Mars conjoined with Saturn), the suggestion of an interruption in education (i.e., not going on to or through college) did not occur for Stern; note the offsetting and intensely focused planet group *in* the 9th.

The western hemisphere emphasis is now perfectly understandable: Stern needs and exploits the public (its acclaim and confirmation) to offset his deep self-worth anxieties and the feeling of not being lovable. He gives himself away to the world, *but on his own terms* (the Moon in Taurus). *He* knows what is right, and *he* will (needs to) prove it. With the powerful Moon in the 12th House, the world does not always agree with him [While Stern is the highest-paid radio personality in the United States, he is also the most fined personality in radio broadcast history].

This is the process of synthesis, key to meaningful horoscope preparation and consultation. The process brings together so many of the guidelines that the Universe offers for the individual. We see the person's orientation with the world, we feel behavioral energies focused through a reigning need, a driving force of Self; we see the developmental patterns as the *inner* environment accosts the *outer* environment, as need tensions interact with family and society for reward, frustration, or change.

SPECIAL BRUSH STROKES

There are special brush strokes that occur in many horoscope portraits, and every astrologer must know these accents in depth.

The first is *Saturn-retrograde phenomenology*: this occurrence usually suggests a legacy of inferiority feelings. These are taken on in the early home life through the relationship (or lack of it) with the father, or the authority figure in the home. The father is taken out of the picture early; or was there but absent or passive most of the time; or was so tyrannical, any one or combination of these, so as not to have provided the guidance of authoritative love.

This crucially formative consideration can also be suggested by strong Saturn-Sun or Moon contacts, the conjunction or square of Saturn (retrograde or not) to the Nodal axis [the mother runs the show], and/or strong aspects to the ruler(s) of the 10th.

With a planet in conjunction or square to the *lunar nodal axis* (recommended 2.5 degree orb), the influence of the mother (or the feminine in general: grandmother, older sister, etc.) is almost always remarkable *through and in terms of the planet so configured*. This can also be suggested through Plutonic contact with the Moon (for male or female).[5]

The *quintile measurement* (72°, a sextile plus 12 degrees) suggests creativity, especially prominent when three or more are present, relating to *any* planets or points. The *quindecile measurement* (165°, a point 15 degrees back from or past an opposition) suggests great intensification, even to the point of obsession.

---

5. My discoveries about Saturn-℞ phenomenology are fully covered in Tyl, *Synthesis & Counseling in Astrology,* pages 38-48; and about the nodal axis, pages 49-64.

Howard Stern has *Uranus (individuation) dramatically quindecile with the Midheaven:* his quest for highest individuation and acclaim is focused pointedly through his professional outreach and status.

How all of this works together, the colors coming together, is the astrologer's art of synthesis.

MEASURING TIMES PAST

In our outline preparation of times past-and-future for the consultation, we must remember always that angles (and their rulers) are all-important! The angles are the *sine qua non* of the rectification process,[6] and symbolic movements of and to the angles trace our development from birth to the present and into the future. This point of view organizes our preparation efficiently; the objective is not to outline *everything* that has taken place in the life, but, rather, the *key* times of development, which almost invariably involve the angles, the Sun, the Moon. In the process, we are also testing the birth time and we are uncovering the places in the horoscope that respond most sensitively and reliably.

We accomplish this, again quite easily, once we understand what we are doing and why.

The solar arcs and transits in the formative years are very, very easy to see in the horoscope; no computations are required.[7] We look for a major Arc, knowing it will apply for six months (one-half a degree) and separate for four to six months (one-third to one-half a degree), *and then we check the ephemeris for a "trigger transit" within that time frame.* This trigger transit will normally "set off" the background arc, and near that date we will discover a major developmental occurrence. The client will react to that event or within those conditions. His or her behaviors will express the individual value system. Reward or frustration is accumulated, and life develops.

The process is not difficult, and the way of notating this and working with it will become crystal clear in the development of this book.

Let us make a quick, confident, cursory overview analysis of what we see within the emerging portrait of Franz Kafka, guided by the preparation guidelines we have studied so far in this book:

---

6. The Midheaven is determined by the time of birth (4m of time=1° of arc over the Midheaven) and the Ascendant reflects the location of birth. Together, the Angles are our orientation to our world.

7. See the 100-year, first-of-the-month ephemeris [Mars-Pluto] in *Synthesis & Counseling in Astrology* and in *Solar Arcs*, access to which is perhaps a thousand times faster than working through the computer!

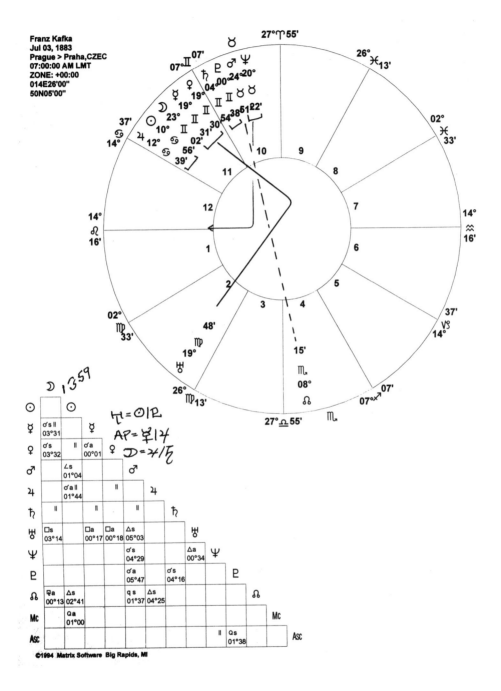

Franz Kafka
Jul 03, 1883
Prague > Praha,CZEC
07:00:00 AM LMT
ZONE: +00:00
014E26'00"
50N05'00"

©1994 Matrix Software Big Rapids, MI

- The southeastern hemisphere orientation suggests that Kafka may very well be swept away by events around him, that he may be pushed around—even victimized—by the world in which he traffics. This can be hurtful indeed to his nascent need to be appreciated, loved, and honored (the Leo Ascendant squared by Neptune); he might feel much suppression.

- Now, in our interpretation of horoscopic guidelines to follow on from assessment of hemisphere emphasis, we are watching for *echoes of this first impression* (they will always be there!). The Sun-Moon blend suggests that much sensitivity could be stirred up (Moon), worrying about emotional/family security (Sun); anxiety and nervous fragility may manifest as Kafka rushes around to find emotional anchor. The nervous system will be highly charged (Uranus square the Moon in Gemini; an intensive intrusion into the Sun-Moon blend).

- There are surely enormous parental problems to deal with, since all four(!) parental rulers are under high developmental tension.

- Kafka's mindset can be jarred deeply by all this self-worth anxiety (Mercury rules the 2nd *and* the 3rd and is squared by Uranus) and by the deep feeling that he is not lovable (Mercury also rules the 11th). The anxieties will all too easily be carried over into adult relationships, his relationship with the world (Uranus rules the 7th).

Please be aware of how much our preparation technique has already uncovered, all of which is most significant in Kafka's astrological portrait!

Now look at Pluto, natally jeopardized through the conjunction with Saturn (a very difficult, hard-work and struggle aspect[8]). Let us just move Pluto forward in generalized solar arc fashion, i.e., one degree for a year.[9]

As arcing Pluto "contacts" natal planets and angles, we *know* there will be major developments in his life, undoubtedly punctuating his vulnerabilities and the rigors of his existence, becoming more and more painful the older he becomes, the more mature he becomes in intelligence and perception. Pluto=Saturn at four and a half years of age.

---

8. This conjunction is certainly a sub-generational signal. All people Kafka's age, give or take three or four years, would have had this signature, and they were all caught up in the dreadful political, social, "racial" persecution tensions in turn-of-the-century central and eastern Europe.

9. Indeed, since Kafka was born between March and September, the arc accumulation will be "slow," accumulating one-degree/one-year error for every thirty years of life, in the degree-year generalization. Please see Tyl, *Solar Arcs* for full development.

Pluto =(semisquare) MC at twelve. Pluto=Mercury-Venus at nineteen. Pluto=Moon at twenty-three. Pluto=Sun at forty-one, when Kafka died.

Of course there were other arcs developing at the same time and those involving the angles will be all-important. For example, see MC=Neptune at twenty-three (at the same time as Pluto=Moon!). Note Uranus=IC-MC at thirty-nine at the same time as Pluto=Sun, coinciding with Kafka's illness with tuberculosis at thirty-nine (toward his death at forty-one). There is Asc=Neptune at age six at the same time as SA Mars=Pluto; Asc=Pluto at sixteen, Asc=Saturn at twenty (along with Pluto=Mercury-Venus, a complete breakdown of idealism).

This is how it works in our preparation. And it is much neater and cohesive when it is noted chronologically on the horoscope paper (as we will see many times later) than just listed textually here.

Let's zero in on Kafka's mortal illness and death period. Of course, this picture would be obvious a month, a year, or more before.

We know that critical illness is very frequently profiled by strong involvement of the Ascendant (the health center), the ruler of the 12th House, the Sun (life-giver), and almost always, the planet Pluto.[10]

For Kafka, those concomitants of critical illness are all present: SA Asc=Moon, ruler of the 12th; SA Pluto=Sun. As well: SA Uranus=IC-MC, and SA Neptune approaches very tightly the Aries Point of 00 Cancer (strong suppression—even defeat—of the ego). And at the same time, *transiting* Pluto at 10 Cancer was conjunct the Sun and *transiting* Saturn was at 27 Libra exactly upon the IC-MC axis.

Kafka had a natal vulnerability to problems with his lungs, which we see suggested through the square of Uranus to *Mercury* and to the Moon in *Gemini*, the Moon ruling the 12th House [developmental tension translated into somatic and systemic significance]. The very powerfully telling arcs and transits all came together upon this point of weakness as his system finally broke down under lifelong depression, extreme anxiety, and self-hate.[11]

---

10. Please see Tyl, *Astrological Timing of Critical Illness* for full development of this thesis.

11. Kafka's final words to his doctor, begging the doctor for an overdose of morphine, were "Kill me, or else you are a murderer."

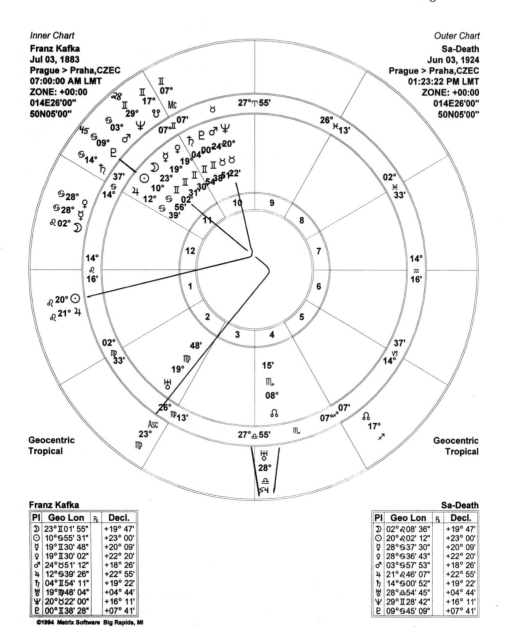

Inner Chart

Franz Kafka
Jul 03, 1883
Prague > Praha,CZEC
07:00:00 AM LMT
ZONE: +00:00
014E26'00"
50N05'00"

Outer Chart

Sa-Death
Jun 03, 1924
Prague > Praha,CZEC
01:23:22 PM LMT
ZONE: +00:00
014E26'00"
50N05'00"

Geocentric
Tropical

Geocentric
Tropical

Franz Kafka

Pl	Geo Lon	℞	Decl.
☽	23°♊01' 55"		+19° 47'
☉	10°♋55' 31"		+23° 00'
☿	19°♊30' 48"		+20° 09'
♀	19°♊30' 02"		+22° 20'
♂	24°♉51' 12"		+18° 26'
♃	12°♋39' 26"		+22° 55'
♄	04°♊54' 11"		+19° 22'
♅	19°♍48' 04"		+04° 44'
♆	20°♉22' 00"		+16° 11'
♇	00°♊38' 28"		+07° 41'

©1994 Matrix Software Big Rapids, MI

Sa-Death

Pl	Geo Lon	℞	Decl.
☽	02°♌08' 36"		+19° 47'
☉	20°♌02' 12"		+23° 00'
☿	28°♋37' 30"		+20° 09'
♀	28°♋36' 43"		+22° 20'
♂	03°♋57' 53"		+18° 26'
♃	21°♌46' 07"		+22° 55'
♄	14°♋00' 52"		+19° 22'
♅	28°♎54' 45"		+04° 44'
♆	29°♊28' 42"		+16° 11'
♇	09°♋45' 09"		+07° 41'

SUBTEXT AND GUIDING THOUGHTS

Our preparation process cannot just be a rote compilation of data. The astrologer's *thought process* is vitally important in the preparation of the horoscopic portrait. *From the very beginning of data organization, we need to think in terms of synthesis, within established patterns of human development.* Let's review part of the Kafka preparation with the mental *subtext* that could be going on as we work to bring the preparation process *to* life.

- SE hemisphere—*Potential victimization here. Getting pushed around. Tough times back then. What's the Ascendant saying? Yes, there's the Neptune square; suppression for sure. The hurting-Leo feel. It holds together.*

- The Sun-Moon blend—*So much nervous preoccupation about emotional/family security; really strong accents from Uranus. Checking self-worth and mindset: Mercury on fire...this tension, maybe a clash with idealism in the background from Mercury-Venus?*

- Parental underpinning—*All four parental rulers are tense! Mars quindecile node, father-mother "at it" too. Tough stuff. Alienation usually follows; echoes of hemisphere emphasis and wounded Ascendant. It all fits.*

- Feeling unlovable—*We can expect this for sure, and there it is: Mercury a major key here, obviously. Also ruling the 11th. Tremendous anxiety about being lovable; and that's carried over to adult relationships...the Uranus factor. It continues to fit.*

- Key midpoints—*There's Moon=Jupiter/Saturn: he's searching for purpose; my goodness! What support and outlet does he have except for this hyperactive mind? Uranus=Sun/Pluto: is he driving for reform, rebellion? AP=Mercury/Jupiter: this is the signature of the writer; the Mercury prominence as well. Does he fight back as a social critic? How does it all fit in with... with idealism? Is that the culprit? Is idealism shattered in his real life? AP=Sun/Mercury-Venus...it gets crushed somehow: the Uranus squares, and the Neptune square to the Ascendant. He's in a subgroup of sufferers: that's what the Saturn-Pluto conjunction must be saying.*

This process of analysis is a long, long way from isolating horoscope parts and dwelling on them, like "What's it mean when you have a stellium in the 11th House?" Or "Won't the Jupiter conjunction with the Sun save the day?" Those questions stop cold our progress to the whole-view. All too often the emerging astrologer finds security in being measurement-bound, enslaved by this-means-that specifics, expecting astrology to tell every detail of life. The measurement guidelines must be brought to the client for humanization; *for the horoscope to have meaning, it must be related to the reality being lived by the client.*

Measurements must never substitute for intelligence, for the active mind following astrological guidelines with sophistication into the patterns of life development. Creative management of measurement routings brings a portrait into being. We know about life, we anticipate behavioral reactions, and we see how they all fit together. *How do a particular horoscope's guidelines fit known patterns of life development,* which we can see from the developmental tension profiles of planets ruling the houses of life experience?

Interaction with Our Parents

We need our parents for three things. First, *nurturance* (shelter and protection, food, caring and love). Second, *modeling* (how man and woman interact, husband-wife, father-mother). Third, *contrast* (with self-contentment and a modicum of fulfillment, we can look back objectively and appreciate the problems from which we have come).

When there is acute or chronic frustration with either the first or second consideration, development tends to become fixated at that stage to get it sorted out. Kafka, for example, was fixated on the second consideration: how to behave with alienating parents alienated from each other; how to function as a despised German Jew in a maelstrom of political and religious upset. *It is very easy for the Self to get lost within the parental model.*[12]

We must remember that we achieve our individual identity through parental filters. Our parents' identities were achieved through *their* parental filters. We are raised to be like them. Very little about us as individuals is respected or even acknowledged, all too often. We long for support, approval, love. We "marry" our mothers and fathers when we must in order to settle unfinished business.

Reigning Need Fulfillment

The Moon in Aries (the need to be *numero uno),* in Leo (the need to be applauded, respected, honored), or in Sagittarius (the need to have one's opinions respected) energizes so very much of all our life behavior. The simple focused statements about these reigning needs have been distilled through thousands and thousands of horoscopes. They are emphatically reliable. *If their registration is not immediately discernible, it is not that the astrology is misguided; instead, there is a "plumbing" problem in the life, so to speak; the behaviors working to fulfill that*

---

12. Kafka's famous story *Metamorphosis,* wherein a man gradually and horrifically becomes a giant insect, a cockroach, is regarded in every detail as autobiographical metaphor.

need are diverted, constricted, suppressed somehow. The need is having difficulty showing itself. In the Fire signs, these needs are indomitably individual (ego-orientated) in reference; they must be freed for fulfillment by the job situation, through improved family recognition, through expanded communication outlet.

The Moon in Libra (the need to be appreciated as fair, attractive, and interesting), in Aquarius (to be socially significant, unusual, helping others), or Gemini (to be bright, clever, scintillating, informed, intense) energizes so very much of our life behavior. In the Air signs these needs focus strongly on other people—they are society-dependent for fulfillment. They must be freed for fulfillment by the job situation, through improved family recognition, through communication outlet.

The Moon in Cancer (the need for emotional security, especially in the family), in Scorpio (the need to be in control, to be regarded as deep, significant, reliable, self-sufficient, right), or in Pisces (the need to identify the ideal, to understand impressions, to work with the intangible) is emotionally based to a great extent. The need pressures in these Water signs must be freed for fulfillment by the job situation, through improved family recognition, through communication outlet.

The Moon in Capricorn (the reigning need to administrate progress, to make things happen), in Taurus (the need to build security, to keep things as they are or to change them to how they are supposed to be…often a passionately determined pursuit), or in Virgo (the need to be correct, exact, insightful) is deeply task-oriented. Moving things along is extremely important because it reflects how effective one is. These Earth sign need behaviors must be freed for fulfillment by the job situation, through improved family recognition, through communication outlet.

Self-Worth Anxiety

When there is strong self-worth anxiety in our lives—in the main, when the significator of the 2nd House (and/or the 11th) is under high developmental tension, probably accompanying the guidelines of Saturn-℞ phenomenology, nodal axis involvements, Pluto in strong aspect to the Sun (stifling) or Moon (mother), the Ascendant ruler jeopardized—we must know that this condition, often strongly self-deprecating, can be dangerous. Self-worth is an aspect crucial to our mental well-being. This is because disturbances in our relationship with ourselves permeate all we do, all we hope to become, all that others see of us.

With the 2nd House always square to the 11th, we know there is a strong dynamic tension between our self-worth profile and our feelings of being lovable, our ability to have friends. If we are awash with problems with ourselves, can we expect others to want to be close with us? If we can't receive love, how can we feel comfortable giving it? There are people who cannot accept a compliment...because they don't trust it. What does that do for socialization? Why is that so? What was the modeling situation in the home that produced this way of behaving? Why so much self-isolating defensiveness?

What do constant put-downs do to one's sexual confidence and response profile? The 2nd House is also square to the 5th and opposed the 8th.

Defensiveness

When we see a Grand Trine among planets in the horoscope, we are seeing a classic defense mechanism: a closed circuit of practical (in Earth), motivational (in Fire), Social (in Air), or emotional (in Water) *self-sufficiency*. The Grand Trine isolates and protects by assembling the symbols of behavioral faculties to form a three-sided moat surrounding our ego castle. Very little traffic comes in or goes out. We are safe.[13]

But, we must know that this defensive construct works particularly *against* relationships. While that may keep us safe, it also keeps us to ourselves. Life implodes.

With the eastern hemisphere emphasis, we also see a defensive posture throughout the life.

We must ask "Why?" The defensive structures are there because they are *needed*. Why are they needed? What are the tie-ins with the parental structures? The Self-worth structures? What is the person afraid of in making relationships?

Mindset, Depression, Siblings

These considerations have a 3rd House focus. How we think emerges in our early development in terms of our natal Mercury and its condition: how we need to think in order to be efficient in helping our behaviors to fulfill our reigning need. That early mind set is influenced enormously by our parents, their modeling, AND by our interaction with our brothers and sisters. Each sibling works to carve out a niche in the family structure. The more parental conflict there is early on, the more the child espouses independent behavior and rebels against authority and leadership in adult life. Sibling rivalry is a very real family phenomenon and can condition our mindset, including our self-worth, for our entire lifetime.

---

13. Full development of the Grand Trine concept is presented in Tyl, *Synthesis & Counseling in Astrology*, pages 284–302. Measurement of the Grand Trine may feature Ascendant, Midheaven, or node at one of the points.

For example, when a strong planet conjoins or squares the Ascendant closely, we can expect birth trauma, a difficult time with the birth, or extremely difficult circumstances surrounding the birth, i.e., the child was not wanted, perhaps there had been attempts to abort the fetus, etc.[14] When our client *knows* this(!), we must ask *how* does he or she know this. We discover that a parent told them *punitively* or told a sibling who passed it on punitively to feather the sibling's nest in the family structure.

Depression is rampant. The World Health Organization estimates that on any given day 121 million people worldwide suffer from depression. Children exhibit depression at nearly ten times the rate of previous generations. Depression is strongly linked with obesity and with cancer.[15]

We must know that negative thoughts disturb heart rhythm, the immune functions, blood pressure, and clotting in ways that correlate with higher chances for heart attack.[16]

Facial muscles that are inert, robbing the face of expression, or the potential for expression, are something to note [that's how we are seen; how we communicate our persona]. How did they get that way? Was this the way of the face the person saw most often as a child? The mother?

Our internal mood set (certainly related to the mindset) is influenced greatly by mimicry; we imitate the moods of others. Our parents. Our siblings.

This knowledge and much more are the basis for making creative connections in horoscope analysis during the consultation discussion. Being prepared to listen for and to make these connections is vital to the artist analyst. Many, many more (several *hundreds* of these considerations) are presented in Tyl, *The Creative Astrologer*, pages 188–204 and 222–234.

MEASURING TIMES TO COME

Times to come are times that were. We develop and carry imprints of our development with us into continual forward passage within future time. Knowing that past developmental imprint and how it is set by events, value judgments, and behavioral patterns reveals individuation.

---

14. Often accompanied by a close Sun-Moon square in the birth horoscope, suggesting that the parents were strongly at odds when the child was born.

15. Persaud, pages 52–54 and more.

16. These findings are reflected in the high developmental tension tie between the 3rd House and the 12th, those zones of experience.

For example, if we have a horoscope with an eastern orientation (defensiveness) and a Mars in the 12th House, say, 8 degrees above the Ascendant, ruling the 10th, we can expect much anger to have been born at age eight. Something occurred at eight, probably in relation to one of the parents, probably the father, that hurt, that threatened emotional security (assuming a Cancer Ascendant here in the example, with an Aries Midheaven).

The arc to the Ascendant would be ever so clear, and we would look into the eighth year for a trigger transit to help us zero in on the month(s) of occurrence. We may see transiting Uranus on the fourth cusp in the summer of the eighth year. This would suggest a major relocation, probably due to the father's change of job, of status. The child would feel uprooted. But why would he or she be so angry about this occurrence?

The answer could well be within the Saturn-retrograde phenomenology or natal Saturn square the Sun, for example, that may be present: an empty, aloof relationship with the father, but a grandfather who took over that fatherly function, who was deeply indulgent with the child. With the grandfather being a father-surrogate, the move, which would take the child away from the grandfather, perhaps quite a distance, represents deprivation and aloneness, etc. That *is* something to be angry about, and the imprint of this event perhaps suggests, for much time to come, that emotional security, for the child/adult, *can never be reliable.*

As another example, with the arcing Mars coming to the Ascendant, say, in the springtime of the eighth year, this Mars could enter a square with natal Pluto, ruling the 5th. The ephemeris could show that, at the same time, transiting Saturn would be conjoining natal Venus! That would be the time when the arc would be activated, as it were. This time would not be a relocation, but a highly probable time of sexual abuse, molestation, something untoward about sexual propriety. Perhaps it involved the father; perhaps the child told the mother, but she did nothing about it. That is something to be hurt and angry about. The imprint of this time could easily suggest much difficulty brought forward with regard to issues of trust, love, relationship, and more.

Our orientation for this preparation work is simply to note on the natal horoscope arcs that leap out clearly, especially within the first twelve to eighteen years. Then we check those years consecutively within the abbreviated ephemeris—and this is done so quickly—watching as well, in between the notated arcs periods, for major transits to angles, the Sun and the Moon, and, as a scenario of development evolves, to the ruler of the House that may be critically emblematic of that development, e.g. the ruler of the 7th if relationship issues dominate the life.

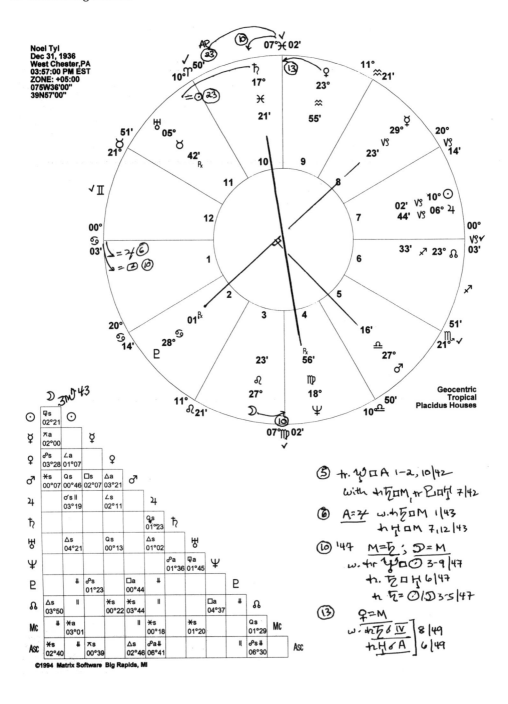

Noel Tyl
Dec 31, 1936
West Chester,PA
03:57:00 PM EST
ZONE: +05:00
075W36'00"
39N57'00"

Geocentric
Tropical
Placidus Houses

©1994 Matrix Software Big Rapids, MI

Case Study: Noel Tyl

Let us look at our preparation technique within my horoscope: for my first, most forma-tive fourteen years of life…how to prepare that quickly and meaningfully…and then for my "future" years as if we were doing the analysis three years ago, in 2002.[17]

The preparation guideline-marks made on the horoscope, with amplified notes below the wheel, are offered for the key ages suggested by strong arcs and transits.

Here are the thoughts behind these parts of the preparation process:

1. We see from our general age markings of major Arcs, ages six, ten (three of them!), and thirteen. Those will be our first targets to include any major transits in parallel time development.

2. [See ephemeris panels for 1942 and 1943.] Transiting Neptune is squaring the Ascen-dant in 2–3, 10/42 [February–March, and October 1942], age six (just before my sixth birthday)]; that's a loneliness-aloneness background (the Neptune transit) but, at the same time, for Asc=Jupiter, a rewarding personal projection (7th House). We can sur-mise that I probably was doing well in school but was bewildered on the home front.]

3. At ages five and six,[18] transiting Saturn squared my Midheaven in July 1942, and then transiting Uranus did the same in July and December 1943 and May 1944, then *with tr Saturn on my Ascendant!* The major suggestion for this time was a major move for my family, with me being bewildered (tr Neptune square Ascendant) at starting school in a town thirty minutes away by bus, taking that ride alone each way every day. I didn't know where I belonged.

   Additionally, undoubtedly, my parents were feuding (Midheaven tensions; the sta-tus of my family). Finally, I excelled at school from the very beginning (Asc=Jupiter).

4. The arcs at age ten—MC=Saturn, Moon=MC, and Asc=Sun—carry much weight. The "significant family development" (MC=Saturn) was my father leaving the home. We can note the trigger transits to that occurrence: which took place in July 1947. [See especially transiting Saturn= (square) Sun/Moon as echo of MC=Saturn.]

---

17. Using my horoscope and these time frames allows us maximum reality corroboration in relation to the measurements.

18. For the horoscope preparation notes made by hand, I recommend putting personal age numbers inside a circle to separate those references from degree numbers or years; Roman numerals for the houses, except A for Ascendant and M for Midheaven.

1942						
MONTH	MARS LONG	JUPITER LONG	SATURN LONG	URANUS LONG	NEPTUNE LONG	PLUTO LONG
Jan	25 ♈	13 ♊	22 ♉	27 ♉	00 ♎	05 ♌
Feb	10 ♉	11	22	26	00	04
Mar	26	12	23	27	29 ♍	04
Apr	15 ♊	16	26	28	28	04
May	03 ♋	21	29	29	27	04
Jun	22	28	03 ♊	01 ♊	27	04
Jul	10 ♌	05 ♋	07	03	27	05
Aug	00 ♍	12	10	04	28	05
Sep	19	18	13	05	29	06
Oct	09 ♎	22	12	04	00 ♎	07
Nov	29	25	11	04	01	07
Dec	20 ♏	25	09	02	02	07

1943						
MONTH	MARS LONG	JUPITER LONG	SATURN LONG	URANUS LONG	NEPTUNE LONG	PLUTO LONG
Jan	11 ♐	22 ♋	07 ♊	01 ♊	02 ♎	07 ♌
Feb	04 ♑	18	06	01	02	06
Mar	24	15	06	01	01	05
Apr	18 ♒	16	08	02	00	05
May	10 ♓	19	11	03	00	05
Jun	03 ♈	24	15	05	29 ♍	05
Jul	25	00 ♌	20	07	29	06
Aug	16 ♉	07	23	08	00 ♎	07
Sep	04 ♊	14	25	09	01	08
Oct	17	19	27	09	03	08
Nov	22	24	26	08	03	09
Dec	15	27	24	07	04	09

The Moon=MC[19] suggests so strongly that my needs were screaming for attention: the reigning need to be appreciated, respected, and helped with ego development and bloom.

The Ascendant=Sun arc suggested that there was certainly some fine reward potential for personal recognition within this time of upheaval. There would be "personality clarification" for sure. One thinks of the phrase, "best thing that ever could have happened at that time."

---

19. Actually the IC, but in solar arc practice we refer to the Midheaven from the IC and to the Ascendant from the Descendant, for simplification.

1948					
	MARS	JUPITER	SATURN	URANUS	NEPTUNE	PLUTO
MONTH	LONG	LONG	LONG	LONG	LONG	LONG
Jan	07 ♍	15 ♐	22 ♌	24 ♊	13 ♎	15 ♌
Feb	04	21	20	22	13	14
Mar	23 ♌	26	18	22	12	13
Apr	18	29	16	23	12	13
May	24	29	16	24	11	13
Jun	06 ♍	26	17	25	10	13
Jul	21	22	20	27	10	13
Aug	09 ♎	19	24	29	11	14
Sep	28	19	28	00 ⊗	11	15
Oct	19 ♏	22	01 ♍	01	13	16
Nov	11 ♐	27	04	00	14	16
Dec	03 ♑	03 ♑	06	29 ♊	15	17

1949					
	MARS	JUPITER	SATURN	URANUS	NEPTUNE	PLUTO
MONTH	LONG	LONG	LONG	LONG	LONG	LONG
Jan	27 ♑	10 ♑	07 ♍	28 ♊	15 ♎	16 ♌
Feb	21 ♒	17	04	27	15	15
Mar	14 ♓	23	02	27	15	15
Apr	08 ♈	29	00	27	14	14
May	01 ♉	02 ♒	29 ♌	28	13	14
Jun	24	02	00 ♍	29	13	14
Jul	15 ♊	00	02	01 ⊗	12	15
Aug	06 ⊗	26 ♑	06	03	13	16
Sep	26	23	09	04	14	17
Oct	15 ♌	23	13	05	15	18
Nov	03 ♍	25	16	05	16	18
Dec	19	00 ♒	19	04	17	18R

5. Then at age thirteen, we see Venus=MC with *transiting Saturn conjunct the fourth cusp* and *transiting Uranus conjunct the Ascendant* (both angles involved simultaneously). See the ephemeris panels for 1948 and 1949.

My life changed completely with my stepfather-to-be moving in to live with us in the late spring in 1949, and his marriage to my mother six days before my thirteenth birthday. This was the biggest reward turn of my young life.

And so the preparation can go. The eye easily sees SA Saturn=Sun (from Saturn's position arced to 10 Aries) at age twenty-three. Additionally, note how adding 23 degrees/years to the Midheaven brings the MC to the Aries Point; and also Venus=Saturn! At that same time, transiting Saturn was crossing my seventh cusp in September 1959 and conjoining my Sun in January 1960. Those measurements signify my change of life course from music management and promotion to becoming an opera singer myself! This decision affected my entire life thereafter.

	1959					
MONTH	MARS LONG	JUPITER LONG	SATURN LONG	URANUS LONG	NEPTUNE LONG	PLUTO LONG
Jan	17 ♉	24 ♏	29 ♐	16 ♌	07 ♏	04 ♍
Feb	26	29	03 ♑	14	07	03
Mar	09 ♊	01 ♐	05	13	07	03
Apr	25	02	07	12	06	02
May	12 ♋	29 ♏	07	12	05	02
Jun	00 ♌	25	06	13	05	02
Jul	18	23	03	14	04	02
Aug	07 ♍	22	01	16	04	03
Sep	27	25	00	18	05	04
Oct	16 ♎	29	01	20	06	05
Nov	07 ♏	05 ♐	03	21	07	06
Dec	28	12	06	21	08	06

	1960					
MONTH	MARS LONG	JUPITER LONG	SATURN LONG	URANUS LONG	NEPTUNE LONG	PLUTO LONG
Jan	20 ♐	19 ♐	09 ♑	21 ♌	09 ♏	06 ♍
Feb	13 ♐	25	13	19	09	05
Mar	05 ♒	00 ♑	16	18	09	05
Apr	29	03	18	17	08	04
May	22 ♓	03	18	17	08	04
Jun	16 ♈	01	18	18	07	04
Jul	08 ♉	27 ♐	16	19	06	04
Aug	29	24	13	21	06	05
Sep	19 ♊	24	12	23	07	06
Oct	05 ♋	26	12	24	08	07
Nov	16	01 ♐	14	25	09	08
Dec	18	07	16	26	10	08

Most quickly, with eye experience, we can jump way into the future as well. For example, by arcing the Sun (and Jupiter) to the Midheaven [20 degrees to complete Capricorn plus 30 through Aquarius, plus 7 into Pisces]: 57 degree/years, we can anticipate a time of enormous "ego recognition, potential glory, unusual success, fulfillment." This was the time when my astrology career was in high gear all over the world and when *Synthesis & Counseling in Astrology* was published, and much more.

In routine preparation, the years would be filled in from the time of my mother's re-marriage, through years of opera performance to my retirement from the opera world, and into full-time work in the world of astrology. The preparation would be guided by *angular transits and major transits to the Sun or Moon.* The eye will not as easily capture the middle years of rapport arc measurements—they get busy and the number-crunching can be difficult—but we learn *to know that those arcs are there behind key angular transits.* The strong angular transits and those transits to the Sun or Moon and key ruling planets guide preparation perfectly. *They all do go together!*

During the consultation, at its climax, as we focus on the present time frame and, say, two years into the future, we need to be more exacting with measurements. We prepare a double-ringed horoscope for the consultation date; it helps us see things dramatically. *From this drawing, we can generalize backward in time and forward in time.*

We are looking at the Tyl horoscope (next page) as if our consultation were taking place early in January 2003. The arced positions of the planets tell us much about the im-mediate past and the immediate future, just as the *natal* horoscope projected so clearly the key developmental events into the early years.

- Mars=Asc (on the 7th cusp) was exact four years earlier than the consultation. [Make sure you see that and understand it perfectly.] This arc that has already taken place makes a clear suggestion about marital tension in 1999, four years earlier (when SA Mars was at 00 Capricorn). This leads us to see SA Uranus opposed the Sun two years later (from 10 Cancer) in 2001. That period of time also saw tr Neptune=Sun/Moon 3–8/99 with transiting Jupiter-Saturn=Venus in spring '00.

We would have had to inquire about the condition of the marriage *leading up to the con-sultation time* and even consider its dissolution around June 2003, with transiting Saturn conjoining the Ascendant. This was a very powerful measurement group.

But, practical reality considerations are vitally important too: the people involved with this situation are sixty-six years old at that time. Does one dissolve a marriage easily at that age? Do values change under duress differently than they would, for example, for a couple in their thirties?

Then, looking ahead, we see the mighty arcs of Sun and Jupiter over Saturn speaking strongly and well about career performance and career longevity. The man with his all-im-portant Moon in Leo would not want to jeopardize that! But the transit of Uranus over the Midheaven (2005–06) would promise another opportunity or necessity for big change—

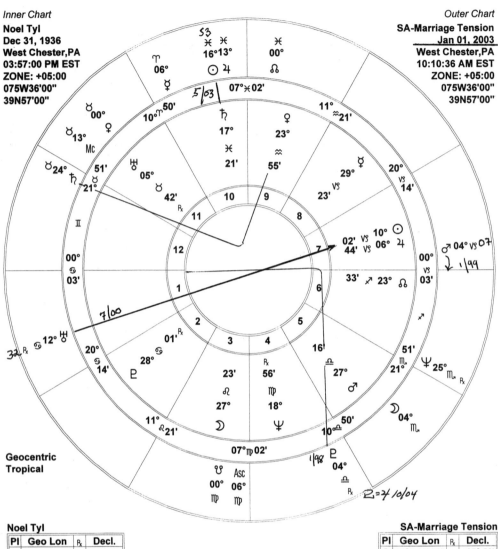

Inner Chart

Noel Tyl
Dec 31, 1936
West Chester, PA
03:57:00 PM EST
ZONE: +05:00
075W36'00"
39N57'00"

Outer Chart

SA-Marriage Tension
Jan 01, 2003
West Chester, PA
10:10:36 AM EST
ZONE: +05:00
075W36'00"
39N57'00"

**Geocentric
Tropical**

Noel Tyl

Pl	Geo Lon	Rx	Decl.
☽	27° ♌ 23' 02"		+07° 58'
☉	10° ♑ 02' 25"		- 23° 04'
☿	29° ♑ 23' 27"		- 21° 05'
♀	23° ♒ 55' 08"		- 15° 11'
♂	27° ♎ 16' 28"		- 09° 04'
♃	06° ♑ 43' 53"		- 23° 12'
♄	17° ♓ 20' 32"		- 06° 55'
♅	05° ♉ 41' 38"	Rx	+12° 59'
♆	18° ♍ 56' 09"	Rx	+05° 21'
♇	28° ♋ 00' 55"	Rx	+23° 04'

©1994 Matrix Software Big Rapids, MI

SA-Marriage Tension

Pl	Geo Lon	Rx	Decl.
☽	04° ♏ 13' 50"		+07° 58'
☉	16° ♓ 53' 13"		- 23° 04'
☿	06° ♈ 14' 15"		- 21° 05'
♀	00° ♉ 45' 56"		- 15° 11'
♂	04° ♑ 07' 16"		- 09° 04'
♃	13° ♓ 34' 42"		- 23° 12'
♄	24° ♉ 11' 21"		- 06° 55'
♅	12° ♋ 32' 26"	Rx	+12° 59'
♆	25° ♏ 46' 58"	Rx	+05° 21'
♇	04° ♎ 51' 43"	Rx	+23° 04'

			1999			
MONTH	MARS LONG	JUPITER LONG	SATURN LONG	URANUS LONG	NEPTUNE LONG	PLUTO LONG
Jan	18 ♎	22 ♓	27 ♈	11 ≈	01 ≈	09 ♐
Feb	02 ♏	27	28	13	02	10
Mar	10	04 ♈	01 ♉	14	03	10
Apr	11	11	03	16	04	10
May	02	18	07	17	04	10
Jun	25 ♎	25	11	17	04	09
Jul	29	00 ♉	14	16	04	08
Aug	11 ♏	04	16	15	03	08
Sep	29	05	17	14	02	08
Oct	19 ♐	03	16	13	02	08
Nov	11 ♑	29 ♈	14	13	02	09
Dec	04 ≈	26	12	13	02	10

			2000			
MONTH	MARS LONG	JUPITER LONG	SATURN LONG	URANUS LONG	NEPTUNE LONG	PLUTO LONG
Jan	28 ≈	25 ♈	10 ♉	15 ≈	03 ≈	11 ♐
Feb	22 ♓	28	11	16	04	12
Mar	14 ♈	03 ♉	12	18	05	13
Apr	07 ♉	09	15	20	06	13
May	28	16	19	21	07	12
Jun	20 ♊	23	23	21	06	12
Jul	10 ♋	00 ♊	27	20	06	11
Aug	00 ♌	06	29	19	05	10
Sep	20	10	01 ♊	18	04	10
Oct	09 ♍	11	01	17	04	11
Nov	28	10	29 ♉	17	04	11
Dec	16 ♎	06	27	17	04	13

and that change was a change of home, which was a critical decision within the marriage climate. That change of home changed the couple's fortunes; it occurred precisely with transiting Uranus' last touch to the Midheaven, November 2005.[20]

In consultation conversation, many details and values come forward, and they are charted throughout the years of life development, with many creative connections made in the process. [We will "hear" five verbatim consultation transcripts later in this book, and all of that will become clear.]

---

20. The full details of that move are presented in the Appendix as highly detailed instruction for making a prediction strategically, for selling a house.

Female

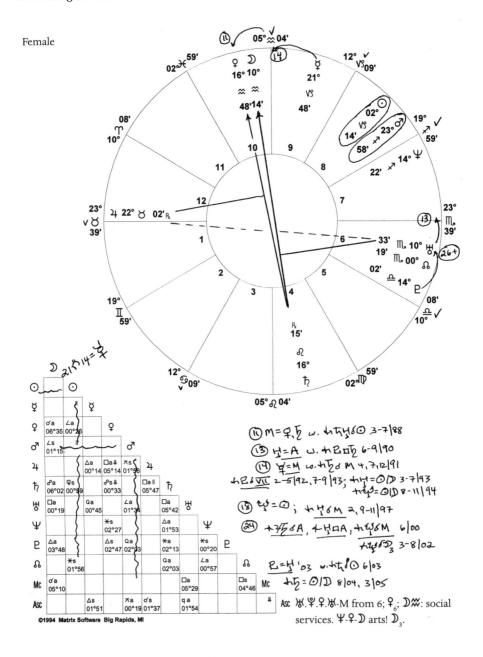

©1994 Matrix Software Big Rapids, MI

We are seeing gradually how to prepare the time development overview, following major arcs in the formative years, then following major transits for the middle years [and with experience, the major arcs that pop into view], then returning to precision coordination of transits and arcs at the time of consultation for strategy into the near future.

The combination search (see pages 14–15) for the horoscope at hand guides us into keen measurement specifics for the two years (the recommended projection interval) ahead after consultation.

The Complete Work-Up

Let's now study the horoscope of a young woman at a major time of life development. What is her make-up? Through her development, what does she bring forward to the opportunities in the near future? What does she need to consider in the midst of the pressure?

- The hemisphere orientation is clearly to the west, perhaps with a lean to the southwest. This orientation is a clear echo of her "humanitarian" reigning need of the Moon in Aquarius. The administrative push behind fulfilling that need is clear through the Sun in Capricorn. *The lady needs to be significant in helping others.*

- The Sun is peregrine: this suggests that she will be quite set apart from the normal flow of things, perhaps easily taken advantage of (with the hemisphere emphasis so pronounced); she will march to a different drummer, not necessarily fully understanding the world as it goes, but surely harboring intense opinions about it (Mars in Sagittarius). This Mars is also peregrine and it is *oriental*[21] and will probably be converted into promotion energy for a "cause," serving the thrust of the Aquarian Moon.

- The altruistic persona emerging here is probably overcompensatory for the developmental tension contained in the Saturn-retrograde phenomenology: Saturn opposed Venus-Moon, the axis squared by Uranus, ruler of one arm of the parental axis [the Sun peregrine ruling the other arm]. The strong involvement of the Moon under this tension from Saturn-℞ and the Sun's highlighting of the 4th House introduce the mother strongly within the father situation we know to expect.

- The ruler of the 9th is under high developmental tension, suggesting that the education will have been interrupted. How will this loss of credentials inhibit the

---

21. Rising last before the Sun does in clockwise motion. See Tyl, *Synthesis & Counseling in Astrology,* page 497.

administrative-promotion push to fulfill the humanitarian needs, the special-service needs of the Moon in Aquarius?

- Three quintile measurements suggest the potential of high creativity, probably in music.[22]

- The quindecile from Uranus to the Ascendant (and, really, to Jupiter; i.e., the orb opens reasonably to admit this) suggests that the special individual appreciation she craves (through the reigning need of the Moon in Aquarius) should be, and will be accomplished sooner or later *through her professional work*: Uranus rules the Midheaven and is dispositor of the all-important Moon and Venus, ruler of the Ascendant. This focus will probably dominate her thoughts and plans.

The client corroborated all of these deductions at the beginning of the consultation. The observation about the parental tensions introduced discussion about the developmental chronology.

The father was "entirely passive," with the mother being dominant. This tells us that the parental modeling situation was poor, out of balance, and quite possibly worse. When my client was nine (Mars=Sun, ruler of the 4th), her mother joined the Navy. It was a terribly bewildering and lonely time.

For age eleven, we talked about her awareness of emotional tightening (the Midheaven "status" measurement coming into the emotional-tightness, deprivation axis, Venus-Saturn). She never ever heard from her parents that they loved her, etc. Her early teenage years were dreadfully alone, no recognition or encouragement whatsoever.

Age thirteen was "hazy" for her. Just dullness; no support; minimal opportunity; contrary to the measurements but consonant with her reality.

At fourteen, the Mercury arc to the Midheaven corresponded to her study of music and an intense study of astrology, finding herself through the astrological symobologies.

Through 1992–94, there was much upset and change, clearly keyed by the Pluto transit of an angle. The concomitant strong transits to the Sun/Moon midpoint promise relationship upheaval and confusion. And at ages sixteen–eighteen here we must be sensitive to her education being interrupted, as suggested by the natal horoscope.

---

22. This routing block with its special shorthand (in this footnote) captures the vocational profiling of the Midheaven Extension Process, presented in Tyl, *Vocations*: ♅.♇.♀.♅-M from 6; ♀₆; ☽♒: social services. Three quintiles, ♇-♀-☽₃, aesthetic communication.

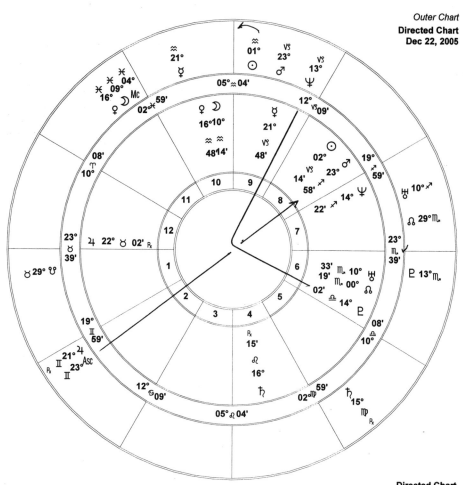

Directed Chart

Pl	Geo Lon	℞	Decl.
☽	09°♓46' 13"		- 12° 50'
☉	01°≈47' 02"		- 23° 25'
☿	21°≈20' 24"		- 22° 41'
♀	16°♓21' 02"		- 17° 40'
♂	23°♑31' 00"		- 23° 51'
♃	21°♊34' 44"	℞	+17° 18'
♄	15°♍47' 48"	℞	+16° 47'
♅	10°♐05' 22"		- 14° 34'
♆	13°♑54' 30"		- 21° 05'
♇	13°♏34' 20"		+10° 02'

Pl	Geo Lon	℞	Decl.
☽	10°≈13' 39"		- 12° 50'
☉	02°♑14' 28"		- 23° 25'
☿	21°♑47' 50"		- 22° 41'
♀	16°≈48' 28"		- 17° 40'
♂	23°♐58' 26"		- 23° 51'
♃	22°♉02' 11"	℞	+17° 18'
♄	16°♌15' 15"	℞	+16° 47'
♅	10°♏32' 48"		- 14° 34'
♆	14°♐21' 56"		- 21° 05'
♇	14°♎01' 46"		+10° 02'

At this time, the young lady quit school, before high school graduation, to get a job "to help with family support." Additionally, in her outreach for love and caring, she had a series of relationships: her first serious boyfriend, and her first girlfriend, beginning her bisexual orientation.

In 1997, individuation was finally starting to emerge: she got her first professional music work, got on stage for the first time. [Transiting Uranus conjunct the Midheaven.]

In 2000, it was a "fuzzy time" because of emotional aloneness (note tr Neptune conjunction the Midheaven), but she enjoyed a protracted music performance success in Tokyo! [Note Saturn's rulership of the 9th.]

This time ushered in two years of affluence. We can see how the Neptune symbology has developed from bewilderment to creativity, something that happens often with artistic people: the isolation turns into/allows artistic inspiration or support.

Now, in 2003, a very, very important measurement takes place, which should signal a tremendous overthrowing of her status quo, a major change of direction, especially with Uranus ruling her Midheaven and being so key within her horoscope. The lady met a businesswoman, a bit her senior, and at the same time, *started a social services nonprofit business designed to protect young women traveling in big cities at night.*

The female mate also provides monies to sustain the nonprofit business.

This is the bare-bones outline of analysis preparation and general consultation record.

Prediction Possibilities

While there *are* generalized energy correspondences that *can* be made with certain major projection measurements—like Uranus contact with the Ascendant (or really, any angle) by transit or arc: major disruption and change in geography and direction in life; secondary progressed Moon quadrature with natal Saturn, and the tr Saturn-return cycle: times of ambition's advance; Neptune and an Angle: aloneness, deep introspective bewilderment, suppression, ego wipe-out; Jupiter-Sun, reward; Uranus-Pluto, revolutionary change; Saturn-Pluto, loss; and more—the key thread that tightens the prediction focus is *common sense*, following along with a *reasonable* extension of the person's reality experience in advancing time.

An insurance executive experiencing a Neptune arc of his Venus is not going to drop everything and go to the Bolshoi theatre in Moscow to study ballet, even though Neptune development in the horoscope "on a good day" will suggest aesthetics and artistic inspiration!

An eight-year-old won't give birth (strong measurements to very young people still under the aegis of their parents are going to manifest more likely than not through the parents and reflect themselves in family status—the MC-IC axis).

Additionally, we must know that no measurement will correspond easily to dislodging someone from inactivity, from hermitic distance from the environment, or depressive boredom; *the individual must be involved with activity and interaction with the environment for things to happen, to develop.*

The key, key question for a client in order to introduce future time is, *"What do you project for yourself in the next six months to a year?"* This question asks about *the individual's involvement with personal progress*, with choice, with plans, with responsibilities, with dreams. Within the reply to this question, *we find the tenable significances of projected measurements.* We see how the future-time measurements enter into the client's plausibly projected reality experience.

In our double-ringed horoscope for this example we are preparing, we are alerted to two key arcs: Neptune=Pluto, ruler of the 7th. This suggests at best "creative enterprise," and at worst, "unusual problems in relationships," often related to peculiar (even otherworldly) experiences. This is a key strategy concern because the lady's mate is sustaining the business financially, but the relationship here is suggested to be "shaky."

The second key arc is Ascendant=Mars: "individual talents put into action."

The question arises—the challenge emerges—"How will/can the two potentials work out with each other?" Ideally, we would hope for creative enterprise with the partner to support individual talents put into action.

The combo-search shown here for our young lady client presents a lucid prediction possibility. With the understanding of the background development of her life which we have been preparing, the reality supporting these measurements is appreciated and the projections gain reliability.

We know that *two occupations* are clarified by the natal horoscope and corroborated by the client: creative work as a musician and overall direction of a program of public service. The consultation took place December 27, 2005.

Search From Nov 14, 2005 to Aug 20, 2006 GMT

Aspect	Date	Time	Event	Type	P1 Pos.	P2 Pos	E/X/L
♅ ---- SD	11-15-2005	09:50 pm	♅ SD	Tr-Na	06°♓51'		
♃ -- □ Mc	11-18-2005	04:18 pm	♃ □ Mc	Tr-Na	05°♏04'	05°♒04'	Exact
♂ -- ☍ ♅	11-21-2005	05:43 pm	♂ ☍ ♅	Tr-Na	10°♉33'℞	10°♏33'	Exact
♄ -- S℞	11-22-2005	06:54 am	♄ S℞	Tr-Na	11°♌19'℞		
♂ -- □ ☽	11-23-2005	02:01 am	♂ □ ☽	Tr-Na	10°♉14'℞	10°♒14'	Exact
♇ ---- □ ☽/♀	12-03-2005	07:07 am	♇ □ ☽/♀	Ar-Na	13°♏31'	13°♒31'	Exact
♇ ---- ☌ ♂	12-07-2005	11:05 am	♇ ☌ ♂	Tr-Na	23°♐58'	23°♐58'	Exact
♂ -- SD	12-10-2005	04:34 am	♂ SD	Tr-Na	08°♉14'		
♃ -- □ ☽	12-14-2005	10:33 am	♃ □ ☽	Tr-Na	10°♏14'	10°♒14'	Exact
♇ ---- ⚻ ♃/Mc	12-15-2005	08:43 pm	♇ ⚻ ♃/Mc	Ar-Na	13°♏33'	28°♓33'	Exact
♃ -- ☌ ♅	12-16-2005	03:43 am	♃ ☌ ♅	Tr-Na	10°♏33'	10°♏33'	Exact
♄ -- □ ♅	12-21-2005	07:51 am	♄ □ ♅	Tr-Na	10°♌33'℞	10°♏33'	Exact
♄ -- ☍ ☽	12-27-2005	02:43 am	♄ ☍ ☽	Tr-Na	10°♌14'℞	10°♒14'	Exact
♂ -- □ ☽	12-28-2005	06:20 am	♂ □ ☽	Tr-Na	10°♉14'	10°♒14'	Exact
♂ -- ☍ ♅	12-29-2005	05:44 pm	♂ ☍ ♅	Tr-Na	10°♉33'	10°♏33'	Exact
♆ ---- ☍ ♄	01-09-2006	06:11 am	♆ ☍ ♄	Tr-Na	16°♒15'	16°♌15'℞	Exact
♂ -- □ ♄	01-17-2006	04:24 pm	♂ □ ♄	Tr-Na	16°♉15'	16°♌15'℞	Exact
♂ -- □ ♀	01-19-2006	04:10 am	♂ □ ♀	Tr-Na	16°♉48'	16°♒48'	Exact
♃ -- □ ♄	01-21-2006	10:14 pm	♃ □ ♄	Tr-Na	16°♏15'	16°♌15'℞	Exact
Asc --- □ ♄/☊	01-23-2006	12:54 pm	Asc □ ♄/☊	Ar-Na	23°♊17'	23°♍17'	Exact
♆ ---- ☌ ♀	01-24-2006	02:17 pm	♆ ☌ ♀	Tr-Na	16°♒48'	16°♒48'	Exact
♃ -- □ ♀	01-26-2006	07:54 pm	♃ □ ♀	Tr-Na	16°♏48'	16°♒48'	Exact
♇ ---- ∠ ♀/♅	01-29-2006	02:19 pm	♇ ∠ ♀/♅	Ar-Na	13°♏41'	28°♐41'	Exact
♂ -- ☌ ♃	01-31-2006	11:10 pm	♂ ☌ ♃	Tr-Na	22°♉02'	22°♉02'℞	Exact
♆ ---- □ ♇	02-04-2006	09:52 am	♆ □ ♇	Ar-Na	14°♑02'	14°♎02'	Exact
♂ -- ☌ Asc	02-04-2006	02:05 pm	♂ ☌ Asc	Tr-Na	23°♉39'	23°♉39'	Exact
♃ -- S℞	03-04-2006	05:37 pm	♃ S℞	Tr-Na	18°♏52'℞		
♄ -- ☍ Mc	03-08-2006	04:26 pm	♄ ☍ Mc	Tr-Na	05°♌04'℞	05°♒04'	Exact
♄ -- ⚻ ☽/☿	03-10-2006	06:35 am	♄ ⚻ ☽/☿	Ar-Na	16°♍01'	01°♒01'	Exact
♂ -- ☍ ♆	03-17-2006	07:45 am	♂ ☍ ♆	Tr-Na	14°♊22'	14°♐22'	Exact
♇ ---- S℞	03-29-2006	10:29 am	♇ S℞	Tr-Na	26°♐45'℞		
♂ -- ☍ ♂	04-03-2006	12:25 pm	♂ ☍ ♂	Tr-Na	23°♊58'	23°♐58'	Exact
♄ -- SD	04-05-2006	12:08 pm	♄ SD	Tr-Na	04°♌23'		
♂ -- ∠ ♂/Asc	04-08-2006	00:42 am	♂ ∠ ♂/Asc	Ar-Na	23°♑49'	08°♓49'	Exact
♃ -- □ ♀	04-10-2006	12:00 pm	♃ □ ♀	Tr-Na	16°♏48'℞	16°♒48'	Exact
☉ - q ♅/Asc	04-14-2006	10:48 pm	☉ q ♅/Asc	Ar-Na	02°♒06'	17°♌06'	Exact
♃ -- □ ♄	04-16-2006	03:18 am	♃ □ ♄	Tr-Na	16°♏15'℞	16°♌15'℞	Exact
♂ -- ☍ ☉	04-17-2006	10:02 pm	♂ ☍ ☉	Tr-Na	02°♋14'	02°♑14'	Exact
♄ -- q ☽/♃	04-22-2006	03:58 am	♄ q ☽/♃	Ar-Na	16°♍08'	01°♈08'	Exact
♃ -- □ ☿/♃	04-23-2006	03:08 am	♃ □ ☿/♃	Ar-Na	21°♊55'	21°♓55'	Exact
♄ -- ☍ Mc	05-03-2006	09:46 am	♄ ☍ Mc	Tr-Na	05°♌04'	05°♒04'	Exact
♄ -- □ ☿/♅	05-06-2006	01:52 pm	♄ □ ☿/♅	Ar-Na	16°♍10'	16°♐10'	Exact
♂ -- □ ♇	05-08-2006	01:01 am	♂ □ ♇	Tr-Na	14°♋02'	14°♎02'	Exact
☊ --- □ ☉	05-08-2006	01:05 pm	☊ □ ☉	Tr-Na	02°♈14'℞	02°♑14'	Exact
♅ ---- □ ♆	05-20-2006	05:39 am	♅ □ ♆	Tr-Na	14°♓22'	14°♐22'	Exact
♂ -- ☍ ☿	05-21-2006	02:43 am	♂ ☍ ☿	Tr-Na	21°♋48'	21°♑48'	Exact
♆ ---- S℞	05-22-2006	09:24 am	♆ S℞	Tr-Na	19°♒49'℞		
♃ -- ☌ ♅	06-03-2006	12:36 pm	♃ ☌ ♅	Tr-Na	10°♏33'℞	10°♏33'	Exact
♂ -- □ ☊	06-04-2006	07:02 am	♂ □ ☊	Tr-Na	00°♌19'	00°♏19'℞	Exact
☊ --- ∠ ♄/♆	06-05-2006	06:23 am	☊ ∠ ♄/♆	Ar-Na	00°♐19'	15°♎19'	Exact
♃ -- □ ☽	06-07-2006	04:25 am	♃ □ ☽	Tr-Na	10°♏14'℞	10°♒14'	Exact
♂ -- ☍ Mc	06-12-2006	04:00 am	♂ ☍ Mc	Tr-Na	05°♌04'	05°♒04'	Exact
♅ ---- S℞	06-19-2006	04:32 am	♅ S℞	Tr-Na	14°♓44'℞		
♂ -- ☍ ☽	06-20-2006	03:48 pm	♂ ☍ ☽	Tr-Na	10°♌14'	10°♒14'	Exact
♂ -- □ ♅	06-21-2006	04:23 am	♂ □ ♅	Tr-Na	10°♌33'	10°♏33'	Exact
Mc --- ⚻ ♂/♄	06-21-2006	04:28 am	Mc ⚻ ♂/♄	Ar-Na	05°♓07'	20°♎07'	Exact
♂ -- ☌ ♄	06-30-2006	12:27 pm	♂ ☌ ♄	Tr-Na	16°♌15'	16°♌15'℞	Exact
♄ -- ☍ ☽	07-01-2006	08:24 am	♄ ☍ ☽	Tr-Na	10°♌14'	10°♒14'	Exact
♂ -- ☍ ♀	07-01-2006	10:07 am	♂ ☍ ♀	Tr-Na	16°♌48'	16°♒48'	Exact
♄ -- □ ♅	07-04-2006	01:43 am	♄ □ ♅	Tr-Na	10°♌33'	10°♏33'	Exact
♃ -- SD	07-06-2006	07:39 am	♃ SD	Tr-Na	08°♏59'		
♂ -- □ ♃	07-09-2006	10:11 pm	♂ □ ♃	Tr-Na	22°♌02'	22°♉02'℞	Exact
♂ -- □ Asc	07-12-2006	12:58 pm	♂ □ Asc	Tr-Na	23°♌39'	23°♉39'	Exact
♅ ---- □ ♆	07-19-2006	11:07 pm	♅ □ ♆	Tr-Na	14°♓22'℞	14°♐22'	Exact
♆ ---- ☌ ♂/Mc	07-30-2006	11:07 pm	♆ ☌ ♂/Mc	Ar-Na	14°♑31'	14°♑31'	Exact
♇ ---- ☌ ♆/♇	08-04-2006	07:58 am	♇ ☌ ♆/♇	Ar-Na	14°♏12'	14°♏12'	Exact
♃ -- □ ☽	08-04-2006	01:34 pm	♃ □ ☽	Tr-Na	10°♏14'	10°♒14'	Exact
♃ -- ☌ ♅	08-08-2006	04:43 am	♃ ☌ ♅	Tr-Na	10°♏33'	10°♏33'	Exact
♂ -- □ ♆	08-14-2006	04:46 pm	♂ □ ♆	Tr-Na	14°♍22'	14°♐22'	Exact
♄ -- ☌ ♄	08-18-2006	11:15 am	♄ ☌ ♄	Tr-Na	16°♌15'	16°♌15'℞	Exact

consultation

♆♇ = ♇₇

tr♄☌IV 2nd "hit"

tr♄☌IV final

tr♄☌♄₉

- There's a suggestion here that much publicity has surrounded your work lately; looks good!—[Paraphrased responses] *Yes, there's been much publicity.*

- Publicity about your music work or the public service company?—*The public service company.* [Is the environment making a decision here?]

- And there it seems that your personal relationship is shaky, right in the middle of all this [SA Neptune=Pluto, ruler of the 7th].—*Yes, that's my business partner, and, as you know, we're also romantically involved. But while the business part is strong, the emotional part is rocky at the moment.*

- Well, the relationship has got to be defined strongly and clearly [offsetting the Neptune] so that the *both of you* are comfortable and productive. Much is at stake now. One of the biggest changes of direction and/or level in your life to date is about to take place (the transiting Saturn conjunction with the fourth cusp and the transiting Saturn return); we don't want anything to jeopardize it. I think this big, life-focus change will take place between May and August next year, 2006. This is the build-up now. *Well, I feel it too, and I'm afraid....*

- Let me suggest that it's not something to be afraid of; it's something to know about and to strategize for: you've got to decide...and you *will now*...to concentrate your life work on the public service dimension, and let the music work slide to hobby status. Your environment—the publicity acclaim, your future plans for the service development—has determined that that's the course to follow. I think you will do this, I think you'll love doing this! *I think you're right.*

- One more question on this, please: is there anything "international" about the public service company outreach? [Saturn, so active here, rules the client's 9th House.] *Yes! Our publicity has reached around the globe! There are plans to...*

This was enormously corroborating dialogue, for both of us. Everything slipped into place. The Saturn return dimension was clarified for highest level fulfillment; the hard work and reward dimensions were clearly and reasonably indicated. We made a date to talk again in three months to follow up (or earlier, of course, should things start to pop).[23]

---

23. Of course, there was considerably more discussion about these points and choices of strategies, especially about clarification of the very important relationship. Only the essential progress of the discussion is noted here for our learning of the process.

In other words, *the client's reality was pushed forward in terms of the astrological guide-lines exhibiting themselves in her life.* At this point in the consultation, much was brought forward about themes of insecurity, aloneness, fractured relationships, and lack of cre-dentialization (interrupted education), undermining vocational confidence. All of these considerations would have to be consciously weighed; *they focused on the business/personal relationship at the heart of things.* How was this to be managed? If the personal dimension destroyed the business dimension, the future would be terribly compromised. This was the danger symbolized within Neptune.

PREPARATION REVIEW

Our preparation process fills in a mechanical frame with the beginnings of subjective sub-stance. The measurement outline begins to become an experiential portrait.

With our understanding of aspects in terms of varying degrees of developmental ten-sion (different colorations), we are able to glean greatest meaning from the aspect grid. We direct our computer to give us measurements that are the most meaningful in life development, groomed within the parameters of orb and punctuated by the incisive, oc-casional statements of peregrination. The measurements give high visibility to classic structures suggesting idealization, defensive self-containment, victimization, over-exten-sion, and unfinished business in the early home, creativity, obsession, rewards, and more. As the measurements are transferred to the chart wheel, we see the first impression of the horoscope portrait finding specific behavioral echoes throughout developmental experi-ence and time.

Midpoints presented in the 90°-sort reiterate the basic aspect structures but often add incidentals that can become major statements in the portrait. Above all, the Sun/Moon midpoint takes its place as a measurement of great importance.

As we begin initial analysis, psychological need theory is easily laid over the patterned symbols, with the life-energy of the Sun blending with the reigning need symbol of the Moon to animate the portrait. Tension networks among the planets introduce interaction patterns among the houses they rule, and we see the networks of experiential concerns that shape development to varying degrees. Special brush strokes of greatest importance come forward: Saturn-℞ phenomenology, the nodal axis, the quindecile aspect, the quin-tile, the Grand Trine defensive structures, and more.

Using *rapport* measurements—the generalized abbreviation of solar arc measurements—we are able to see times past in earliest development. We quickly take in considerations of parental interaction, self-worth anxiety, sibling relationships, defensiveness, relationship tensions, mindset disturbances, education, and much more.

We extend these abbreviated measurements into times to come as well.

Then a finer tuning of measurements takes place using the abbreviated Ephemeris to relate major transits to background arc pictures. Holistically, knowing much about life and behavior, we begin to see the developmental extensions that bring measurements literally and figuratively to life.

This preparation process is conducted *the same way with every horoscope*. It becomes a routine of expertise that supports great analytical security. With experience, the process can be put into a forty-minute time frame quite easily for a life-overview of fifty to sixty years. The process is shorter for younger clients, a bit longer for older clients.

3 PRE-CONSULTATION IMAGE-MAKING
—WHAT CAN BE ACCOMPLISHED

When someone calls an astrologer for an appointment, the person usually has special concerns about something in their experience, past, present, or future. Clients are not just "curious" any more; curiosity about astrology has faded, as circumspection and appreciation of astrology and what it "does" have become more known to the public, more responsibly represented.

MAKING THE APPOINTMENT

The person calling is particularly sensitive—it is a significant moment to telephone an astrologer for an appointment. The person is perhaps strongly preoccupied with worries, with pressures to make a decision; the person is entering uncharted territory with feelings, questions, and apprehensions; the person is always vulnerable, emotionally and intellectually. The only security the person has in phoning the astrologer could be attributed to a referral or could have been established through familiarity with the astrologer's reputation, public appearance, or writings.

The first interaction with the astrologer is extremely important. The person may have spent hours or days trying to find the accurate birth time, knowing this would be needed; then several days deciding whether or not to call the astrologer; anticipation about the astrological process is highly charged.

What does the person want to "hear" from the astrologer when they first come together by phone or in person? The nervously distraught person will certainly want to hear kindness and understanding—even within the appointment making process, even when nothing specific about what motivated the call is covered! The businessman may listen for something else, perhaps authority and experience, in addition to courtesy. In our language, we talk about our need for others to "lend a kind ear."

After the appointment is made, the person may then mention it to a friend or two (for reinforcement, for sharing the tension leading to the meeting). The consultation will have become an event to look forward to; there is a new energy of more specific anticipation. A friend will ask, "Tell me, what did she/he say? What did he/she sound like?"

I have thought much about this over the years and many, many thousands of consultation experiences. I feel that the astrologer must establish the following image: *being specially informed, seasoned in life, and adept with conversation.* We could say: informed, experienced, and articulate. *That* image is professional and secure for the caller. Those attributes build toward a profile of wisdom and effective communication.

The communication moment of making the appointment establishes the image of the astrologer so very quickly. The astrologer is already performing.

And it is not always smooth as silk. Some people phoning for an appointment are embarrassed that they are doing so, or they need desperately to establish their ego strength in the light of whatever it is that is on their mind, that may be depleting them, making them vulnerable. They sometimes cover that with know-it-all braggadocio about their knowledge of astrology, having "read a few books about it." I quietly counter with, "Please know that we will not be talking about astrology when we have our consultation. I'll do my work ahead of time, of course, but we'll be talking about you and your development. I look forward to that." This establishes that the consultation will not be loaded with jargon, that the discussion will be centered on the individual, and that the astrologer is ready to be involved.

Callers sometimes strongly request information about "What's actually going to happen in the consultation?" I've learned to say simply, "I do a lot of preparation using your birth data, organizing the thoughts and datelines that we'll talk about—things I think are very important about your development, throughout your whole life—and we have a very good discussion together. It's not a performance by me. You and I work together to appreciate who you are, and we take all that into the future."

Notice what that statement establishes: preparation work, good organization, my specialized discernment about the person's life development, and the necessity for the discussion to be just that…*a discussion*…toward understanding and planning strategy.

The caller is getting a clear impression of who the astrologer is, how she or he will communicate during the consultation. Just as when meeting the astrologer in person at a lecture or at a dinner party, clues about the astrologer are flooding the prospect's sensibility: the sound of the voice, the choice of words, one's sense of humor, etc. On the phone, the senses reach farther for more information since nothing visual is involved to help with the image-making process.[1]

This image-making process happens very quickly. Think how you react to the sound of another person's voice, especially one with which you are going to be dealing with some degree of confidential intimacy. Think how you react to the words you hear in your introductory conversation. Think how all your intelligence and senses work to establish a value judgment of the person!

And, we must know that this image-making process *works both ways: the client-to-be is making an impression on the astrologer as well.* The caller is under pressure and will also want to make a fine impression. The caller knows that this impression can color the consultation to come—that's only human.

The astrologer must listen for the person's image as it forms during the call. Is the caller courteous, careful and their word choices thought-out, using correct grammar—a major index about education and sociometric level; is there responsiveness to humor? Perhaps the first question the astrologer should ask is, "Yes, this is he (or she) speaking. Thank you for calling...May I ask, please, how you got my name and number?" This is important information for the astrologer's marketing efforts, to learn what efforts are producing business contacts, and being correct with grammar immediately says so much to the caller; whether or not the caller is tuned into grammar and word choice, *the caller reacts to it*; the image is built.[2]

When the astrologer takes the birth data from the caller, there is a further opportunity for the astrologer to establish image during initial interaction with the client-to-be. Naturally, these data are critically important, and the astrologer can show this: "May I have your birth data, please?" The caller will often blurt out the data very quickly,

---

1. I often ask the caller, "Have you visited my website?" If the caller has, I add, "Good! Thank you. And you've seen my picture?" This establishes that they will have already stored up many impressions that should be working in my favor.

2. "This is him or her" is wrong—the verb "to be" cannot take a direct object, the accusative case. Learning proper use of pronouns, the verbs "lie" and "lay," the conjunctions "as" and "like," and more are essential points of fine speech, which must be correct to reflect well upon all that is being said conversationally in the consultation.

e.g., "three–eleven–forty-six." The astrologer should reply, "Thank you, but please, let's be sure: is it March 11, or is it November 3?"[3]

The caller will say, March 11. The astrologer should clarify: 'March one-one." Yes.

Then, with the year, "19 four-six." Stating the all-important numbers like that shows how careful the astrologer is being; a very important part of the image that should be put forward.

With the birth time, there is another opportunity: the astrologer asks about the time, and the caller says, 2:06 AM. The astrologer should say, "Thank you: that's 2 zero-six *in the morning,*" and wait for corroboration.

Then, the astrologer should ask, with a touch of inquisitiveness in the voice, "How do you know?"

This opportunity for response by the applicant often clarifies the birth time importantly or reveals a problem with it, but it *always* stimulates further conversation, a further opportunity to build impressions of the caller within the image-creating process.

In short, the telephone exchange says so very much about the astrologer as well as about the client-to-be. I like to remind myself with every call—especially when I am very tired, perhaps harassed, perhaps in an argumentative frame of mind—"If you *feel* kind, you *will* be kind. If you *think yourself* correct and impressive, you *will* be correct and impressive. If you are consciously determined to be patient and tolerant, *you will be.*"

There is a decided difference in the tone and often in the productivity of the consultation that is related to how much the client knows about the astrologer *ahead of time*. If the client is calling the astrologer from a listing in the Yellow Pages, the air is quite different from what it is when the client is calling with the security of a prestigious referral, with knowledge of the astrologer from different sources. The more the caller can know and feel ahead of time—and then have established or corroborated in the telephone call by what is heard—the closer is the meeting of minds forming between the caller and the astrologer.

All of this affects the expectations the client has about the consultation. Those expectations will be framed in interpersonal terms, emotional terms, because the client has in most cases never experienced an astrological consultation before, and really does not know what to expect. Sometimes on the telephone—or in the personal meeting to set up the consultation—the astrologer will need to calm things down if the client betrays much

---

3. Most of the world puts the day of the month first; the month second. The United States and a few other countries are exceptions. The month should always be spelled out.

anxiety about the "unknown process;" or assuage earnest curiosity if the client articulates interest in the specifics ahead. I have distilled some words that work extremely well to set the scene: "I appreciate your faith in me and this process." [*This is an assumptive statement; nothing may have been discussed about "faith," but by assuming that it is important—that the client should* know *that it is important—the astrologer is able to inject a graceful, personable, softening touch into the client's regard for the appointment.*]

"I appreciate your faith in me and this process. We're going to have [not "we're gonna have"] a fine discussion together. [*Again, so important: the client is notified that the consultation will be a discussion, not a one-sided magical performance by the astrologer. This relaxes many pressures, I assure you.*] The patterns of the planets at the moment of your birth—fascinatingly—have an extraordinary correlation with the patterns in life development. We will be discussing those behavioral event patterns in your past...and project them strategically into the near future...We'll talk together for about an hour. You'll understand so much; I look forward to it."[4]

That is enough. The client now knows what to expect: a discussion for which the astrologer is specially prepared, and a lot of new understanding forthcoming.

YOUR WORK AREA

When you go to someone's home, to your doctor's office, to the salon or barbershop for a haircut, you make instant assessments, instant impressions. *These impressions are for your security*: is there anything there that is threatening, what *is* there that *is* comforting? The impressions condition how you will feel during your visit; they clarify how much attention is being paid to your coming there, to your sensitivities, often when you are emotionally preoccupied and vulnerable.

When someone arrives at your home, they are instinctively "sizing things up," and the astrologer must anticipate this. Preparation for the astrological consultation includes having a private, comfortable place clearly set aside for your work with the client. [One cannot conduct an astrological consultation with dignity at the kitchen table, except if the client is a friend of some fifty years standing!]

No cats, no dogs, no food or drink or smoking or chewing gum, no music. Clearly, a sense of privacy must be established, free from telephone interruption, from children

---

4. The words "correlation" and "patterns" are subtle introductions of being "scientific" and "sure"; "behavioral event patterns" promises much, as do "strategy" and "understanding."

jumping in and out, calling from afar. Cleanliness, neatness, order must be immediately obvious.

The most important dimension that will establish client security and astrologer preparedness is *a display of books*. Books speak of authority. They calm things down. Encase your books beautifully and prominently; let the colors of the bindings brighten the room. Your pride in them will communicate itself and say much.

The chair for your client across the astrologer's desk (or a coffee table if the consultation is taking place in a living room setting—which opens up a great deal of space for interruption) must be strong, comfortable, but not soft and swallowing. The client must stay supported and alert. (Sit in the chair yourself, spend some time in it, and feel it as your client will feel it.)

Every person has a "best distance" in face-to-face communication. The astrologer should measure the distance from his/her face to her/his client's face to determine this "best distance." Test it with someone; discover it. It is very subtle: one inch more or less can affect the *rapport* with your client…and the astrologer's confidence with communication. Set the chairs for that distance to be automatic.

Check the lighting: a lamp for the astrologer may be a glaring distraction for the client, just because of the tilt of the shade or a reflection from a mirror. Make the adjustment. Check temperature. Balance the room.

Whenever we enter into someone else's territory, we instinctively look around for something about which to pay a compliment. Our instincts tell us that this will please our host and lessen any tensions of "newness" that may be in the air. To attract this process, it is a good idea to have something eminently notable in the work area: a special picture on the wall, a piece of sculpture, an award or two, a book display, or a beautiful artifact brought back from a faraway vacation. This will attract the small talk that is part of the human socialization process.

[Should the client *not* comment favorably on anything about the work area or the astrologer's person, the astrologer will know that there is keen self-worth anxiety, notably within the 2nd–8th House axis, or involving the rulers of those Houses. The client feels that giving a compliment somehow diminishes him- or herself. This is an obvious cramp in the socialization process, the founding and maintaining of relationships.]

Part of the astrologer's preparation during this process is to start bringing the client's astrology into the client's reality experience. The astrologer has prepared the horoscope completely (chapters 1 and 2); now, the astrologer should observe *what within the client's astrology is becoming obvious as client and astrologer come together*? Punctuality, lateness; speech patterns and word choice, i.e., educational background; direct or indirect gaze; smiles; graciousness with compliments or the lack of them; color choice in clothing; neatness or sloppiness; is the client a nail biter, a foot-wiggler; did the woman wash her hair that morning? Did the man have his shoes shined? What about jewelry accents?

And we must remember that, at the same time, the client is doing the same kind of evaluation of the astrologer! How do *we* look? What is *our* image saying…now, face to face?

The beginning moment of the consultation ideally should emerge out of the small talk. The astrologer will have an open file folder on the desk. The horoscope will be in view and the notations around it or on other pieces of paper will be obvious to the client and indicate technical preparation. Talk should best begin about "the patterns of the planets at your birth, at the time and place you were born, are so significant. Fascinatingly, they correlate with patterns in life development. To begin our discussion, *one of the patterns here suggests…*"

This is an all-important statement: "One of the patterns here suggests…" The astrologer conveys the sense of patterns *objectively measured*. What is coming in the consultation is not going to be a *subjective evaluation* of any kind; no criticisms, no preaching [for some clients, this brings about an immediate sense of relief.] The verb "suggests" is of extreme value: "Your horoscope *shows* or *indicates*" suggests that portents of fate are cast in stone! It paints the client back into a corner, and the client becomes self-protecting. Using the verb "suggests" allows the client to adjust things as he or she discloses to the astrologer personal reality experience in development. This is the beginning of the client's trust of the astrologer.

The astrologer, talking to Franz Kafka, might say, "And one of the patterns here suggests quite a lot of defensiveness…When we see something so pronounced, we look around to find its cause, and here, we should talk about your relationship quality with your parents…each one individually. That's what's behind the defensiveness. Please tell me about that; there's quite a lot of tension there."

Talking to Howard Stern, the astrologer might say, "And one of the patterns suggests quite a strong, perhaps indomitable drive to reach the public, to give yourself over to others to make a point, *a point that is your life*…and when we see something so pronounced, we want to find out why it is so…there *has* to be a reason for it…a mission, if you will. Here the indication is that the keys are your enormous needs to establish self-worth, to prove yourself lovable…those *are* the keys. What are those anxieties underneath your public onslaught?"

The consultation has begun, and the client is invited into discussion. The astrologer is revealing the portrait.

Gradually, with experience, the astrologer learns to begin the consultation in different ways, flowing out of introductory conversation, with different weight given to hemisphere emphasis and the Sun-Moon blend, or a dominating aspect focus tied to Saturn-retrograde phenomenology or contact with the lunar nodal axis, or other such powerful keys. But the essential guidelines are that the astrologer uses *absolutely no astrological jargon.*[5] Listening posts are established in the conversation as the client reacts to the discussion points presented by the astrologer. Creative connections are made, and more and more, the client's unconscious is allowing trust of the astrologer to build and more and more truthful evaluations of development to emerge.

GREATER EXPECTATIONS

From the outset, the time of making the appointment, the client will be accumulating impressions of the astrologer that should accumulatively reflect a strong professionalism. Personal presentation upon first meeting will augment this image. And within the first few sentences of discussion, the client will be startled and impressed with the depth at which the consultation is pitched.

As the consultation develops, the client will start to see patterns of behavior from earliest developmental times that more than likely will be coloring what is being brought to the table in the present, the issues of pressure, choice, anxiety that are of strategic concern. Adjustments are made through this recognition, through objectification, and through behavioral modification. Patterns *can* be changed.

Perhaps the coloring of the present in development has been established well. The projection into the near future commands highly focused attention at the closing of the consultation, and discussion eases into projection of the now-familiar horoscope symbology for the months ahead.

---

5. The use of jargon only confounds the client, who understands none of it. Jargon uses up time and space for saying something significant. The use of jargon is a device used by the insecure astrologer with nothing humanistically substantive to say.

This is a moment of high analytical tension. The astrologer is fitting measurement guidelines into reality plans and hopes for the future. Does the sheer fact of talking about these projections with accumulated insight *guarantee* reality occurrence? The client would certainly like that to be so. Even with a transitory dismal projection, the client will feel forewarned, and therefore well armed. In retrospect, often, that kind of weathering-the-storm period will be viewed as an essential turning point, a clearing of the air, a new start forced into being.

The phrasing of things must be carefully chosen: talking about *probabilities* is highly recommended over projecting facts to come. Talking about *what is reasonable* is the sense that must prevail: it is *reasonable* that one's father, battling lung cancer for six months already, may die in three months with the Pluto and Saturn measurements tied into the Midheaven of the client's horoscope. The strategic questions become: What will that death mean? How does one prepare for it in many different avenues of concern?

It is reasonable that a long-distance relocation (or even a shorter one outside the present school district) will challenge the family, with their three children, corresponding to the strong Uranus contacts with the husband's Ascendant, involving the ruler of the Midheaven as well. His corporation has already broached the subject, and we see that reality suggested vividly in the horoscope portrait. It is a high-probability projection. What becomes extremely important is keeping peace within family progress, acknowledging the children's school peer-group disruptions and shifts to a new location, timing the move for the summer months, finding rewards for the children at the new location, involving them with the reward potentials of the decision, etc.

It is reasonable that a woman's affair will die out with the Saturn transit to her Sun/Moon midpoint, also involving the rulers of her 5th and 7th. But is she seeing the hidden message about the threat to her marriage as well? Of what is the affair a symptom in terms of the marriage? How can the marriage be strengthened as the affair dissolves? Is this being seen as well? The client may not be expecting these layers of significances tied to probable event development. The astrologer is broadening the spectrum of expectations within the astrological consultation.

But, uncannily often, after business strategy for an improved job situation or relocation plans or extended family reorganization or management of a problematic brother or sister situation, or a court case or an affair, etc., is illuminated and agreed to by the client and the astrologer—really big considerations—even greater expectations can raise their heads! This is natural: so much trust has been built up between client and astrologer that wishful thinking is now free to be heard, and, to one degree or another, what the astrologer has to say may just "make it so"!

The question most often heard in the midst of professional, geographic, or status change is, "Will I ever meet someone?" or "*When* will I meet someone?" This is a query from someone unmarried, having just broken up within a relationship (part of the larger change, clearly) or about to be divorced, afraid of transient insecurity, aloneness, or an extension of heretofore-protracted aloneness, seeking rescue. Rarely is resolution of change strategies accompanied *simultaneously* with realization of romance, unless, of course, romance is at the core of the change.

The astrologer's very good answer, judging from near unanimous agreement of clients when they think it out, is "I'd like to suggest, *first things first.* You are going to go through quite a change here, as we've seen. It's possible. It's probable; and we see that the change will probably stretch out over eight months to be settled.

"What will probably be happening at the same time is that you will become *quite a different person!* Your values will probably change; your confidence level will change; your appreciation of yourself and your work in life will be greatly enhanced. You will be a different person and *you will probably attract a different kind of relationship!* You will probably leave behind those old vibes and no longer attract the same kind of unproductive relationships that we've seen so often over the last twenty years. Maybe it's best to wait for the changes now to take place *and then see what the 'new you' starts to attract!*"

This is stick-to-the-business-at-hand reasoning. It is supportive reasoning. It is an idea with which it is very comfortable to live. It can temper any overly extended expectations formed within the consultation.

4 CASE STUDY: ALICE

Our technical preparation work has been well choreographed. This process should take place the exact same way every time we prepare a horoscope for consultation; the repetition of the process anchors the mechanics of deduction and the thrust of interpretation; our mind discovers and routinizes ways to manage measurements. The preparation process itself supports a library of deductive techniques that become instinct.

Let's put all the preparation work together for actual cases, conducted by telephone, with the consultation dialogue recorded here precisely as it occurred. And, along with that transcribed dialogue, let's follow *"thought guides"* in analysis (printed in italics). The thought-guide insertions will capture what I was thinking as the consultation developed.

HOROSCOPE ORIENTATION

For "Alice," four major observations should reveal the portrait (chart, page 66).

1. NW hemisphere emphasis suggests unfinished business in the early home *[how much, how strong, from where?]*, echoed by Saturn conjunct Sun, and Pluto opposed Jupiter, ruler of the parental 4th. *[Mercury, ruler of the Ascendant and the parental 10th, is retrograde, disposited by Saturn in conjunction with the Sun. Things hold together here with the NW hemisphere deduction.]*

2. The Sun in Aquarius and the Moon in Pisces: Introspection drives the personality. Emotional vulnerability, while trying to be special. *[Saturn conjunction with the Sun*

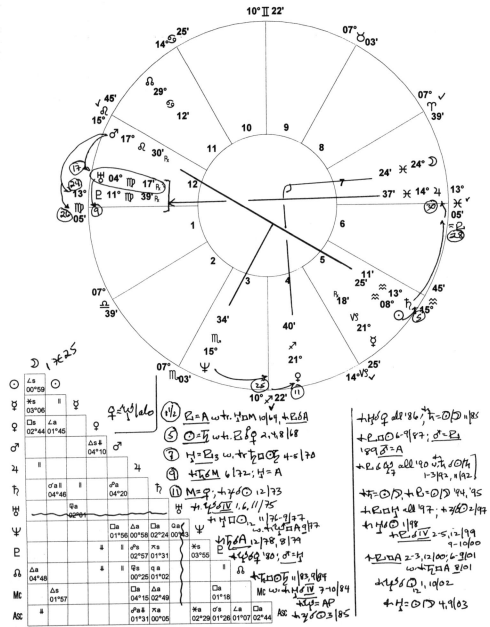

Midpoint Sort: 90° Dial

☿/Mc	000°50'	☿	021°18'	♄/☊	036°11'	☊/Asc	051°09'	♂/♃	061°03'	♃	074°37'
♂/♆	001°32'	♅/Mc	022°19'	☽/♀	038°02'	☉/♅	051°21'	☽/☉	061°25'	♀/Mc	076°01'
☊/Mc	004°47'	☿/☊	025°15'	♂/☊	038°21'	♃/☊	051°54'	♀/♆	063°37'	☽/♇	078°02'
☿/♀	006°29'	♇/Mc	026°00'	☉	038°25'	☽/☿	052°51'	☽/♄	063°47'	☿/♆	078°26'
☉/Mc	009°23'	Mc/Asc	026°44'	☉/♄	040°48'	♄/♅	053°44'	♅	064°17'	☽/Asc	078°45'
♅/♆	009°56'	♃/Mc	027°29'	☿/♅	042°48'	☉/♇	055°02'	☽/♂	065°57'	☽/♃	079°30'
♀/☊	010°26'	♀/♅	027°59'	☉/♂	042°58'	☉/Asc	055°45'	♅/♇	067°58'	♀	081°40'
♄/Mc	011°46'	☊	029°12'	♄	043°11'	♂/♅	055°54'	♅/Asc	068°41'	♆/☊	082°23'
♆/♇	013°37'	☉/☿	029°52'	♂/♄	045°20'	☉/♃	056°31'	♃/♅	069°27'	☽	084°24'
♂/Mc	013°56'	♀/♇	031°40'	♆	045°34'	☽/☊	056°48'	Mc	070°22'	☉/♆	087°00'
♆/Asc	014°20'	☿/♄	032°14'	☿/♇	046°29'	♄/♇	057°25'	♇	071°39'	♄/♆	089°22'
☉/♀	015°02'	☽/Mc	032°23'	♅/☊	046°45'	♆/Mc	057°58'	♇/Asc	072°22'		
♃/♆	015°05'	♀/Asc	032°23'	☿/Asc	047°12'	♄/Asc	058°08'	Asc	073°05'		
♀/♄	017°25'	♀/♃	033°08'	♂	047°30'	♃/♄	058°54'	♃/♇	073°08'		
♀/♂	019°35'	☉/☊	033°48'	☿/♃	047°58'	♂/♇	059°35'	♃/Asc	073°51'		
☽/♆	019°59'	☿/♂	034°24'	♇/☊	050°26'	♂/Asc	060°18'	☽/♅	074°21'		

clamps down on avant-garde free-making behaviors. But Uranus is peregrine, perhaps offsetting the pull-back.]

3. Retrograde pair at the Ascendant focus strongly on Pluto, a counterpoint (℞ Pluto and Uranus) to personal power expression. *[And is this related somehow to sibling rivalry, with Pluto ruling the 3rd, holding Neptune; with Pluto squaring the parental axis?]* And we can expect difficulties carried over into adult relationships *[since Neptune, ruler of the 7th, is squared by Saturn and by Mars].*
4. With Saturn quindecile the nodal axis, the key is the mother, her position and activity in the home, her model. [Whenever Saturn is configured strongly with the nodal axis, the probability of the mother "running the show" is extremely high. *What happened to the father? Things are out of balance.*]

The *rapport* arcs generalized and noted on the natal horoscope guide us into the chronology of development written out below the wheel. Major transits are included to vivify events and focus date development. This flow will guide the consultation dialogue. During that dialogue, creative connections will be made and significances will form. [To appreciate this preparation presentation thoroughly, one should actually look into the 100-year ephemeris in *Synthesis & Counseling in Astrology* or in *Solar Arcs* and see the trigger transits visually, related to the arc formations that I have already noted. Study these preparation notes.]

It is always good to see where the development into the near future is going; it helps to set a "target time." The combo-search (pages 69–70) shows this dramatically in March

Inner Chart

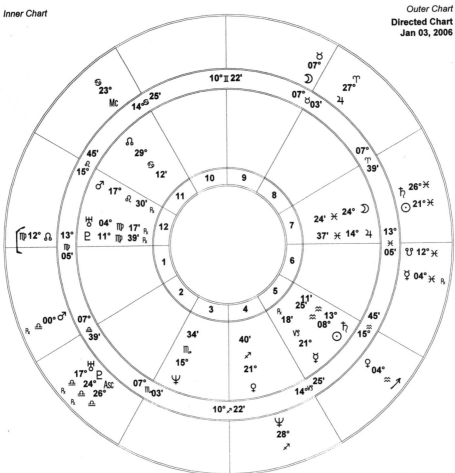

Pl	Geo Lon	R	Decl.
☽	24° ♓ 24' 09"		- 06° 11'
☉	08° ♒ 24' 51"		- 18° 10'
☿	21° ♑ 18' 20"	℞	- 18° 36'
♀	21° ♐ 40' 08"		- 19° 49'
♂	17° ♌ 30' 11"	℞	+19° 53'
♃	14° ♓ 36' 43"		- 07° 03'
♄	13° ♒ 10' 35"		- 17° 37'
♅	04° ♍ 16' 59"	℞	+10° 41'
♆	15° ♏ 34' 15"		- 14° 49'
♇	11° ♍ 39' 21"	℞	+19° 54'

Directed Chart

Pl	Geo Lon	R	Decl.
☽	07° ♉ 40' 15"		- 06° 11'
☉	21° ♓ 40' 57"		- 18° 10'
☿	04° ♓ 34' 26"	℞	- 18° 36'
♀	04° ♒ 56' 14"		- 19° 49'
♂	00° ♎ 46' 17"	℞	+19° 53'
♃	27° ♈ 52' 49"		- 07° 03'
♄	26° ♓ 26' 41"		- 17° 37'
♅	17° ♎ 33' 05"	℞	+10° 41'
♆	28° ♐ 50' 21"		- 14° 49'
♇	24° ♎ 55' 27"	℞	+19° 54'

Search From Oct 30, 2005 to Jan 31, 2007 GMT Page: 1

Aspect	Date	Time	Event	Type	P1 Pos.	P2 Pos	E/X/L
♂ -- □ ♂	10-31-2005	07:02 am	♂ □ ♂	Tr-Na	17°♉30'℞	17°♌30'℞	Exact
♅ ---- q ☽/Mc	11-02-2005	11:37 am	♅ q ☽/Mc	Ar-Na	17°♎23'	02°♉23'	Exact
♂ -- ☍ ♆	11-05-2005	06:05 pm	♂ ☍ ♆	Tr-Na	15°♉34'℞	15°♏34'	Exact
♂ -- □ ♄	11-12-2005	04:30 pm	♂ □ ♄	Tr-Na	13°♉11'℞	13°♒11'	Exact
♅ ---- SD	11-15-2005	09:58 pm	♅ SD	Tr-Na	06°♓51'		
♅ ---- □ ♀/♄	11-17-2005	03:51 pm	♅ □ ♀/♄	Ar-Na	17°♎25'	17°♑25'	Exact
♄ -- SR℞	11-22-2005	06:56 am	♄ SR℞	Tr-Na	11°♌19'℞		
☊ --- ☌ ♇/Asc	11-29-2005	05:31 am	☊ ☌ ♇/Asc	Ar-Na	12°♍22'	12°♍22'	Exact
♃ -- q ☿/♅	12-03-2005	07:57 am	♃ q ☿/♅	Ar-Na	27°♈48'	12°♏48'	Exact
♃ -- □ ☉	12-05-2005	00:41 am	♃ □ ☉	Tr-Na	08°♏25'	08°♒25'	Exact
♂ -- □ ☉	12-05-2005	01:18 am	♂ □ ☉	Tr-Na	08°♉25'℞	08°♒25'	Exact
♂ -- SD	12-10-2005	04:00 am	♂ SD	Tr-Na	08°♉14'		
♂ -- □ ☉	12-15-2005	10:04 am	♂ □ ☉	Tr-Na	08°♉25'	08°♒25'	Exact
♆ ---- □ ♆	12-18-2005	09:34 am	♆ □ ♆	Tr-Na	15°♒34'	15°♏34'	Exact
♇ ---- □ ☽	12-18-2005	10:13 pm	♇ □ ☽	Tr-Na	24°♐24'	24°♓24'	Exact
☉ - □ ♀	12-29-2005	07:38 pm	☉ □ ♀	Ar-Na	21°♓40'	21°♐40'	Exact
♃ -- □ ♄	12-31-2005	05:28 am	♃ □ ♄	Tr-Na	13°♏11'	13°♒11'	Exact
♆ ---- q ♃/Asc	01-08-2006	04:36 am	♆ q ♃/Asc	Ar-Na	28°♐51'	13°♊51'	Exact
☿ - ⚼ ♀/♂	01-08-2006	06:18 am	☿ ⚼ ♀/♂	Ar-Na	04°♓35'	19°♎35'	Exact
♂ -- □ ♄	01-08-2006	02:08 pm	♂ □ ♄	Tr-Na	13°♉11'	13°♒11'	Exact
☊ --- ⚼ ♃/Mc	01-09-2006	12:45 pm	☊ ⚼ ♃/Mc	Ar-Na	12°♍29'	27°♈29'	Exact
☽ □ ☿	01-11-2006	04:12 pm	☽ □ ☿	Pr-Na	21°♎18'	21°♑18'℞	Exact
♂ -- ☍ ♆	01-15-2006	07:05 pm	♂ ☍ ♆	Tr-Na	15°♉34'	15°♏34'	Exact
♃ -- ☌ ♆	01-16-2006	11:06 am	♃ ☌ ♆	Tr-Na	15°♏34'	15°♏34'	Exact
♂ -- □ ♂	01-20-2006	11:57 pm	♂ □ ♂	Tr-Na	17°♉30'	17°♌30'℞	Exact
♄ -- ☍ ☉	01-21-2006	05:04 am	♄ ☍ ☉	Tr-Na	08°♌25'℞	08°♒25'	Exact
Mc --- ∠ ♅/Asc	01-25-2006	06:10 am	Mc ∠ ♅/Asc	Ar-Na	23°♋41'	08°♍41'	Exact
♃ -- q ☉/♂	02-01-2006	12:09 pm	♃ q ☉/♂	Ar-Na	27°♈58'	12°♏58'	Exact
♃ -- □ ♂	02-02-2006	10:21 pm	♃ □ ♂	Tr-Na	17°♏30'	17°♌30'℞	Exact
♆ ---- q ♂/Mc	02-06-2006	01:50 pm	♆ q ♂/Mc	Ar-Na	28°♐56'	13°♋56'	Exact
♆ ---- ☍ ♂	02-11-2006	11:22 pm	♆ ☍ ♂	Tr-Na	17°♒30'	17°♌30'℞	Exact
♅ ---- □ Mc	02-23-2006	04:51 am	♅ □ Mc	Tr-Na	10°♓22'	10°♊22'	Exact
♂ -- □ ♅	02-26-2006	10:05 am	♂ □ ♅	Tr-Na	04°♊17'	04°♍17'℞	Exact
♃ -- SR℞	03-04-2006	05:46 pm	♃ SR℞	Tr-Na	18°♏52'℞		
♂ -- ☌ Mc	03-09-2006	10:43 pm	♂ ☌ Mc	Tr-Na	10°♊22'	10°♊22'	Exact
♂ -- □ ♇	03-12-2006	08:23 am	♂ □ ♇	Tr-Na	11°♊39'	11°♍39'℞	Exact
♂ -- □ Asc	03-14-2006	11:47 pm	♂ □ Asc	Tr-Na	13°♊05'	13°♍05'	Exact
♂ -- □ ♃	03-17-2006	06:32 pm	♂ □ ♃	Tr-Na	14°♊37'	14°♓37'	Exact
♅ ---- ☍ ♇	03-17-2006	10:14 pm	♅ ☍ ♇	Tr-Na	11°♓39'	11°♍39'℞	Exact
♃ -- ⚼ Asc	03-21-2006	06:52 pm	♃ ⚼ Asc	Ar-Na	28°♈05'	13°♍05'	Exact
♄ -- q ♇	03-22-2006	02:32 am	♄ q ♇	Ar-Na	26°♓39'	11°♍39'℞	Exact
♇ ---- SR℞	03-29-2006	10:34 am	♇ SR℞	Tr-Na	26°♐45'℞		
♂ -- ☍ ♀	03-30-2006	10:44 am	♂ ☍ ♀	Tr-Na	21°♊40'	21°♐40'	Exact
♂ -- q ♀/Mc	04-02-2006	07:52 pm	♂ q ♀/Mc	Ar-Na	01°♎01'	16°♓01'	Exact
♃ -- □ ♂	04-03-2006	04:59 pm	♃ □ ♂	Tr-Na	17°♏30'℞	17°♌30'℞	Exact
♂ -- □ ☽	04-04-2006	06:31 am	♂ □ ☽	Tr-Na	24°♊24'	24°♓24'	Exact
♄ -- SD	04-05-2006	12:14 pm	♄ SD	Tr-Na	04°♌23'		
♃ -- ∠ ♃/♇	04-06-2006	04:13 pm	♃ ∠ ♃/♇	Ar-Na	28°♈08'	13°♊08'	Exact
♅ ---- ☍ Asc	04-14-2006	03:53 pm	♅ ☍ Asc	Tr-Na	13°♓05'	13°♍05'	Exact
♃ -- ☌ ♆	04-22-2006	00:09 am	♃ ☌ ♆	Tr-Na	15°♏34'℞	15°♏34'	Exact
Asc --- ∠ ♇	04-22-2006	01:35 pm	Asc ∠ ♇	Ar-Na	26°♎39'	11°♍39'℞	Exact
♇ ---- ☌ ☿/☊	05-04-2006	12:34 pm	♇ ☌ ☿/☊	Ar-Na	25°♎15'	25°♎15'	Exact
♃ -- □ ♄	05-11-2006	01:13 am	♃ □ ♄	Tr-Na	13°♏11'℞	13°♒11'	Exact
☽ □ ☽/♀	05-17-2006	10:26 am	☽ □ ☽/♀	Ar-Na	08°♉02'	08°♒02'	Exact
Asc --- □ Mc/Asc	05-17-2006	11:39 pm	Asc □ Mc/Asc	Ar-Na	26°♎44'	26°♋44'	Exact
♂ -- ☍ ☿	05-20-2006	06:56 am	♂ ☍ ☿	Tr-Na	21°♋18'	21°♑18'℞	Exact
♆ ---- SR℞	05-22-2006	09:16 am	♆ SR℞	Tr-Na	19°♒49'℞		
♅ ---- ☌ ♃	06-02-2006	07:33 am	♅ ☌ ♃	Tr-Na	14°♓37'	14°♓37'	Exact
♂ -- ☌ ☋	06-02-2006	10:57 am	♂ ☌ ☋	Tr-Na	29°♋12'	29°♋12'℞	Exact
Asc --- q ♄/Mc	06-02-2006	05:11 pm	Asc q ♄/Mc	Ar-Na	26°♎46'	11°♈46'	Exact
☿ - ∠ ☽/♆	06-04-2006	00:31 am	☿ ∠ ☽/♆	Ar-Na	04°♓59'	19°♑59'	Exact
♇ ---- ⚼ Mc	06-12-2006	09:44 am	♇ ⚼ Mc	Ar-Na	25°♎22'	10°♊22'	Exact
♄ -- ☍ ☉	06-14-2006	10:17 pm	♄ ☍ ☉	Tr-Na	08°♌25'	08°♒25'	Exact
♂ -- ☍ ☉	06-17-2006	04:18 pm	♂ ☍ ☉	Tr-Na	08°♌25'	08°♒25'	Exact
♅ ---- SR℞	06-19-2006	04:37 am	♅ SR℞	Tr-Na	14°♓44'℞		
♂ -- ☍ ♄	06-25-2006	11:47 am	♂ ☍ ♄	Tr-Na	13°♌11'	13°♒11'	Exact
♂ -- □ ♆	06-29-2006	09:43 am	♂ □ ♆	Tr-Na	15°♌34'	15°♏34'	Exact
♂ -- ☌ ♂	07-02-2006	01:19 pm	♂ ☌ ♂	Tr-Na	17°♌30'	17°♌30'℞	Exact
♀ - q ♇/☊	07-02-2006	08:19 pm	♀ q ♇/☊	Ar-Na	05°♒26'	20°♌26'	Exact
♃ -- SD	07-06-2006	07:43 am	♃ SD	Tr-Na	08°♏59'		
♅ ---- ☌ ♃	07-06-2006	12:30 pm	♅ ☌ ♃	Tr-Na	14°♓37'℞	14°♓37'	Exact
♆ ---- q ☽/♅	07-07-2006	05:31 am	♆ q ☽/♅	Ar-Na	29°♐21'	14°♊21'	Exact
☊ --- ∠ ♀/♅	07-08-2006	00:29 am	☊ ∠ ♀/♅	Ar-Na	12°♍59'	27°♎59'	Exact

★ ☉=♀

SP☽□☿

♄♅□M

★ ♄♅☌VII

♄♅☌♃

Search From Oct 30, 2005 to Jan 31, 2007 GMT   Page: 2

Aspect	Date	Time	Event	Type	P1 Pos.	P2 Pos.	E/X/L
Ψ ---- σ ♄/Ψ	07-18-2006	12:33 pm	Ψ σ ♄/Ψ	Ar-Na	29°♐22'	29°♐22'	Exact
♄ -- □ ☉/Ψ	07-23-2006	11:04 am	♄ □ ☉/Ψ	Ar-Na	27°♓00'	27°♐00'	Exact
♄ -- ♂ ♄	07-25-2006	09:59 am	♄ ♂ ♄	Tr-Na	13°♌11'	13°♒11'	Exact
♂ -- σ ♅	07-29-2006	03:45 pm	♂ σ ♅	Tr-Na	04°♍17'	04°♍17'℞	Exact
♀ ---- □ ☽	07-30-2006	07:26 pm	♀ □ ☽	Tr-Na	24°♈24'℞	24°♓24'	Exact
♂ -- □ Mc	08-08-2006	08:20 am	♂ □ Mc	Tr-Na	10°♍22'	10°Ⅱ22'	Exact
♂ -- σ ♀	08-10-2006	09:44 am	♂ σ ♀	Tr-Na	11°♍39'	11°♍39'	Exact
♂ -- σ Asc	08-12-2006	04:20 pm	♂ σ Asc	Tr-Na	13°♍05'	13°♍05'	Exact
♄ -- □ Ψ	08-13-2006	02:57 am	♄ □ Ψ	Tr-Na	15°♌34'	15°♏34'	Exact
♂ -- ♂ ♃	08-15-2006	02:08 am	♂ ♂ ♃	Tr-Na	14°♍37'	14°♓37'	Exact
☊ -- σ Asc	08-18-2006	10:34 pm	☊ σ Asc	Ar-Na	13°♍05'	13°♍05'	Exact
♂ -- □ ♀	08-26-2006	04:42 am	♂ □ ♀	Tr-Na	21°♍40'	21°♐40'	Exact
♅ -- ♂ Asc	08-27-2006	07:45 pm	♅ ♂ Asc	Tr-Na	13°♓05'℞	13°♍05'	Exact
♄ -- σ σ	08-28-2006	08:57 am	♄ σ σ	Tr-Na	17°♌30'	17°♌30'℞	Exact
♃ -- □ ♄	08-30-2006	10:17 am	♃ □ ♄	Tr-Na	13°♏11'	13°♒11'	Exact
♂ -- σ ☽	08-30-2006	11:19 am	♂ ♂ ☽	Tr-Na	24°♍24'	24°♓24'	Exact
☊ -- □ ♃/♀	09-03-2006	08:00 pm	☊ □ ♃/♀	Ar-Na	13°♍08'	13°Ⅱ08'	Exact
♀ ---- SD	09-04-2006	07:58 pm	♀ SD		24°♐05'		
☽ □ σ/☊	09-10-2006	10:53 am	☽ □ σ/☊	Ar-Na	08°♉21'	08°♌21'	Exact
☽ □ ☊	09-11-2006	08:00 am	☽ □ ☊	Pr-Na	29°♎12'	29°♋12'℞	Exact
♃ -- σ Ψ	09-14-2006	06:49 pm	♃ σ Ψ	Tr-Na	15°♏34'	15°♏34'	Exact
Ψ -- ♂ σ	09-16-2006	05:27 pm	Ψ ♂ σ	Tr-Na	17°♒30'℞	17°♌30'℞	Exact
σ -- ∠ ☿/♀	09-20-2006	02:04 pm	σ ∠ ☿/♀	Ar-Na	01°♎29'	16°♏29'	Exact
♃ -- □ σ	09-25-2006	04:45 pm	♃ □ σ	Tr-Na	17°♏30'	17°♌30'℞	Exact
♃ -- q Ψ/♀	09-29-2006	07:07 am	♃ q Ψ/♀	Ar-Na	28°♈37'	13°♎37'	Exact
☽ □ ☉	10-03-2006	01:52 am	☽ □ ☉	Tr-Na	08°♉25'	08°♏25'	Exact
☊ -- σ ☽	10-03-2006	01:41 pm	☊ σ ☽	Tr-Na	24°♍24'℞	24°♓24'	Exact
♅ -- ♂ ♀	10-04-2006	10:46 am	♅ ♂ ♀	Tr-Na	11°♓39'℞	11°♍39'℞	Exact
♀ ---- □ ☽	10-10-2006	03:41 am	♀ □ ☽	Tr-Na	24°♈24'	24°♓24'	Exact
σ -- □ ☿	10-10-2006	05:01 pm	σ □ ☿	Tr-Na	21°♎18'	21°♑18'℞	Exact
σ -- σ σ/Ψ	10-11-2006	05:17 am	σ σ σ/Ψ	Ar-Na	01°♎32'	01°♎32'	Exact
σ -- □ ☊	10-22-2006	12:12 pm	σ □ ☊	Tr-Na	29°♌12'	29°♋12'℞	Exact
Ψ -- SD	10-29-2006	05:07 am	Ψ SD		17°♒02'		
Mc -- ∠ ♃/♅	10-30-2006	09:10 pm	Mc ∠ ♃/♅	Ar-Na	24°♋27'	09°Ⅱ27'	Exact
□ ☉	11-05-2006	02:21 am	□ ☉	Tr-Na	08°♏25'	08°♒25'	Exact
σ -- □ ♄	11-12-2006	01:11 am	σ □ ♄	Tr-Na	13°♏11'	13°♒11'	Exact
☿ -- q ♀/☊	11-12-2006	11:29 pm	☿ q ♀/☊	Ar-Na	05°♏26'	20°♌26'	Exact
σ -- σ ♀ Ψ	11-15-2006	12:36 pm	σ σ Ψ	Tr-Na	15°♏34'	15°♏34'	Exact
σ -- □ ☊	11-18-2006	07:41 am	σ □ ☊	Tr-Na	17°♏30'	17°♌30'℞	Exact
♅ -- SD	11-20-2006	03:55 am	♅ SD		10°♓49'		
☊ -- □ ♀	11-24-2006	04:36 am	☊ □ ♀	Tr-Na	21°♓40'℞	21°♐40'	Exact
♄ -- SR	12-06-2006	02:00 am	♄ SR	Tr-Na	25°♌04'℞		
Ψ -- ♂ σ	12-09-2006	12:42 pm	Ψ ♂ σ	Tr-Na	17°♒30'	17°♌39'℞	Exact
♄ -- q ♀/Asc	12-09-2006	08:34 pm	♄ q ♀/Asc	Ar-Na	27°♓22'	12°♍22'	Exact
σ -- □ ♅	12-12-2006	06:18 am	σ □ ♅	Tr-Na	04°♐17'	04°♍17'℞	Exact
♃ -- □ ♅	12-13-2006	02:00 pm	♃ □ ♅	Tr-Na	04°♐17'	04°♍17'℞	Exact
σ -- σ Mc	12-20-2006	06:55 pm	σ σ Mc	Tr-Na	10°♐22'	10°Ⅱ22'	Exact
σ -- □ ♀	12-22-2006	02:20 pm	σ □ ♀	Tr-Na	11°♐39'	11°♍39'℞	Exact
σ -- □ Asc	12-24-2006	02:18 pm	σ □ Asc	Tr-Na	13°♐05'	13°♍05'	Exact
♃ -- ∠ ♃/Asc	12-25-2006	10:23 am	♃ ∠ ♃/Asc	Ar-Na	28°♈51'	13°Ⅱ51'	Exact
σ -- ∠ ♅/☊	12-25-2006	12:40 pm	σ ∠ ♅/☊	Ar-Na	01°♎45'	16°♌45'	Exact
σ -- □ ♃	12-26-2006	05:04 pm	σ □ ♃	Tr-Na	14°♐37'	14°♓37'	Exact
♅ ---- ♂ ♀	01-04-2007	06:32 am	♅ ♂ ♀	Tr-Na	11°♓39'	11°♍39'℞	Exact
σ -- σ ♀	01-05-2007	11:15 am	σ σ ♀	Tr-Na	21°♐40'	21°♐40'	Exact
♀ ---- □ ☽	01-09-2007	05:22 am	♀ □ ☽	Tr-Na	24°♈24'	24°♓24'	Exact
Asc -- ∠ ♀/Asc	01-10-2007	07:52 am	Asc ∠ ♀/Asc	Ar-Na	27°♎22'	12°♍22'	Exact
♃ -- ♂ Mc	01-11-2007	07:49 am	♃ ♂ Mc	Tr-Na	10°♐22'	10°Ⅱ22'	Exact
♃ -- □ ♀	01-18-2007	03:35 pm	♃ □ ♀	Tr-Na	11°♐39'	11°♍39'℞	Exact
♃ -- □ Asc	01-26-2007	03:16 pm	♃ □ Asc	Tr-Na	13°♐05'	13°♍05'	Exact
☽ q ♄/♅	01-26-2007	03:40 pm	☽ q ♄/♅	Ar-Na	08°♉44'	23°♏44'	Exact
♅ ---- ∠ ♀/Ψ	01-30-2007	04:15 am	♅ ∠ ♀/Ψ	Ar-Na	18°♓37'	03°♐37'	Exact

(handwritten marginal notes:)

♄ ⚷ ♂ ♀
♄ ♂ ☊ ☽

also = A
♄ ♅ σ VII 2nd "hit"

SA ☽ □ ☉

8/07 SA ♄/♀ = A
with ∠
the accumulated
SA SEMISQUARE

2006 with SA Sat$_q$=Pluto$_3$.[1] That's the first target *[quite possibly a sibling crisis if the consulta-tion reveals that potential. Why would that be so important to Alice?]*. Leading up to it we see tr Uranus square the MH *[usually a major job development]*, and just a bit earlier SP Moon square Mercury, ruler of the MH and the Ascendant *[tied in with the job development immediately thereafter]*. A bit earlier before the consultation, which occurred on January 8, 2006, we see the partile SA Sun=Venus, with tr Neptune squaring Neptune, ruler of the 7th *[normally an affair; the two together increases probability]*. We are getting a feel of development into future time.

Beyond March 2006, we have another target set in February 2007, with the final transit of Uranus over the seventh cusp. This suggests that much tension *[during the first two transit contacts with the angle]* will be resolved at that time, or just before, in the marriage, one way or another. Granted, there is a year between time targets, and that time span will be filled in in terms of probabilities, as the consultation unfolds.

THE CONSULTATION

N: Good morning, hi!

A: (Most cheerfully) Hi! How are you?

N: (Laughing) Well, that's a short question for a long answer!

A: (Teasing) Oh NO! I'm sorry.

N: You sound so chipper!

A: Well, I just got out of the shower! I feel refreshed!

N: All righty; good! Alice, thanks very much for being on time; I appreciate it a lot. What do you do for a living?

> The Midheaven Extension Process[2] reads: ☿.♄.♅.♀;♇$_3$□ M;♃□M;♃.♆3;☽7□♀: *"Innovative communications administration with big business, public image orientation with aesthetic touch."* This is what I thought Alice needed to do with her energies and talents.

---

1. This reads: solar arc Saturn is quindecile to natal Pluto, ruler of the 3rd House.

2. Please see Tyl, *Vocations* for full development and presentation of the Midheaven Extension Process for vocational profiling. The "code line" for the vocational deduction is included here as part of the complete preparation of the horoscope consultation. The specialization of the technique cannot be included in this text.

A: Um, I am currently a content-webmaster…I do a lot of the graphics, a lot of editing…I do this for large organizations…

N: That's what you've been doing for a long time?

A: No, dear…(much laughter) I've been with the same organization for about fourteen years in a variety of capacities…Um…most of these rely on my communication ability one way or another and my ability to organize information. In the beginning of my career, I had a few odd jobs, and uh, then I worked in television production for several years.

> *With the mention of "fourteen years" I quickly found "1992" in the preparation notes and made a note of "job change."*

N: Hm mn…(assent).

A: Um, and then I floated around for a while; I didn't really know what I was going to do…

N: I see a lot of that floating around in this horoscope (laughter); this is why I asked you!

> *Neptune can easily work to dilute the power of the Mars-Saturn relationship when it aspects both.*

A: (Laughing) Yeah!

N: Sure. The background aesthetic is there; you know, the management of information is begging to be disciplined…

A: (Strong laughter)

N: Are you with me?

A: (Still laughing) Yes I am; as a matter of fact, I'm writing it down!

N: Well (purposeful pause), start writing the word *"mother."*

A: (A pause) OK.

N: I need to know about this relationship you had with her.

> *Clearly we are pursuing Saturn quindecile the node, the node semisquare the Ascendant: very, very strong maternal influence; the mother ran the show.*

A: OK…hold on…."information"…

N: (Firmly, wanting her emotional involvement) Come on; come on! We have to talk.

A: OK. *My mother.* My mom and I have a very difficult relationship.

N: Write that word down: "difficult." It's all over this horoscope, the difficulty with your mother. She ran the show. She was the dominant force in the family.

A: Um. Yes, she was. Um. And not in a very direct way. Um. She's very indirect; it's very manipulative; it's very, um, smothering and controlling, and um…just one of those things: I know she means well, but *she just doesn't get it!*

N: Yes. But when you're that young, you don't think in those terms.

A: No. And I actually *do* have really, really fond memories of, uh, my very young childhood with her at home, when it was the two of us.

This is a common occurrence: immediately defending the parent, the relationship, in the shock of its being brought up; the unconscious is now processing the observation and determining how much to reveal.

N: Hm mn. Well, how did the father handle the victimization by his wife?

A: Well, I never thought of victimization; he was pretty, uh, he was pretty disruptive himself! He had a very violent temper…um…he was very verbal.

Saturn conjunct her Sun; the Mars intensification.

N: But you see all the suffering he had with her.

A: I, I, you know, I thought…Yeah, I was the only person who empathized with him at all, and when they split up, he was the bad guy. Um, but I was old enough to sort of see that it was a two-way street.

N: Well, in those early years…Yeah. Well…That's nice. But you're still responding. You're responding to a power struggle around you.

A: Hm mn. (assent)

N: …and it's not comfortable.

A: No.

N: And a lot of this carried over into some of the difficulties with your adult relationships on your own.

A: (Laughing lightly in recognition; sarcastically) Imagine that!

N: Yeah. Imagine. But you're so vulnerable, so sensitive, you know; you need to have things have meanings, and sometimes, these intrusions from reality, these bombastic things get in the way.

> *The Moon in Pisces.*

A: Hm mn (assent).

N: Do you have any brothers or sisters?

> *This was a key question, I hoped; to settle the Pluto symbolism, ruling the 3rd and squaring the Midheaven.*

A: I do. I have a younger brother; he's about three years younger than me; four years behind me in school.

N: Well, I'm just saying, that this sibling situation—I have written down here possibly being born in 1968.

A: He was born in 1966.

N: But he somehow comes to the foreground here [in 1968]. Was there any kind of jealousy going on…here?

A: (Aggressively) Yeah. There was! There was a lot! There was a lot. Um. I very quickly became the "bad child," the "disruptive child," the…uh…child with unrealistic expectations, and uh, and who…uh…you know…and you know when you're little kids together…you know…kids will try to get responses out of each other. And, uh, and John…was…is a very active, dynamic person. And you know…what I saw him doing was pushing, pushing, pushing me, and then I would react and then I would be blamed for whatever happened.

> *Of course the evaluations that she was "bad, disruptive," etc., came from the mother.*

N: All right. So you see what you're saying: isn't it amazing, first of all, that astrology can see this. I mean, I'm sitting here thousands of miles away from you, and I'm seeing the birth of this sibling who comes to the foreground…. In a bombastic household that's very, very unsettled.

A: Hm mn (assent).

N: And you say, "Well, I became the bad child."

A: Hm mn (assent).

N: And becoming the bad child suppresses those very, very sensitive, artistic, aesthetic dimensions about you.

A: Yeah. Well, I spent a lot of time in my room.

N: And closed the door…and read a book.

A: Right.

N: But hear what I'm saying: you are not being supported for that special, special sensitivity that you have.

> *This lack of support for her birthright will be there in her life, to one degree or another, for so much of her life. And it was linked to her favored brother.*

A: (Firmly) Right!

N: Got it?

A: Yeah.

N: Yeah. And this gets very, very strongly felt when you're seven years old, and this is *really* a disruptive period of time.

> *The Arc Uranus=Pluto, Pluto ruling the 3rd.*

A: Yes, it was.

N: 1970…as was 1972.

A: "Also 1972," yeah! 1972, really bad. My dad lost his job that year.

> *I note the powerful arc of Uranus=Asc with tr Saturn conjunct the Midheaven!*

N: Yes. Probably around June.

A: Hm mn…It was in the spring. It was Marchish, and um, and um, after school was out, um, I believe he got a job in San Antonio.

N: But I'm just saying to you: you see how messed up it is?

A: Yes. It's messed up.

N: And they're…they're thinking about this split…

A: Oh yeah, early…

N: …that is pending, and he has no compunction about going far away to San Antonio to get a job.

A: Right…. He took us with him that time.

N: But you know what I'm saying: he's trying to "get out of Dodge."

A: Hm mn (assent).

N: Now, something very, very nice should have happened here in '73; when you were eleven, toward the end of the year.

A: Actually, that's when we ended up…that's when we moved to San Antonio. In '72, we moved from our community in one part of Maryland to another community that was completely different.

N: Do you hear what I'm saying? This trip to San Antonio somehow comes off beneficial for you.

>*The tr Jupiter conjunction with the Sun.*

A: Oh yeah! In a lot of ways it does! Uh…It does. There's a few really important people I met, um…I feel like there's one friend in particular that…you know…was basically the reason I needed to be in San Antonio.

>*This is very interesting; the sense is that she is talking about a friend "now" related to the meeting back then in '73. It almost sounds fatalistic. How will this be explained? Is it a problem NOW?*

N: Hm mn. Did their marriage last past 1975?

A: Yes. But not by much.

N: I'm amazed, because it is really highly pressured. And then again in, around September '77, toward the end of the year.

A: Yeah.

N: Now we're in a position here for 1980, where you are probably experiencing your first swoons of love!

A: It was earlier than that, actually.

N: There's a serious relationship here.

A: What time in 1980?

N: I'm not sure; I didn't jot that down. It's a clear period of relationship importance. And it's critical, because at this point, you're considering about going on to college.

A: Yeah. Well, actually, I…um…this relationship with this important friend, a boy in high school, and…he and I…were not dating, but we were considering going to the same college. And, he was under extraordinary pressure to go to this particular college, and it probably wasn't the right school for him.

The friend is emerging.

N: But I see this all wrapped up together. It's very important in your development here. So, how did it come down?

A: So he ended up going off to this school and struggling there and being miserable, um, and I went off to another college, and um, we went on a date once in 1981 and had a wonderful time, and, for whatever reasons, things didn't work out, and, we're actually dealing with that right now *[twenty-five years later!]*.

N: We are actually *dealing with that right now!?*

A: We're talking again.

N: The young man.

A: Yeah, he's not young anymore (a slight giggle).

N: All right: do you understand? I bring this up because it is so punctuated in your horoscope. *This relationship factor with that young man then.*

A: Oh yeah. Yeah.

N: It's totally caught up with the college experience and decision-making, and you're saying *now it is still alive!*

A: Yeah! (whimsically)

N: It's very interesting, isn't it?

A: Hm mn.

N: I feel like a Buddha on a mountaintop without enough clothing! (Laughter.) Remember all those shaggy dog jokes where you get the secret of life at the top of a mountain? [Both laughing] OK. In 1984, is that the year you graduated from college?

I couldn't yet get her to open up emotionally about this relationship from long ago that still existed.

A: 1984 I graduated from college. Correct.

N: And then immediately it looks like there's a job for you somewhere, that you get.

The Uranian transit.

A: Um. I actually did have a freelance job that summer, working as a production assistant.

N: I can see it, almost before you graduate…set up for September 1984.

A: Well, it's funny, that would have been late August, but, uh, it was the Republican National Convention and I worked for a couple weeks, you know, as a production person. Um, and then did another really cool job, actually that summer—maybe that's what you mean about being immediately set up—I had a wonderful job that summer writing curriculum guides for the San Antonio Museum of Art.

N: It's an excellent time, and I just wanted to point that out to you. Now, uh, all the way from July through October, it's excellent. Then, there's a change: does more aesthetic work come to you, work with art?

A: Are we '84 or '85 with this?

N: Late '84, leading to March '85, in which there's a very conspicuous opportunity. And new job…

A: No. Actually at that time I was working for…at a very low wage, at a very sub-standard [job] far below my abilities.

N: All right: "Far below your abilities." Why do you think that happened?

A: Because I wasn't feeling very good about myself, I guess.

N: But you see my point? My point is: all the potential is swirling around you, and this is the first time that, positive or negative—if you want to look at it that way—that it didn't keep schedule.

A: Hm mn.

N: There's a definite opportunity early in '85 that should have kicked in.
The Jupiter transit.

A: Yeah. I did get to do some on-air, uh, I was an on-air presenter for the local public TV station in San Antonio. At that time, they had an auction, and they needed auctioneers.

N: Did you do well with that?

A: I did fairly well with that; yeah!

N: Was that in March, by any chance?

A: It was in the spring.

N: There you go! That's what I'm seeing. Now, you might look back on this and say that is was a small thing…in the scheme of things…*but it wasn't!*

A: No it wasn't. No it wasn't!

N: There is a significance here begging to be born!

A: (Silence) OK. I've got to write that down; keep talking.

N: No, I'm not going to keep talking. Please respond to me right away.

A: Um. I think my uh…Well, I don't exactly know how to put this; I'm having a hard time with the verbs…and nouns…actually. Um…It was important to me; it was incredibly important in terms of…I got up there in front of somebody, and I did my thing, and it went down all right!

N: That's right. Now why did it not necessarily lead directly to further development?

A: Because I didn't pursue it.

N: And, may I ask, "Why?" Were you not confident?

A: I was *not* confident! And, I felt like, you know, I don't really want to be in front of people. I would rather be behind the scenes telling the people up front what to do.

N: *While your brother is out front getting all the glory.*
   This was a major statement, delivered with impact, to start bringing themes together in the analysis.

A: (Strong nervous laughter spurts out) Which he was, by the way!

N: You understand what I'm saying.

A: Yes. Uh-huh.

N: If you had this reinforcement of your sensitive, dramatic, public portrayal, you would have seen this as an open door to great reward. I'm pointing that out to you. Do you hear me? (with kindness)

A: Yes, I do.

N: At the same time, there seems to be a lot of bewilderment and confusion in a personal relationship too.
   Tr Saturn=Sun/Moon

A: (Perfunctorily) Oh, yeah.

N: (Startled by the minimal answer; responding in humor) Listen: say something nice to your astrologer, because we are hitting all these very important points!

A: You rock!! (giggling)

N: What did you say?

A: You rock!!

N: I rock. That's pretty good—I just had my sixty-ninth birthday…

A: Well, congratulations!

N: Thank you…and I got a card from a thirty-two-year old…one of my students, and he said to me, "Happy birthday for the umpteenth time!" And I replied, "How much is 'umpteenth,' and 'does it show'?"

A: (Big laugh) Can I get some wrinkle removal with that (laughing)?

N: All right, in 1986, there's another major love affair that…is, is strong, strong, strong…it should have been.

   Tr Uranus conjunct Venus, fitting into her scheme of development.

A: Uh, yeah, it was; and I'm still friends with him too.

N: OK. You're "collecting"!

A: Well, um, there's one other guy I dated, um, you know, later, then there is my husband…

   I ignored this tangent. I wanted to stay on the track about the brother: his prominence and her suppression, echoing the early labels of her as the "bad" child.

N: In 1987, please tell me how the brother comes into the foreground again.

   Clearly the Mars=Pluto arc, Pluto ruling the 3rd with tr Pluto square the Sun.

A: My brother um…my brother is a talented athlete who…uh…became a professional football player. He…um…graduated from college in 1988, so in 1987, he was, you know, it was obvious he was going to turn pro. At this point I had moved away to Washington D.C. Um…partly to get away from the pressure of that friendship and partly to make something happen from the major love affair of 1986 and partly to get away from my high school boyfriend, because I just couldn't bear to keep running into him…

N: Get back to your brother, now…

A: Brother! My brother's going pro...getting ready to go pro. He wanted to get engaged to be married. My mother...um...My parents...um...My father gave [had given] my mother a very nice diamond ring for an engagement ring...sold his car...blah blah blah...the diamond was [then] supposed to be...*mine.*

N: There's our key; you see that. That diamond ring was reserved for you, for your marriage...

A: Or for whatever...you know...Whatever...And, *my mother gave it to my brother.*
   And what does this do to Alice; this constant comparative undermining?

N: ...and again we see the shift of preference.

A: Oh yes. Absolutely. Very strong.

N: Not comfortable. In 1989, there seems to be a major break, and...uh...this is a time when I think you probably started to step forward for yourself for the first time, strongly.
   Mars=Asc

A: Yeah, and it was hard.

N: Yes. Very difficult. Did you get some psychotherapeutic help at the time?
   I saw the transit of Pluto onto the Neptune applying in 1989.

A: Oh, most definitely.

N: We're doing very well here. It takes a psychotherapist how long to get to these points?
   I tried to relax the tension for a moment.

A: Yeah. Well, I've been interested in astrology all my life [in other words, this accuracy and depth are not a surprise].

N: All right, there's anger here, there's upset, change. Everything. The whole year of 1989. Tremendous relationship problems, the whole year of 1990.
   Tr Pluto conjunct Neptune, ruler of the 7th, all being fit into the developmental scenario.

A: Hm mn (assent).

N: And there seems to be *a radical shift in your professional level and pursuit direction*...at the end of '92, and I would suggest perhaps [you're] working it out by November 1992.

Here we are at the change-of-career period I noted earlier from her initial work description; perfectly in the sense of the Saturn return, of course: a strong alteration of direction and/or level in the profession.

A: Hm mn…

N: Please tell me about that

A: Um…I basically decided that television wasn't working for me; that I needed to give it up; that it's too hard…I was a minnow in a shark tank…you know, in terms of the kind of resilience and toughness it takes to be in that business…and I decided that I would just, uh, work at temp jobs until I could figure out what to do. And in, uh, September of that year, I took a job with my current organization. It was, uh…I got to use, you know, a lot of my production skills. You know, I was doing…um…I was still supervising the production of video material…um…as well as books and newsletters and…

N: OK. Good. So you're settling down, just as I said.

A: Right.

N: Changes of direction and level, and there it is…and you're still with that firm. Now, in '94 and all of '95, there seems to be lots more of these relationship problems, power struggles, depression about them…

   The strong transits to Sun/Moon.

A: Hm mn (assent)

N: You know why?

A: (Pause) Um…I think that…my take on it is that, you know, trying to make something happen…um…I did not see myself as being single, and I didn't want to be single, and I didn't want to be an old maid or whatever…

N: …**and you didn't see yourself as eminently lovable either.**

A: No, I didn't, and so I saw myself in a series or…you know…one- to three-month relationships…that were really messy and…but which ultimately showed me that…uh…*I knew I deserved better, and I just couldn't tell myself; I had to show myself.*

N: Gotcha. Thank you. I'm glad you understand it so nicely. In early '97, there must have been a raise or a promotion in this work.

Again, testing the Jupiter transit, with the very strong tr Pluto square Uranus (peregrine) in effect simultaneously.

A: Yes, and I also got married!

N: Good. All of this is so clear. The horoscope all works. In 1998, I think, at the very beginning of the year, did the people at your work offer you a little more autonomy, a little more responsibility, a new direction for yourself?

A: YES! Somewhat.

N: You should have started feeling better about yourself: a stabilized relationship situation because you are married; number two, the job has been on the ascendancy since you took it; there's some autonomy; you're feeling good...

A: Hm mn...

N: Was there a new home for you at the end of '99?
   Tr Pluto at the 4th cusp.

A: Well, uh, actually it was, uh, a new home...uh...at the *beginning* of 1999.
   I had noted a later contact time of tr Pluto at the 4th cusp.

N: ...Yes, between February and May, but then it comes back around December, and I thought it took you that long to get settled in...

A: Yeah. We bought a house in late 1998, around Christmas time.

N: Very good. Right on schedule. Then in 2000, there's more development at work that should have been favorable for you.

A: *Very* favorable!

N: Especially, I think August, September, something like that?

A: EXACTLY! I took a new job in the organization in August; a new position was created, and that's how I ended up starting doing the web stuff. I was the assistant webmaster.

N: Terrific! Congratulations. That's nice. Then we come into 2002 and...uh...I have to ask you a research question first: were you ill in 2002?
   I framed this as a research question since I wasn't sure. I was pursuing tr Neptune conjunct the Sun, ruler of the 12th.

A: VERY ill.

N: Very ill. How come?

A: Well, it goes back to 2000, actually…

>*When the tr Pluto was square the Ascendant, the health center.*

N: Well, OK…I was…

A: I uh…I uh…After about a series of miscarriages and really not feeling well, I finally fig-
ured out in 2002, um, that I was suffering from hyperthyroidism, which of course is a loss
of your energy, the loss of your voice, um, and the symptoms for that were—and I had
been tested for that several times in high school, and…um…nobody really picked it up.

>*The thyroid is ruled by Venus, and here, there is no challenging Venus accentuation natally or
in development.*

N: Do you *really* think…Has it been diagnosed that you had a deficient thyroid at that time?

A: Yes. Um…but at that point I was…I was pretty ill from the effect of it. I was extremely
depressed, losing hair, um, infections, self-medicating with sugar and alcohol…and everything else.

N: Gotcha. Yes, indeed. I'm sorry you were very ill. The signs are there, it was like a two-
year period of the blahs…

>*But not necessarily from the thyroid.*

A: Hm mn…

N: What's happening to your brother?

>*I need to bring this issue to a peak, in the light of the powerful target arc in March 2006: SA
Saturn quindecile Pluto, ruler of the 3rd, peaking as we were having the consultation.*

A: My brother, um, is retired from football, and he's working, and he's had his own…it's
been a struggle for him!

N: Yes, it has. And it's getting worse, right now.—I know this is a call [consultation] about
you, but we see from the time he is born—'66–'68—you have a tie in parallel with him
in his ascendancy and the preference over you and things like that, which stimulate a
great deal of sibling jealousy, rivalry, and self-deprecation. We know that. *It's hard to
outgrow that!*

A: Hm mn (in agreement).

N: And, uh, I'm seeing some very very strong suggestion that he is having a very difficult time right now.

A: Hm mn. (in agreement)

N: How difficult is it?

A: Well, he recently received a promotion that's really really really stretching his abilities. Um…And he needs to make it work, but, you know, he's behind. He got paid to "hit" people, you know, for twenty years. And, you can't, uh, make a living at that income level [his present job], um, by "hitting people" [with that attitude]. He's very bright, but he has some information processing deficits that make it really hard for him to assimilate and spit out information again very quickly…

N: All right. Part of that is the professional athlete's profile…

A: But part of that too is that, you know, that he came into business late; he has a high-level position but he doesn't have twenty years of office politics [behind him]…

N: But what is the link with you?

A: The link with me?

N: Why is this showing up so poignantly in your horoscope?

A: Is it that I'm starting to worry what his mid-life crisis is going to look like?

N: Yes. I guess so. But anyhow, it is very very clear here that I'm seeing him again through you, and I don't see the tie this time. Is he asking you for help?

A: Um…If he knew he could, he would. There was a time I needed help, and he offered it, and I turned it down, because I was too proud. And that could be the dynamic that's happening here.

I certainly had alerted her to the brother situation, chronically in terms of their competition, and acutely in terms of his very difficult time now on his job and, probably, throughout his life at the moment.

N: I understand. Let's go back to *you,* now. At the end of the year, 2005, things should have been going very positively for you, in your work especially.

I felt good about Uranus$_q$ = Moon/MC and tr Jupiter square Sun, etc. [See page 69.]

A: OK (anticipating something).

N: Are you still married?

A: Yes (strongly).

N: (Pause) I have to suggest that there might have been some sort of extra-curricular activity here.

> *Assimilating Sun=Venus and tr Neptune square Neptune, ruler of the 7th.*

A: Yes, there was.

N: All right. Boy! Was I diplomatic (laughter)!

A: I *like* your diplomacy (laughter).

N: Does your husband know that it took place?

A: He doesn't know the details of the situation.

N: He knows you had an affair?

A: (Pause) No.

N: All right. He doesn't know.

A: He knows that this high school friend of mine has been facing some tough times and had some questions about…

> *The friend is found…recalling the early references during her school years.*

N: All right. We don't need the details.

A: Yeah.

N: Now, in February there's going to be a shift, I think, in your job situation.…

> *Tr. Uranus square the Midheaven*

A: Oh, I'll tell you what else also happened in '05: um, we received a referral on the daughter we're adopting.

> *Not unfamiliar to the Sun-Venus arc; add on tr Jupiter square Saturn, ruler of the 5th. [Conception, fertility, delivery, management of birth/children are classically difficult with Saturn ruling the 5th and/or the ruler of the 5th under high developmental tension. Both conditions are present here. Recall her series of miscarriages.]*

N: In December.

A: Uh…November.

N: You're adopting a daughter. How old is the daughter?

A: She's currently about two and one-half months old.

N: All right. *But there's tension in your marriage here.*

> *Again: tr Neptune square Neptune, ruler of the 7th.*

A: Yeah; there is (wistfully). There is.

N: Do you think that adopting the child is going to somehow be something to mend the marriage?

A: No.

She clearly had given this question some thought quite some time before our discussion.

N: You're under a lot of pressure, my dear, with this marriage; I have to point that out to you. *Do you know why?*

So important: find out the client's explanation, the client's value judgments first.

A: (Forthrightly) **Because it buys into a system that I no longer believe in.**

N: Would you illuminate that for me, please?

A: Um…(pause) When I married this guy, I didn't understand myself the way I do now.

N: All right. So, you've changed and, uh, the relationship is different.

A: The relationship is different, and it works on a lot of levels—but on *some* levels, it doesn't.

N: Have you talked it over with your husband?

A: We have.

N: And the bottom line of that, especially in the light of adopting a child two and one-half months old?

A: Um…(long pause) We're willing to take it as far as it goes.
This sounded ominous.

N: All right. Are there any plans for a new home that you're projecting for the spring?
Again—as with the brother situation—the important point had been made. There is little value in taking it further. Alice will have to do that.

I was projecting to tr Uranus conjunct the 7th and conjoining Jupiter, ruler of the 4th. These two conditions would go together, quite obviously; in time as well as in reality.

A: No, not really a new home. We have work to do to get ready for her arrival.

N: That's probably what I'm seeing; some kind of remodeling, changes like that…
Not unusual: hard to tell the difference between a new home and remodeling.

A: Yeah, we do: we've got to paint the room and…

N: What's this new stuff at the job? It looks awfully good here, and they're going to tell you about it within the next three weeks. Do you know about it yet?

> *This is a specific anchor to the transit of tr Uranus square the Midheaven.*

A: Well, uh, I have a new position that I got offered last spring, um, where I'm now in charge.

N: But there's more to it than that. In the next month, I believe very strongly that they're going to advise you of another step of independence and strength in your work. And I should think you would look forward to that.

> *I'm beginning a build-up of her individuality here, accentuating Uranus peregrine in her horoscope, at the time of tr Uranus square her Midheaven, all in the wake of her lifelong self-deprecation in the wake of her brother's success.*

A: More independence…

N: I don't know the exact words; I'm not in your cubicle, so to speak…

A: (Light laughter)

N: You know what I'm saying: you really and truly are going to get a new ramification of your job responsibilities. And I should think that the first tracking of that would have been in your awareness [back] in the first week of December [2005].

> *Tr Jupiter square the Sun*

A: I did get a very positive job review…

N: That's what it is. Sometimes when we get to the future, people get very hesitant to involve their creative projections. But I'm just telling you: that's what it is. I'm also telling you, that I believe from how I've been tracking this that your brother is really suffering. And it can be very difficult for him in March and April.

> *This reminder is part of the wrap-up, the recapitulation of major points covered in the consultation.*

A: He turns forty in April.

N: OK. I think your husband…is he planning something new in his work? Is there a promotion or change setting up for him?

> *This is tr Uranus conjunct the 7th being interpreted derivatively, i.e., seeing the 7th as her husband's Ascendant.*

A: He is getting promoted pretty much every six months.

N: Is one due in April?

A: Possibly.

N: Well, I think it will come through. All of that looks good. Looks good. The only thing I worry about is the health of the marriage, the stability of the marriage.

A: Yeah. I understand that.

> *The point here had been made strongly.*

N: I think you're going to need to work it out, and I think you're going to take some time to work it out because you have this responsibility now of the young baby.

A: Hm mn.

N: And I think that you are probably going to aim in your reality development for a time to have all this settled probably in late summer 2007. [*SA Saturn q=A with accumulated SA semisquare.*]

> *That's about a year and a half when these problems have to gestate, refine themselves, adjust themselves;* **perhaps you and your husband could improve the values within your marriage that will suit the values in you as a changed lady.** [*This statement had strong impact.*]

A: Yeah. Well, that's been happening! That's been happening!

N: Good! Well, I think that's a wonderful path, and I think the child is taking a position on that path.

A: Hm mn.

N: That's a good way to look at it, isn't it, Alice?

A: It is. (emphatically) *It is.* You know, I think one of the things we just have to under-stand—my husband and I—is sort of realize that we just need to give each other a lot of space.

N: OK. Just a few words, but you're saying a lot.

A: Oh really?

N: You're saying that there are individuation factors that have to be factored into this relationship...

A: And it's true for both of us...

N: That's what "giving each other space" means.

A: Right. Right.

N: All right. Now, you have a streak in you that is delightful: it's adventurous; it's rebellious; it's flying naked upside down in airplanes on Saturday afternoons, you know? It's taking risks! And I think *that's* one of the factors that has to be put into this marriage development package. *[Uranus peregrine]*

A: Hm mn...

N: That you have to be able to express yourself with excitement and uh, a bit of *joie de vivre...*

A: (Delighted) Hm mn!

N: Because you've been stultifying...You've been suppressed in that special dimension of behavior.

A: You mean, in other words, *I've been trying to stick to a pattern that's not what I am....*

N: It's incarcerating. It's confining.

A: Yes.

N: That's not an opinion I'm giving you; I'm giving you a measurement.

A: Right.

N: And everything I've said to you, you've corroborated, and everything you've said to me I've corroborated...so we're "lookin' good!" All right. Now, I'm not a medical doctor, but may I ask you a few questions about health?

A: Sure!

N: How's your diet?

A: It could be better, but it's not bad.

N: There seems to be an inefficiency here with metabolic management of nutritional intake.

    The Plutonic-Virgo tensions at the Ascendant.

A: (Light laughter) You're right. I definitely have a weight problem.

N: How tall are you and how much do you weigh?

A: Um, I'm 5'8" and I currently weigh about 220 pounds.

N: That's too much.

A: It is indeed too much, and it doesn't seem to matter what I eat or don't eat!

N: I think you need to get that fixed. It's not easy. Do you suffer from constipation?
[Pluto situation here.]

A: Not very often, but occasionally.

N: I think you need to address this. It's a major, major concern in this horoscope. And it's tied to your self-worth image profile appreciation.

A: Of course it is! [in confirmation]

N: Sometimes I have to bring out the obvious.

A: But I've been noticing a shift, actually. I must say.

N: Now, you are a determined lady! Somebody tells you that you can't build a house by yourself on Malibu Beach with two Popsicle sticks and a tea-bag (laughter), you say, "You can bet on it; I'll do it; and I'll do it in twenty-six days!" That's the kind of person I think you are!! *[The indomitableness of Mars-Saturn hard relationships.]*

A: (Laughing) Generally speaking, yeah!

N: Generally speaking. You have to apply this strength you have, *up front!* **Because you're out in front of your brother...now.**

A: (Long pause) Hm mn.

N: *And I've got a spotlight on you!*

A: Hm.

N: You hear? (friendly)

A: Yes, sir.

N: Doesn't that feel good?

A: Uh huh! (in agreement)

N: Somebody far away telling you, uh, **"I've got *a preferential ring for you; it's your dia-mond,"*** and I want you to earn it. I want you to earn it by getting your body in shape, by talking to your husband about improving the values in your relationship, and realizing that they love you on your job and you're ever doing well. [This was a powerfully ordered summary.]

A: Yeah, I'm pretty hard on myself there [on the job].

N: Well that's because you don't want to be hard on yourself personally. You see, it's a displacement. Say, you're angry; you go into the bathroom and kick your bathtub, rather than kicking your child.

A: Right.

N: There's a displacement here…a displacement of aggression [onto, about the job].

A: Understood. Understood!

N: Now, I'd like you to keep me posted on this. I'd like to hear about the arrival of your child, and I'd like to hear happiness in your voice about the work on the job, AND the work on yourself! You've got to lose fifty pounds. And I think that will tie in with even further job ascendancy, and you'd be a happy mother. OK!

A: I will do my very best.

N: We've had a good, good exchange, and I'm proud of you!

A: Oh good! I have a question for you, though, about improving the values…What kind of values do you…

N: I think the values *of togetherness, of trust, of empathy.*

A: Hm mn.

N: You know, it's very very hard when, for so long, you've been second fiddle…to allow yourself to be *first* fiddle! And your mate must help you. In turn, you've got to be able to say to your mate, without feeling that you're diminishing yourself, all kinds of supportive stuff for your mate's strength as well.

A: Right! Correct! OK. I understand what you're saying.

N: All righty?

A: Yeah. I think actually we've been doing a lot there, although some of this weird stuff that's been going on here is shaking out very interestingly. I have an opportunity to start writing music with the friend of mine.

N: OK. Well, there it is. Be careful.

> *The "friend" has been haunting her for some twenty-five years.*

A: Of course!

N: Know this: *first things first.*

A: What?

N: Know that first things come first…

A: Oh, yeah yeah yeah!

N: When did this opportunity to write the music come to your consciousness?

A: The first offer—we started talking about this in high school—
Amazing: the pervasion of the influence of the bond.

N: But now…

A: Uh, the first offer was…oh gosh…the middle of November or so.

N: Yes. I see it. Fine. Fine.

A: We decided that if we're going to be friends, we need to be constructive about it!

N: All right. Let's see how that works out. Just be waiting at your firm for some sort of improvement within the next three weeks!

A: Wow. OK! I'll definitely let you know what happens there.

N: Thank you, dear Alice.

A: OK. Nice speaking with you!

N: Bye-bye.

A: Bye.

(Approximately forty-two minutes.)

OVERVIEW: STRUCTURE AND TECHNIQUE

In practically all cases, the start of a consultation is founded best upon a broad base, and this base is most often built upon the sense of hemisphere emphasis. This establishes the frame of mind, if you will, for the discussion points that will follow. In this case with Alice, with her horoscope emphasis to the west—giving herself away to others, being taken advantage of, getting lost herself—while I absorbed the signal, I chose not to present that view to her as a starter. Another thought interceded as I began the discussion: I had seen Neptune in the 3rd as the major signal of developmental concern, a suppressed-ego mindset probably formed out of sibling considerations, then further reflected in her work with communications, perhaps her underachievement there somehow, and then carried over into relationships, with Neptune ruling the 7th; I wanted to clarify the focus of all that right away.

This would allow us then to illuminate the Pluto square with the Midheaven, Pluto ruling the key 3rd[3] and then to focus much of the discussion on the mother (Saturn quindecile the nodal axis).

The short vocational discussion helped to do this well. It corroborated much about her work, including the sense and actuality of "floating around." And this allowed the next step of addressing the mother issue, the key into *creative connections* among sibling concerns, relationships, and her job feelings. Her mentioning of "I'm writing it down" allowed me a dramatic, strong entrance of the subject with "Well, start writing the word 'mother'."

Understandings emerge in the consultation as the astrology is brought to the reality experiences disclosed by the client. With Alice, we saw emerge a great deal of unfinished business in the early home, i.e., the detrimental evaluation comparisons with her brother, judged so strongly by her mother (and probably father, although this was not covered). This undermined Alice's young years, and stayed with her. It was a suppressive force.

The very bright spot in the young-years period was her meeting the school friend: "I feel like there's one friend in particular that…you know…was basically the reason I needed to be in San Antonio." [Quite a statement. We hear the adult perspective—the predestination "feel"—flavoring the youthful occurrence.] AND this friend was still intimately in the picture twenty-five years later. It had not been resolved; it was a tie with the unfinished business era in the past. I thought—and I felt from our conversation—that those things bothered, haunted Alice, consciously and unconsciously.

The objective growing during our discussion was certainly to help Alice see her way to a place beyond her brother, in terms of pride, confidence, and talent deployment. This would be accomplished not through further competition for evaluation; rather, it would be done through a focus on self-approving energies that, for everyone, are essential in a productive life. Alice needed to see clearly that she was talented, that her job rewarded that, that there was more to do *and*, should the occasion arise, that she would gain in stature by being helpful to her brother. It was a quest for refreshed values.

---

3. And echoed in present time by the most difficult arc of Saturn quindecile Pluto, ruler of the 3rd, with tr Uranus conjunct the 7th.

Of course, audience, companion, partner to all of this was her husband, and *that* was now adjusted crucially by the adoption of a child. And all of *that* was perhaps being challenged by the reappearance of the "friend" from the past. It was heartening to hear that Alice and her husband were talking these things over, that she realized she was becoming a different person at this stage in her life (and I'm sure she saw the adoption of the child as the signal for that).

An important impact moment took place with the partial summary I offered: "That's about a year and a half when these problems have to gestate, refine themselves, adjust themselves; **perhaps you and your husband could improve the values within your marriage** *that will suit the values in you as a changed lady.*" Alice agreed strongly with this; an objective had been fulfilled. The phrase "as a changed lady" acknowledges that the value changes have indeed already taken place: *that's* accomplished; *now*, the same thing *should* take place in the marriage.

This was reiterated and followed up with, "Somebody far away [I, the astrologer] telling you, **"I've got** *a preferential ring for you; it's your diamond,*" and I want you to earn it. I want you to earn it by getting your body in shape, by talking to your husband about improving the values in your relationship, and realizing that they love you on your job and you're ever doing well."

Powerful turns of phrase happen *if the astrologer respects the communication powers of language,* cultivates these in his or her own life discourse, and becomes sensitive to opportunities to speak beautifully, poignantly, dramatically, authoritatively, etc. There should be something of the actor about the astrologer in consultation, not in any sense insincere, but alert to the opportunity to make impact. The time for this most often occurs toward the end of the consultation, when some kind of summary must take place; it must be memorable for the client. The client will take the words long into the future.

You may think of a power phrase early on in the consultation. I suggest you make a quick note of it, write it down, and let it rest within you as you speak further. As the consultation develops, that phrase will mature in your mind. Then, when the time is right, you can deliver it strongly, with a sense of how it might be delivered in a movie or on the final page of a fine book! These power phrases are important because *they are capsules of feeling and understanding achieved in the consultation;* they are short, they are memorable, and they will be taken away by the client into times to come.

A final observation is importantly in order: nothing was said in the consultation—except with regard to her job improvements (a very secure projection based upon past responses)—that this or that *was going to happen*. Basically, the entire consultation was about values: past, present, and future. The discussion was framed to get through the 3rd House filters and to achieve distance from those old problems. Understanding establishes distance, and distance establishes objectification. Routined hurts can be minimized.

The "job" is up to Alice. *People* do things, planets *don't*. When difficulties are understood, they become motivation for growth. Astrology guides us to that level with highly probable time frames.

5 CASE STUDY: "BRETT"

HOROSCOPE ORIENTATION

Five strong, clearly cut observations orient us well to Brett's horoscope.

1. The eastern hemisphere, tilting to the north, suggests much defensiveness related to unfinished business in the early home.

2. The Sun-Moon blend suggests energy and need for administrative leadership and control—with keen focus on personal projection (the Moon in the 1st House conjunct the Ascendant and square the Midheaven), but this appears importantly conditioned somehow through the maternal influence: the Moon is square the nodal axis, which is conjunct the parental axis. There is a conspicuous imbalance of parental influence.

3. The strong Jupiter-Saturn conjunction in the 11th suggests a drive for a special purpose in life, to improve the societal situation somehow; and with Saturn in the 11th, a great need for love (and acclaim), accentuated by Mercury, the ruler of the 11th being squared by the Great Conjunction. Jupiter-Saturn square the Sun-Mercury conjunction clearly calls attention to parental tension: the Sun rules the Midheaven.

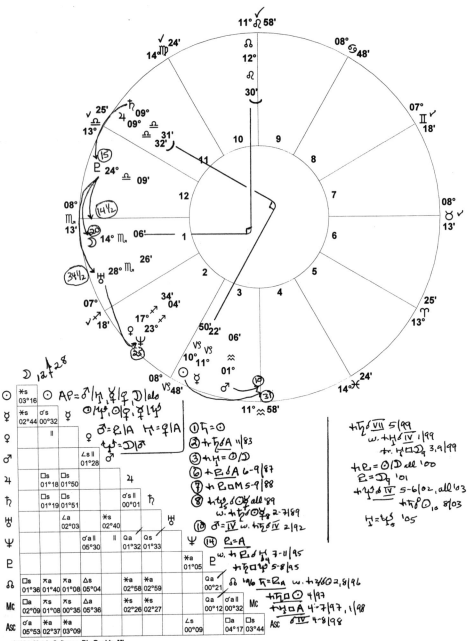

Jan 01, 1981 02:03:00 AM CST 087W13'01" 30N25'16"

Midpoint Sort: 90° Dial

☉/♆	001°57'	♆/Mc	017°31'	♃/♅	033°59'	♀/♇	050°51'	♀/♅	068°00'	☿/♅	079°54'
☿/♆	002°13'	♆/☊	017°47'	☽/♇	034°08'	☽/♅	051°16'	☉/Asc	069°31'	♀/♆	080°19'
♅/Mc	005°12'	☉/♂	020°58'	♂/Mc	036°32'	♆/♇	053°37'	☿/Asc	069°48'	☽/♂	082°36'
♅/☊	005°28'	☿/♂	021°14'	♂/☊	036°48'	☉/♄	055°10'	♄/Mc	070°44'	♆	083°04'
♀/♂	009°20'	♄/Asc	023°52'	Asc	038°13'	☉/♃	055°11'	♃/Mc	070°45'	Mc/Asc	085°05'
♄	009°31'	♃/Asc	023°52'	☽/Asc	041°10'	☿/♄	055°26'	♅/♆	070°45'	☊/Asc	085°22'
♃/♄	009°31'	♇	024°09'	♅/♇	041°17'	☿/♃	055°27'	♄/☊	071°00'	☽/Mc	088°02'
♃	009°32'	☉/Mc	026°24'	Mc	041°58'	♀/Asc	057°53'	♃/☊	071°01'	☽/☊	088°18'
☉	010°50'	☿/Mc	026°40'	☊/Mc	042°14'	♅	058°26'	☽/☉	072°28'	☉/♀	089°12'
☉/☿	011°06'	☉/☊	026°40'	☊	042°30'	♆/Asc	060°38'	♂/♇	072°38'	☿/♀	089°28'
☿	011°22'	☽/♄	026°48'	♀/♄	043°32'	☽/♀	060°50'	☽/☿	072°44'	♂/♅	089°46'
♂/♆	012°05'	☽/♃	026°49'	♀/♃	043°33'	☉/♇	062°30'	♀	077°34'		
♀/Mc	014°46'	☿/☊	026°56'	☽	044°06'	☿/♇	062°46'	♇/Mc	078°03'		
♀/☊	015°02'	♂	031°06'	♄/♆	046°17'	☽/♆	063°35'	♇/☊	078°20'		
♄/♇	016°50'	♇/Asc	031°11'	♃/♆	046°18'	♂/♄	065°18'	☉/♅	079°38'		
♃/♇	016°51'	♄/♅	033°58'	♅/Asc	048°19'	♂/♃	065°19'	♂/Asc	079°39'		

4. Four quintiles suggest the need for conspicuous creative outlet and are included in the vocational profile [**Mc**.☉☿ [3].♄♃.♀.♆E;☽□**Mc**,☽.♇.♀<>♃;4Q;AP=☿/♀: aesthetic persuader; need to sell/administer beautiful, artistic, or idealistic ideas.][1]
5. There is a sense of "the world doesn't understand me" suggested by the Pluto position in the 12th House, and this is quite possibly linked to considerations of the sexual profile, keyed by Neptune, ruler of the 5th, conjunct Venus and Mercury, ruler of the 8th, squared by Saturn; additionally, Venus conjoined by Neptune rules the 12th.

The particular House references of tensions are suggested by the checkmarks on select cusps. The education does not seem threatened (the Moon, ruler of the 9th, is not under high developmental tension).

The rapport arcs for the first ten years of life are few: we see at age one year that Saturn-Jupiter complete the square to the Sun, ruler of the Midheaven. This suggests tremendous upheaval in the home, around the child, very, very early on. This is accompanied by tr

1. Please see Tyl, *Vocations* for full development and presentation of the Midheaven Extension Process for vocational profiling. The "code line" for the vocational deduction is included here as part of the complete preparation of the horoscope consultation. The specialization of the technique cannot be included in this text.

Saturn conjunct the Ascendant at two, tr Uranus=Sun/Moon at three (at this age, strong activation of the Sun/Moon midpoint usually suggests a parental relationship problem), and then tr Pluto conjoins the Ascendant and soon squares the Midheaven at age seven. Clearly, there is much upheaval in the home.

That developmental period is immediately followed by tr Neptune conjoining Sun-Mercury at age eight, suggesting a lonely, perhaps bruised time, which is followed by the Mars=MC arc at age ten with tr Saturn conjunct the fourth cusp.

We can see these first ten years as most difficult, most formative.

We can ask, *"How deeply did things hurt Brett? What defensive behaviors, because of it all, were born and how much of that continues into adulthood? How did he try to escape, to extricate himself from the upset?"*

The major objective within the consultation will be to bring Brett into control of his gifts, to help him find purpose, to create distance with the past influences as soon as he can.

It is easy to see in the solar arc, double-ringed horoscope that a future target-time would be in three years, when SA Jupiter-Saturn comes to the Ascendant, followed by SA Sun-Mercury=MH two years later (accompanied by Brett's tr Saturn return).

Line-by-line study of the combo-search (with practice, it goes very quickly), looking especially for strong contacts with the angles, gives us this picture: tr Saturn makes its final square to the Ascendant in June 2006 and goes on immediately to transit the Midheaven. This should be a peak time, a time when ambition gains new focus. It is preceded by tr Jupiter conjunct the Moon, ruler of Brett's 9th, in May 2006, repeating again in September along with SP Moon conjoining Pluto, ruler of the Ascendant. Could this be a time to get more education, specialized education, for better career strength?

In March 2007, Brett shows SA Node=Pluto, probably a fine romantic liaison, and the strong arc of MC=Pluto building in the summer of 2007: recognition, probably; change of status. And by November 2007, Sun= Ascendant with SP Moon conjunct the Ascendant simultaneously.

Brett

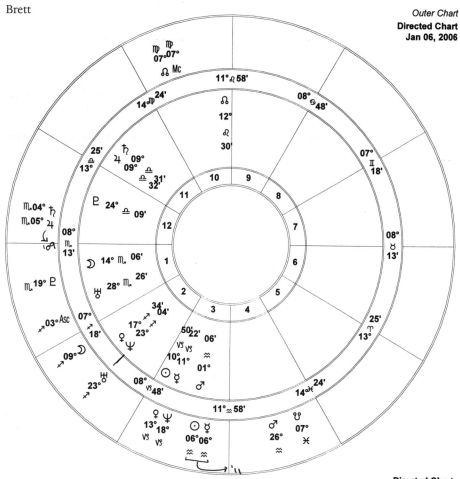

Pl	Geo Lon	℞	Decl.
☽	14°♏06' 05"		- 11° 06'
☉	10°♑49' 47"		- 23° 00'
☿	11°♑22' 12"		- 24° 45'
♀	17°♐33' 31"		- 22° 01'
♂	01°♒05' 47"		- 21° 01'
♃	09°♎31' 52"		- 02° 34'
♄	09°♎30' 47"		- 01° 36'
♅	28°♏25' 41"		- 19° 35'
♆	23°♐03' 53"		- 21° 58'
♇	24°♎09' 15"		+06° 28'

©1994 Matrix Software Big Rapids, MI

Directed Chart

Pl	Geo Lon	℞	Decl.
☽	09°♐34' 33"		- 11° 06'
☉	06°♒18' 15"		- 23° 00'
☿	06°♒50' 40"		- 24° 45'
♀	13°♑01' 59"		- 22° 01'
♂	26°♏34' 15"		- 21° 01'
♃	05°♏00' 20"		- 02° 34'
♄	04°♏59' 15"		- 01° 36'
♅	23°♐54' 09"		- 19° 35'
♆	18°♑32' 21"		- 21° 58'
♇	19°♏37' 43"		+06° 28'

Search From Dec 31, 2005 to Dec 31, 2007 GMT Page: 1

Aspect	Date	Time	Event	Type	P1 Pos.	P2 Pos	E/X/L
♂ -- □ Mc	01-04-2006	09:43 am	♂ □ Mc	Tr-Na	11°♉58'	11°♌58'	Exact
♃ -- ☌ ☽	01-06-2006	02:27 am	♃ ☌ ☽	Tr-Na	14°♏06'	14°♏06'	Exact
♂ -- □ ☊	01-06-2006	07:37 am	♂ □ ☊	Tr-Na	12°♉30'	12°♌30'℞	Exact
♂ -- ☍ ☽	01-11-2006	12:00 pm	♂ ☍ ☽	Tr-Na	14°♉06'	14°♏06'	Exact
☊ --- □ ♀/♅	01-14-2006	01:41 am	☊ □ ♀/♅	Ar-Na	08°♍00'	08°♐00'	Exact
♆ ---- ∠ ☽/♆	01-22-2006	12:49 pm	♆ ∠ ☽/♆	Ar-Na	18°♑35'	03°♐35'	Exact
♄ -- □ Asc	01-23-2006	02:51 pm	♄ □ Asc	Tr-Na	08°♌13'℞	08°♏13'	Exact
♂ -- ☍ ♅	02-14-2006	05:51 pm	♂ ☍ ♅	Tr-Na	28°♉26'	28°♏26'	Exact
♃ -- SR	03-04-2006	05:31 pm	♃ SR	Tr-Na	18°♏52'℞		
♂ -- ☍ ♀	03-23-2006	02:34 am	♂ ☍ ♀	Tr-Na	17°♊34'	17°♐34'	Exact
☽ ☌ ☿/Asc	03-26-2006	06:16 am	☽ ☌ ☿/Asc	Ar-Na	09°♐48'	09°♐48'	Exact
☉ - □ ♂/Mc	03-28-2006	02:18 am	☉ □ ♂/Mc	Ar-Na	06°♒32'	06°♏32'	Exact
♇ ---- SR	03-29-2006	10:22 am	♇ SR	Tr-Na	26°♐45'℞		
♂ -- ☍ ♆	04-01-2006	09:58 pm	♂ ☍ ♆	Tr-Na	23°♊04'	23°♐04'	Exact
♄ -- SD	04-05-2006	12:04 pm	♄ SD	Tr-Na	04°♌23'		
♃ -- ∠ ♀/♆	04-26-2006	06:53 pm	♃ ∠ ♀/♆	Ar-Na	05°♏19'	20°♐19'	Exact
♂ -- □ ♄	04-30-2006	09:08 am	♂ □ ♄	Tr-Na	09°♋31'	09°♎31'	Exact
♂ -- □ ♃	04-30-2006	09:52 am	♂ □ ♃	Tr-Na	09°♋32'	09°♎32'	Exact
♂ -- ☍ ☉	05-02-2006	02:53 pm	♂ ☍ ☉	Tr-Na	10°♋50'	10°♑50'	Exact
♄ -- ∠ ♀/♆	05-03-2006	07:21 am	♄ ∠ ♀/♆	Ar-Na	05°♏19'	20°♐19'	Exact
♂ -- ☍ ☿	05-03-2006	12:53 pm	♂ ☍ ☿	Tr-Na	11°♋22'	11°♑22'	Exact
♃ -- ☌ ☽	05-03-2006	06:34 pm	♃ ☌ ☽	Tr-Na	14°♏06'℞	14°♏06'	Exact
♃ -- □ ☊	05-16-2006	12:29 pm	♃ □ ☊	Tr-Na	12°♏30'℞	12°♌30'℞	Exact
♃ -- □ Mc	05-21-2006	01:13 am	♃ □ Mc	Tr-Na	11°♏58'℞	11°♌58'	Exact
♆ ---- SR	05-22-2006	09:33 am	♆ SR	Tr-Na	19°♒49'℞		
♂ -- □ ♇	05-25-2006	01:17 am	♂ □ ♇	Tr-Na	24°♋09'	24°♎09'	Exact
♂ -- q Mc	05-26-2006	09:38 am	♂ q Mc	Ar-Na	26°♒58'	11°♌58'	Exact
♀ - ∠ ♅	05-28-2006	04:55 pm	♀ ∠ ♅	Ar-Na	13°♑26'	28°♏26'	Exact
♂ -- ☍ ♂	06-05-2006	02:21 pm	♂ ☍ ♂	Tr-Na	01°♌06'	01°♒06'	Exact
♄ -- □ Asc	06-13-2006	00:31 am	♄ □ Asc	Tr-Na	08°♌13'	08°♏13'	Exact
♂ -- □ Asc	06-17-2006	08:34 am	♂ □ Asc	Tr-Na	08°♌13'	08°♏13'	Exact
♅ ---- SR	06-19-2006	04:31 am	♅ SR	Tr-Na	14°♓44'℞		
♂ -- ☌ Mc	06-23-2006	11:58 am	♂ ☌ Mc	Tr-Na	11°♌58'	11°♌58'	Exact
♂ -- ☌ ☊	06-24-2006	09:10 am	♂ ☌ ☊	Tr-Na	12°♌30'	12°♌30'℞	Exact
♂ -- □ ☽	06-27-2006	00:05 am	♂ □ ☽	Tr-Na	14°♌06'	14°♏06'	Exact
☉ - □ ♂/☊	07-03-2006	00:22 am	☉ □ ♂/☊	Ar-Na	06°♒48'	06°♏48'	Exact
♃ -- SD	07-06-2006	07:33 am	♃ SD	Tr-Na	08°♏59'		
♂ -- ∠ ♂/♆	07-08-2006	11:28 pm	♂ ∠ ♂/♆	Ar-Na	27°♒05'	12°♑05'	Exact
♄ -- ☌ Mc	07-15-2006	05:18 pm	♄ ☌ Mc	Tr-Na	11°♌58'	11°♌58'	Exact
♄ -- ☌ ☊	07-20-2006	01:06 am	♄ ☌ ☊	Tr-Na	12°♌30'	12°♌30'℞	Exact
♂ -- □ ♅	07-20-2006	06:10 am	♂ □ ♅	Tr-Na	28°♌26'	28°♏26'	Exact
Mc --- □ ♀/♅	07-26-2006	09:45 pm	Mc □ ♀/♅	Ar-Na	08°♍00'	08°♐00'	Exact
♇ ---- ∠ ♅/Mc	07-28-2006	08:25 pm	♇ ∠ ♅/Mc	Ar-Na	20°♏12'	05°♎12'	Exact
♄ -- □ ☽	08-01-2006	03:59 pm	♄ □ ☽	Tr-Na	14°♌06'	14°♏06'	Exact
♂ -- □ ♀	08-19-2006	05:44 pm	♂ □ ♀	Tr-Na	17°♍34'	17°♐34'	Exact
♃ -- □ Mc	08-21-2006	06:09 am	♃ □ Mc	Tr-Na	11°♏58'	11°♌58'	Exact
♃ -- □ ☊	08-25-2006	11:37 am	♃ □ ☊	Tr-Na	12°♏30'	12°♌30'℞	Exact
♂ -- □ ♆	08-28-2006	09:08 am	♂ □ ♆	Tr-Na	23°♍04'	23°♐04'	Exact
♂ -- q ☊/Mc	08-31-2006	07:46 am	♂ q ☊/Mc	Ar-Na	27°♒14'	12°♌14'	Exact
☽ ☌ ♇	09-01-2006	09:58 am	☽ ☌ ♇	Pr-Na	24°♎09'	24°♎09'	Exact
♇ ---- SD	09-04-2006	08:18 pm	♇ SD	Tr-Na	24°♐05'		
♃ -- ☌ ☽	09-05-2006	04:23 pm	♃ ☌ ☽	Tr-Na	14°♏06'	14°♏06'	Exact
♂ -- ☌ ♄	09-22-2006	07:50 pm	♂ ☌ ♄	Tr-Na	09°♎31'	09°♎31'	Exact
♂ -- ☌ ♃	09-22-2006	08:30 pm	♂ ☌ ♃	Tr-Na	09°♎32'	09°♎32'	Exact
♂ -- □ ☉	09-24-2006	08:07 pm	♂ □ ☉	Tr-Na	10°♎50'	10°♑50'	Exact
♂ -- □ ☿	09-25-2006	03:54 pm	♂ □ ☿	Tr-Na	11°♎22'	11°♑22'	Exact
☿ - ∠ ☽/♂	10-04-2006	10:30 pm	☿ ∠ ☽/♂	Ar-Na	07°♒36'	22°♐36'	Exact
♂ -- ☌ ♇	10-14-2006	11:34 pm	♂ ☌ ♇	Tr-Na	24°♎09'	24°♎09'	Exact
♂ -- □ ♂	10-25-2006	07:38 am	♂ □ ♂	Tr-Na	01°♏06'	01°♒06'	Exact
☊ --- □ ♆	10-28-2006	08:02 pm	☊ □ ♆	Tr-Na	23°♓04'℞	23°♐04'	Exact
♆ ---- SD	10-29-2006	04:49 am	♆ SD	Tr-Na	17°♒02'		
♇ ---- ∠ ♅/☊	11-02-2006	06:37 pm	♇ ∠ ♅/☊	Ar-Na	20°♏28'	05°♎28'	Exact
♂ -- ☌ Asc	11-04-2006	07:28 pm	♂ ☌ Asc	Tr-Na	08°♏13'	08°♏13'	Exact
♂ -- □ Mc	11-10-2006	06:40 am	♂ □ Mc	Tr-Na	11°♏58'	11°♌58'	Exact
♂ -- □ ☊	11-11-2006	01:31 am	♂ □ ☊	Tr-Na	12°♏30'	12°♌30'℞	Exact
♂ -- ☌ ☽	11-13-2006	09:27 am	♂ ☌ ☽	Tr-Na	14°♏06'	14°♏06'	Exact
♃ -- ☌ ♅	11-17-2006	03:05 am	♃ ☌ ♅	Tr-Na	28°♏26'	28°♏26'	Exact
♅ ---- SD	11-20-2006	03:56 am	♅ SD	Tr-Na	10°♓49'		
☊ --- ∠ ♄/Asc	11-23-2006	02:51 pm	☊ ∠ ♄/Asc	Ar-Na	08°♍52'	23°♎52'	Exact
☊ --- ∠ ♃/Asc	11-26-2006	09:06 pm	☊ ∠ ♃/Asc	Ar-Na	08°♍53'	23°♎53'	Exact
♂ -- ☌ ♅	12-03-2006	11:24 pm	♂ ☌ ♅	Tr-Na	28°♏26'	28°♏26'	Exact
♄ -- SR	12-06-2006	01:42 am	♄ SR	Tr-Na	25°♌04'℞		
♂ -- q ☊	12-06-2006	05:59 am	♂ q ☊	Ar-Na	27°♒30'	12°♌30'℞	Exact

+♄□A 2nd "hit"

+♃☌☽q

SA♂q = M

+♄□A final

+♄☌M

Search From Dec 31, 2005 to Dec 31, 2007 GMT Page: 2

Aspect	Date	Time	Event	Type	P1 Pos.	P2 Pos	E/X/L
♂ -- ☌ ♀	12-30-2006	07:07 pm	♂ ☌ ♀	Tr-Na	17°♐34'	17°♐34'	Exact
♂ -- ☌ ♆	01-07-2007	09:18 am	♂ ☌ ♆	Tr-Na	23°♐04'	23°♐04'	Exact
♂ -- □ ♄	01-29-2007	06:03 pm	♂ □ ♄	Tr-Na	09°♑31'	09°♎31'	Exact
♂ -- □ ♃	01-29-2007	06:38 pm	♂ □ ♃	Tr-Na	09°♑32'	09°♎32'	Exact
♂ -- ☌ ☉	01-31-2007	12:35 pm	♂ ☌ ☉	Tr-Na	10°♑50'	10°♑50'	Exact
♂ -- ☌ ☿	02-01-2007	06:01 am	♂ ☌ ☿	Tr-Na	11°♑22'	11°♑22'	Exact
☊ --- □ ♀	02-09-2007	07:31 pm	☊ □ ♀	Tr-Na	17°♓34'℞	17°♐34'	Exact
♂ -- □ ♇	02-18-2007	07:45 am	♂ □ ♇	Tr-Na	24°♑09'	24°♎09'	Exact
♃ -- ☌ ♀	02-26-2007	01:17 pm	♃ ☌ ♀	Tr-Na	17°♐34'	17°♐34'	Exact
♂ -- ☌ ♂	02-27-2007	12:18 pm	♂ ☌ ♂	Tr-Na	01°♒06'	01°♒06'	Exact
☽ □ ♄/Mc	02-27-2007	07:49 pm	☽ □ ♄/Mc	Ar-Na	10°♐44'	10°♍44'	Exact
☽ □ ♃/Mc	03-03-2007	02:04 am	☽ □ ♃/Mc	Ar-Na	10°♐45'	10°♍45'	Exact
☽ ☌ ♅/♆	03-03-2007	12:13 pm	☽ ☌ ♅/♆	Ar-Na	10°♐45'	10°♐45'	Exact
☊ --- ∠ ♇	03-07-2007	07:07 am	☊ ∠ ♇	Ar-Na	09°♍09'	24°♎09'	Exact
♂ -- □ Asc	03-08-2007	09:24 pm	♂ □ Asc	Tr-Na	08°♒13'	08°♏13'	Exact
♅ ---- □ Mc/Asc	03-09-2007	04:30 am	♅ □ Mc/Asc	Ar-Na	25°♐05'	25°♍05'	Exact
♂ -- ☍ Mc	03-13-2007	07:12 pm	♂ ☍ Mc	Tr-Na	11°♒58'	11°♌58'	Exact
♂ -- ☍ ☊	03-14-2007	12:10 pm	♂ ☍ ☊	Tr-Na	12°♒30'	12°♌30'℞	Exact
♂ -- □ ☽	03-16-2007	02:33 pm	♂ □ ☽	Tr-Na	14°♒06'	14°♏06'	Exact
☿ - ∠ ♆	03-21-2007	09:37 am	☿ ∠ ♆	Ar-Na	08°♒04'	23°♐04'	Exact
♇ ---- ☌ ♀/♇	03-24-2007	01:51 am	♇ ☌ ♀/♇	Ar-Na	20°♏51'	20°♏51'	Exact
♇ ---- SR	03-31-2007	08:12 pm	♇ SR	Tr-Na	28°♐58'℞		
☽ □ ♂	04-02-2007	06:55 pm	☽ □ ♂	Pr-Na	01°♏06'	01°♒06'	Exact
♂ -- □ ♅	04-04-2007	07:39 am	♂ □ ♅	Tr-Na	28°♒26'	28°♏26'	Exact
♃ -- SR	04-06-2007	00:30 am	♃ SR	Tr-Na	19°♐47'℞		
☉ - ∠ ☽/♂	04-17-2007	01:34 am	☉ ∠ ☽/♂	Ar-Na	07°♒36'	22°♐36'	Exact
♄ -- SD	04-19-2007	08:35 pm	♄ SD	Tr-Na	18°♌09'		
♂ -- □ ♀/Asc	04-25-2007	10:21 am	♂ □ ♀/Asc	Ar-Na	27°♒53'	27°♏53'	Exact
♂ -- □ ♀	04-29-2007	06:26 am	♂ □ ♀	Tr-Na	17°♓34'	17°♐34'	Exact
♅ ---- □ ♀	04-30-2007	03:09 pm	♅ □ ♀	Tr-Na	17°♓34'	17°♐34'	Exact
♂ -- □ ♆	05-06-2007	11:26 am	♂ □ ♆	Tr-Na	23°♓04'	23°♐04'	Exact
♃ -- ☌ ♀	05-14-2007	10:03 pm	♃ ☌ ♀	Tr-Na	17°♐34'℞	17°♐34'	Exact
☿ - □ Asc	05-15-2007	04:08 pm	☿ □ Asc	Ar-Na	08°♒13'	08°♏13'	Exact
♆ ---- SR	05-24-2007	10:19 pm	♆ SR	Tr-Na	22°♒02'℞		
♂ -- ☍ ♄	05-28-2007	04:24 am	♂ ☍ ♄	Tr-Na	09°♈31'	09°♎31'	Exact
♂ -- ☍ ♃	05-28-2007	04:58 am	♂ ☍ ♃	Tr-Na	09°♈32'	09°♎32'	Exact
♂ -- □ ☉	05-29-2007	10:30 pm	♂ □ ☉	Tr-Na	10°♈50'	10°♑50'	Exact
♂ -- □ ☿	05-30-2007	03:48 pm	♂ □ ☿	Tr-Na	11°♈22'	11°♑22'	Exact
☽ □ ♄/☊	06-04-2007	06:14 pm	☽ □ ♄/☊	Ar-Na	11°♐00'	11°♍00'	Exact
Mc --- ∠ ♄/Asc	06-05-2007	11:35 am	Mc ∠ ♄/Asc	Ar-Na	08°♍52'	23°♎52'	Exact
☽ □ ♃/☊	06-08-2007	00:30 am	☽ □ ♃/☊	Ar-Na	11°♐01'	11°♍01'	Exact
Mc --- ∠ ♃/Asc	06-08-2007	05:50 pm	Mc ∠ ♃/Asc	Ar-Na	08°♍53'	23°♎53'	Exact
♅ ---- □ ☊/Asc	06-14-2007	02:56 am	♅ □ ☊/Asc	Ar-Na	25°♐22'	25°♍22'	Exact
♂ -- ☍ ♇	06-16-2007	09:07 pm	♂ ☍ ♇	Tr-Na	24°♈09'	24°♎09'	Exact
♅ ---- SR	06-23-2007	01:04 pm	♅ SR	Tr-Na	18°♓42'℞		
♂ -- □ ♂	06-26-2007	09:48 am	♂ □ ♂	Tr-Na	01°♉06'	01°♒06'	Exact
♂ -- ☍ Asc	07-06-2007	08:20 am	♂ ☍ Asc	Tr-Na	08°♉13'	08°♏13'	Exact
♃ -- ☌ ♂/Mc	07-07-2007	09:49 pm	♃ ☌ ♂/Mc	Ar-Na	06°♏32'	06°♏32'	Exact
♂ -- □ Mc	07-11-2007	03:28 pm	♂ □ Mc	Tr-Na	11°♉58'	11°♌58'	Exact
♂ -- □ ☊	07-12-2007	09:56 am	♂ □ ☊	Tr-Na	12°♉30'	12°♌30'℞	Exact
♄ -- ☌ ♂/Mc	07-14-2007	10:19 am	♄ ☌ ♂/Mc	Ar-Na	06°♏32'	06°♏32'	Exact
♂ -- ☍ ☽	07-14-2007	04:57 pm	♂ ☍ ☽	Tr-Na	14°♉06'	14°♏06'	Exact
☊ --- □ ☉/Asc	07-18-2007	07:10 am	☊ □ ☉/Asc	Ar-Na	09°♍31'	09°♐31'	Exact
♂ -- ☍ ♅	08-04-2007	08:21 pm	♂ ☍ ♅	Tr-Na	28°♉26'	28°♏26'	Exact
♃ -- SD	08-07-2007	00:40 am	♃ SD	Tr-Na	09°♐56'		
Asc --- ☌ ♂/♄	08-09-2007	02:08 am	Asc ☌ ♂/♄	Ar-Na	05°♐18'	05°♐18'	Exact
Asc --- ☌ ♂/♃	08-12-2007	08:23 am	Asc ☌ ♂/♃	Ar-Na	05°♐19'	05°♐19'	Exact
♇ ---- ☌ ☽/♅	08-17-2007	08:12 pm	♇ ☌ ☽/♅	Ar-Na	21°♏16'	21°♏16'	Exact
♅ ---- □ ♀	08-18-2007	08:15 pm	♅ □ ♀	Tr-Na	17°♓34'℞	17°♐34'	Exact
♄ -- □ ♅	08-21-2007	04:31 am	♄ □ ♅	Tr-Na	28°♌26'	28°♏26'	Exact
♂ -- ☍ ♀	09-04-2007	09:53 pm	♂ ☍ ♀	Tr-Na	17°♊34'	17°♐34'	Exact
♇ ---- SD	09-07-2007	10:24 am	♇ SD	Tr-Na	26°♐18'		
♂ -- ☍ ♆	09-14-2007	10:49 pm	♂ ☍ ♆	Tr-Na	23°♊04'	23°♐04'	Exact
Mc --- ∠ ♇	09-17-2007	04:05 am	Mc ∠ ♇	Ar-Na	09°♍09'	24°♎09'	Exact
♀ - □ ♀/Mc	09-19-2007	02:45 am	♀ □ ♀/Mc	Ar-Na	14°♑46'	14°♎46'	Exact
☉ - ∠ ♆	10-01-2007	01:03 pm	☉ ∠ ♆	Ar-Na	08°♒04'	23°♐04'	Exact
♆ ---- ∠ ♂/♄	10-03-2007	08:43 am	♆ ∠ ♂/♄	Ar-Na	20°♑18'	05°♐18'	Exact
♆ ---- ∠ ♂/♃	10-06-2007	02:59 pm	♆ ∠ ♂/♃	Ar-Na	20°♑19'	05°♐19'	Exact
♃ -- ☌ ♂/☊	10-12-2007	08:22 pm	♃ ☌ ♂/☊	Ar-Na	06°♏48'	06°♏48'	Exact
♄ -- ☌ ♂/☊	10-19-2007	08:53 am	♄ ☌ ♂/☊	Ar-Na	06°♏48'	06°♏48'	Exact
♃ -- ☌ ♀	10-21-2007	04:29 am	♃ ☌ ♀	Tr-Na	17°♐34'	17°♐34'	Exact
☽ ∠ ☉/Mc	10-22-2007	12:24 pm	☽ ∠ ☉/Mc	Ar-Na	11°♐24'	26°♎24'	Exact
☊ --- □ ☿/Asc	10-23-2007	08:58 am	☊ □ ☿/Asc	Ar-Na	09°♍48'	09°♐48'	Exact

Search From Dec 31, 2005 to Dec 31, 2007 GMT   Page: 3

Aspect	Date	Time	Event	Type	P1 Pos.	P2 Pos	E/X/L
♂ -- □ ♄	10-24-2007	10:27 pm	♂ □ ♄	Tr-Na	09°♋31'	09°♎31'	Exact
♂ -- □ ♃	10-25-2007	00:08 am	♂ □ ♃	Tr-Na	09°♋32'	09°♎32'	Exact
♂ -- ☍ ☉	10-30-2007	04:10 pm	♂ ☍ ☉	Tr-Na	10°♋50'	10°♑50'	Exact
♆ ---- SD	10-31-2007	04:45 pm	♆ SD	Tr-Na	19°♒15'		
♂ -- ☍ ☿	11-02-2007	03:19 pm	♂ ☍ ☿	Tr-Na	11°♋22'	11°♑22'	Exact
♂ -- □ ♅	11-05-2007	08:42 am	♂ □ ♅	Ar-Na	28°♒26'	28°♏26'	Exact
☽ ☌ Asc	11-07-2007	09:37 pm	☽ ☌ Asc	Pr-Na	08°♏13'	08°♏13'	Exact
♂ -- SR	11-15-2007	08:41 am	♂ SR	Tr-Na	12°♋27'℞		
♃ -- ☌ ♆	11-17-2007	06:56 pm	♃ ☌ ♆	Tr-Na	23°♐04'	23°♐04'	Exact
♅ ---- SD	11-24-2007	08:26 am	♅ SD	Tr-Na	14°♓46'		
☉ - □ Asc	11-25-2007	07:41 pm	☉ □ Asc	Ar-Na	08°♒13'	08°♏13'	Exact
♂ -- ☍ ☿	11-27-2007	04:10 pm	♂ ☍ ☿	Tr-Na	11°♋22'℞	11°♑22'	Exact
♂ -- ☍ ☉	11-30-2007	10:32 am	♂ ☍ ☉	Tr-Na	10°♋50'℞	10°♑50'	Exact
♂ -- □ ♃	12-05-2007	03:27 pm	♂ □ ♃	Tr-Na	09°♋32'℞	09°♎32'	Exact
♂ -- □ ♄	12-05-2007	04:59 pm	♂ □ ♄	Tr-Na	09°♋31'℞	09°♎31'	Exact
♄ -- SR	12-19-2007	01:21 pm	♄ SR	Tr-Na	08°♍34'℞		
♀ - □ ♀/☊	12-25-2007	01:24 am	♀ □ ♀/☊	Ar-Na	15°♑02'	15°♎02'	Exact

SP ☽ ☌ A ⎤

☉ = A ⎦

THE CONSULTATION

N: Good morning!

B: Good morning, sir.

While this consultation was by telephone, I had met Brett casually some months before during a professional engagement he attended. Southern courtesies prevail with him; he is respectful of the senior astrologer, to a fault!

N: Thank you for being on time!

B: Of course.

N: You know, you're a *young* man and you're so incredibly intelligent. We just have to work for you to understand that. And to understand some of the crooks in the road and what have you.

I was immediately addressing the support objective I knew was essential, to get him out from the defensive postures, whatever they were. Indeed, Brett shows intelligence and poise—as well as defensiveness—through his communication skills and presence.

B: (Quietly) Yes.

N: This is not a Nirvana revelation; there's a defensive curtain around you that is very hard to penetrate: withdrawal, self-protection. You understand that, don't you?

B: (Several times during the last sentence) Yes…Yes.

N: And what about the depression dimension? Have you ever been treated clinically for depression?

B: Uh. No. Um...My...When I was a teenager, I told my mother I wanted to see a therapist, but she said I was "just fine."

N: All right. But you know, there is an awful lot here that is, uh, that is begging for attention, of which you have been deprived for a long time. I think that's a fair assessment... it's not a critique.

I was so careful not to fall into the routine of people criticizing Brett.

B: Yes. Of course.

N: And you mentioned the magic word "mother" here. You've heard in my lectures, there's a tremendous statement here of maternal influence.

B: Yes.

N: How...uh...do you adjust to that? What was this relationship like with her?

B: Well, uh...she ended up having custody of me when my parents separated when I was...five (?).

N: Well, I have six here. It was in the spring-summer of 1987.

Tr Pluto conjunct the Ascendant.

B: That's when they were fully divorced.

N: All right. That's what I'm seeing.

B: ...but they separated, I think a year before that.

N: OK.

B: And the circumstances of their divorce...uh...were fraught with drama, I guess I'll say, and so the relationship between the two of them was extremely poor.

N: It always was beforehand, too; you grew up in those first four or five years in a *milieu* of bombast, don't you think?

B: Yes. Yes. But it was shielded from me by my mother in a very strong way. And, uh, my father was a very, very boisterous man back then. He was involved in everyone's favorite entrepreneurial project then...the product of the '70s–'80s, which was...uh...cocaine. And it...uh...infected the family in a tremendous way. Uh...It affected my mother's first daughter, who was fourteen at the time, I think...

N: Your father was a dealer in cocaine?

B: Yes. In addition to his computer job, his sales job...

N: Well, did he ever get hauled in for this…you know what I'm saying: pulled in by the police, and…?

B: No. He never had to serve any sort of jail time. My mother could have pressed charges, but she and my sister decided they didn't want to for my sake. Um…They didn't want me to have a father who was in jail.

N: Yes. I appreciate that. There are all sorts of stuff going on here right after their split, their formal divorce, for about the next four years. That's what the horoscope suggests.

I'm trying to get over the home scene upset and explain the Mars=MC with tr Saturn conjunct the 4th very early in 1992.

B: My mother remarried in 1989.

N: Yes. Between February and July; something like that.

B: April 29, exactly in between. I was not enthusiastic about it at all, at first. My stepfather and I now get along, um, but at the time it was a very different environment than what I was used to; he was so very the opposite of my father, and he took more of a hard line disciplinarian approach with me that I completely despised.

N: All right. This "stuff" you are sharing with me, with eloquence, is…is painful.

Again: complimenting him; an intentionally complimentary, "excessive" word-choice: "eloquence."

B: Yes.

N: It's lonely. *It causes your intelligence to fabricate a defensive posture.* You know that and I know that.

B: Yes, of course.

N: The, uh, bombast in the earliest home was replaced by the disciplinarian, authoritarian bombast of the stepfather. Fair?

B: Yes. Quite.

N: And uh, astrologically—since you know some astrology for sure—this all coincides with the solar arc of Mars on the fourth cusp. That enters your life and sets you up to be vulnerable to exploitation and the authoritarian statements of everybody you meet thereafter. *It's an open door to this vulnerability.* Does it help to see it that way?

B: Yes. I believe so. Yeah. Yeah.

N: And it was triggered by transiting Saturn on that fourth cusp as well in early 1992. All right: he has moved in and the remarriage takes place, and for two or three years, everybody is jockeying for position, and it comes up that he is running the show. And you are becoming a scapegoat for an awful lot of tensions around you.

B: Yeah. But I don't think he ran the show as far as my mother is concerned.

N: There is "omnipotence" here, that we see in the nodal axis situation.

B: Really?

N: Square the Moon and on the Midheaven. This is a lady who runs the show.

B: Yeah.

N: But the point I'm talking about is the relationship with you. Your stepfather was a strong-armer.

B: Yeah…uh, and he was the one who…uh…My mother made the money. My stepfather's professional career was more or less non-existent. He was attempting to write novels that never went anywhere, but he was the person I had to be around when I was at home all the time, and though I was very much on guard a large portion of my childhood…

N: You hear the words "on guard"? This is the defensiveness that we're seeing here.

B: Yes.

N: And this is how it all evolves. And it's a damn shame! I think what we need to understand is that you're born with this extraordinary, perceptive, keen intelligence and the reaction positive to things beautiful and spiritual even…Dare I say that?

B: Oh yes. That is *completely* spot-on!

N: And what happens is that…NOBODY CARES!

B: [High response level] YES! Exactly!! [Nervous laughing]

N: Nobody cares about that. They *sense* it…and this is why perhaps your mother did not press charges on your father—your sire—for the cocaine dealing and all that "jazz". You said, "Because they wanted to protect my sensibilities." You see?

B: Yes.

N: So people around you even then knew you were a sensitive, vulnerable, highly aesthetic child; impressionable…You see?

B: Yes. Exactly.

N: And you are. I mean…you know…You're *exquisite!* And people see that and they don't quite know what to do with it, **because you haven't *matched it* with reality experience…YET.**

B: Yes!

N: And so what we are seeing in the remarriage is the very strong possibility that, in his frustrations, the stepfather is…is taking things out on the family…onto you.

B: Yes, yes. I recall very strongly one time when we were in the library…he is a book collector, and the bottom floor of my mother's house was…he turned it into his library. He built shelves…books up everywhere. They're still there to this day. Um…But…I remember, we were standing in the library one time; we were fighting over—I don't even remember what—and, I said something, I guess, that he found disrespectful or sassy, and he clean slapped me across the face.

N: Hmm.

B: And that was…um…that had never happened to me before, and I remember growing cold against him. Instantly; the second his hand touched my face. I thought, "Fuck you for the rest of your life!" And I held on to that for such a long time.

N: It's a darn shame. I really want to establish between us here, since we are both trying to enjoy your…your potential: we want to appreciate the short circuits that were inflicted upon you! By your family environment. Is that fair?

B: Yes. Definitely. I have always found that my home life has been a bane.

N: All right. It's not that we're just blaming something "out there." We're saying that your special—dare I use the word in the best sense—precious talents and sensitivity were not recognized, they weren't supported, and you are left with a self-worth anxiety that is so deep…even today…

B: Yeah.

N: …with this tremendous need to feel that you're lovable…and you haven't begun to fight, to show yourself. You are a powerfully insightful dealer of ideas. Now I alluded earlier to things idealistic or spiritual; and even now your response shows me that that allusion is on target.

B: Yes, yes, it definitely is.

N: And I need for you please to share with me a little amplification of that because I don't think anyone in the world would sit here and bring that up to you, Brett, except this way through astrology and great sensitivity.

B: Well, uh…I don't come from a religious family…at all. Um…I was sent to a Christian elementary school, um, a private school of course, when I was a small child, because my father who was a racist didn't want me going to public school with quote-unquote "niggers."

N: Your father or your stepfather?

B: My father.

N: But your father was not there in the school years.

B: I started reading when I was three, and he and my mother agreed that I would go to the Catholic school, which was very close to my house, um, and the public school that was nearby was mostly black.

N: So, you are talking about the first year of school, practically…

B: Yeah, when I started in pre-school, they started me there…but I stayed there until I was ten, in fifth grade, and then I went to public school after that.

N: And that was when this awareness that you were being pushed around pretty strongly and had to defend yourself really set in, in your mother's re-marriage.

B: Yes, but I was also being pushed around by my peers at this school.

N: Absolutely! Now, we mentioned this earlier—remember?—*this continues today*, people taking advantage of you…

B: Yeah.

N: …and this is why [we have] the pervasive defensiveness. *It's a habit!*

B: Yes.

N: It's a vulnerability portrayal that is a shame. **This is what we have to adjust and erase:** *the habit; the perpetuation of being so vulnerable.*

B: [A pause] What...wh...What is the best thing to do?

N: Look at what we've ascertained here in...what...six minutes!

B: Yeah!

N: It's amazing. Now the thing is that, especially among young people who can smell it, somebody who's vulnerable *gets it! You know?*

B: Yes. Definitely.

N: It's like water finding its level somehow around the rocks, and as soon as it finds a nice place to go, it just goes swoooooooosh, you see.

B: The way the kids treated me at that school, um, was pretty awful. They said my gender was different from theirs!

N: Were you aware of homosexuality at that time?

B: No. No. Not until puberty.

N: Uh-huh (acknowledgement).

B: And then, I didn't have any choice but to be faced with the fact that I could associate a sexual physical response with males, and then I would say, "Oh, I am gay! Damn it! They were right!"

N: That's terrible. What do you think tipped them off?

B: Well, uh, I had three older half-sisters who I really really idealized and loved—and still do to this day—and I never attempted male things; I never cared about sports...and I uh...

N: The softer ways were adopted; that's what you're saying.

B: Yeah. Yeah.

N: Let's get back to the spiritual thing, please; I didn't want us to lose that...

B: OK. Well, uh, I decided I was an atheist when I was at eleven, in fifth grade, I guess. My family never talked to me about this. They had grown up with Catholic education their whole lives, and that's the first thing that kills Catholicism! That's a Catholic education! (in my joking experience). And so I was never encouraged to find a spiritual path of my own, um...When I got into middle school, I started following the pop music, the Grateful Dead and stuff like that, and my mother, she gave me Tarot cards when I was eight. I started explaining symbology, you know, in that way, and it was…um…very potent to me, and it seems true, you know, and very believable, and I ran around a little bit in Tampa's New Age community, but it was always sniffed at…

N: Let's just stop there for a minute.

B: OK.

N: When you say, "I determined that I was atheist, when I was eleven"…Now, *why do you think that happened in your mind?*

   I thought Brett was searching for special considerations that would give prestige to his lone position away from the mainstream.

B: Well, uh, part of it, I think, would have to do with the rejection I suffered at school, where I was mercilessly harassed for seven years, to escape it…

N: Right. And I think it's also a way *to make you special to yourself!*

B: Yeah. And, I don't believe in this [religion] so I'm immune to it. I'm a step above all of that.

N: Hm mn (encouragingly). You're really telling me that you started to search around and that you changed your mind.

B: Yeah. Definitely. Definitely. I don't consider myself an atheist now, but also, I don't consider myself a Christian. I studied some Wicca; it was nice to read about it, I found some value in it, but there never was anyone around who appreciated it the same way. I mean, I knew other "pagans" in my middle school, but they really weren't pagan, they just didn't like Christians, and I knew I really wasn't *that* pagan…

N: Let's not get into a detailed discussion of this; we have to follow the principles of the channel. The principle of the channel [of discussion] is that *it defines you as being special*; you could read the books that nobody else was reading.

B: Yeah. Definitely! And I continue to read about it, but I don't bring it up in my day-to-day life; I don't know what to do with it…The practical applications…

N: Just as I think the awareness of a sexual bent, if you will, in 1995—that's when I think it was…

B: (Pause) Yes! That's when I came out!!

N: And that again is *the badge of being special!* You're searching for things to define you in a special way. Because you *are* special! And they just didn't come out right. In 1996, you're fifteen years old: did you get any kind of conspicuous honor? I'm sure you did well in school, and I hope you got some recognition for it. Tell me about it.

Hoping the Jupiter transit of the Sun would prevail in spite of the background "loss" arc of Saturn=Pluto.

B: Yeah, I did. Fifteen, junior year…Um, I was doing pretty well in my German class…I was the best drama student…every year…

N: This is what I'm pointing out to you: no matter what you touch at this stage of your development, it defines you as special, and you are rewarded for it. You see that?

B: Yeah. Yeah.

N: Now, there's a very difficult time here suggested in late '96 into the summer of '97. This is hard. First of all I need to know, were you sick, ill?

Now I wanted to pay attention to the Saturn-Pluto possibility further, leading to the angular transits of mid-1998.

B: No. I don't think so.

N: What was this intense love feeling?

Neptune=Sun at seventeen, Neptune ruling the 5th.

B: My "first" love!!! My first love completely never returned anything, because he was terrified to death of coming out, and denied it even to me and I knew it. Um…I confronted him directly with my extreme affection—at the time—for him, and he shut me out completely.

N: So nothing was consummated?

B: Never at all.

N: Was there any move in your family near summer to December of '98?

Checking angular responsiveness.

B: Um, that's when I graduated and went to college…and didn't stay.

N: And that's our next point of focus: this college sojourn should *not* have been interrupted. I think it was, though, taking on a lot of [unintelligible] in the spring of your first year…May of '99…

B: I didn't even make it that far.

N: January–May 1999 is a real big problem. Why did you not stay? When you realized down deep that you needed this desperately? *To take your specialness to a higher level.*

B: I dropped my classes; I was suicidally depressed and paranoid.

N: You were suicidally depressed and paranoid because you realized you were LOST in this huge university atmosphere?

> *Brett was anonymous in the big new environment. The school years of being pushed around were gone. The routine of negative recognition had been broken. What defined him now?*

B: Yes, exactly, and I didn't feel that there was any kind of way for me to break through to anybody. Um. To top it off, I lived in the international dorm…and I had thought it would be really really cool; it was, but…I don't know. It never felt comfortable for me. My classes were three miles apart from one another

N: All right. What did you do when you got *out* of college?

B: I moved to Memphis for the first time. Um, but there is something very specific, the reason why. On December 28 of '98, my grandmother died. After, you know, intense and years-drawn-out illness, etc., but the day that she died, I was in Memphis visiting my father, and that night I went out to a coffee shop and met the woman who works for a record label, an R & B [rhythm and blues] label. But anyway, I sat there, and they said they wanted to get me on their label, and they filled me and my not-quite eighteen-year old head with "You're gonna be famous," and that's all I'd wanted for a long time. Or that's how I thought I would be the most vindicated would be a sudden jump, especially after having just quit college. A sudden jump to fame, and I thought, "Oh God, yes!" So I went back to Tampa and recorded a really careful demo—and not in any sort of professional circumstances—

> *I was startled by this. Brett had not mentioned anything about his aspirations as a performer (not a strong part of his vocational profile).*

N: What's the bottom line on that?

B: Nothing.

N: All right. Let's get stabilized with dates here. In the first three months of '99, where are you?

B: I was still in Tampa, working on the demo.

N: All right. The world falls apart the next year, though; it really does.

B: Yeah, you're right. I moved up to Memphis, stayed for a year, and just kinda worked... um...dated a couple people and then I came back to Tampa.

N: And for the next two or three years, though, you are really wandering.

  Seeing Brett's empty life and the build-up of tr Neptune to the fourth cusp.

B: That's when I got into drugs.

N: Right. I would say in the springtime of 2002 and all of 2003.

B: Exactly right. That is completely accurate.

N: Now, I lament this objectively for you...and you do too. But I think it is important to understand here that the reason for the wandering and the bewilderment is simply because that train of yours didn't get into the right station!

B: Yeah. Right.

N: And the train should have been in college for four or six years with people being supportive around you and building your intelligent aesthetic sensibilities to a beautiful level at which you could be very proud.

B: (Long pause).

N: Fair? (softly).

B: Quite fair (with sadness).

N: Was there any kind of theatre experience in 2005?

B: 2005? Last year? No.

N: No? Was it banging on the door? Nearby? Did you want it?

B: I wanted it. What happened in 2005 was I really didn't make that much music...No... OHH! Oh, do you know what happened in 2005? *I went to recording school.*

N: Yes, that's what I was seeing; something like that; "entering the theatre situation."

  SA Uranus=Neptune, ruler of the 5th.

B: Yes. Well, the thing is, it's...it's...it's the support staff of the performer, rather than the performer himself (with a quiet resentment).

N: (Firmly, but not harshly) Well, you're not going to make it as a performer. You know that, and I know that.

This may have sounded like a tyrannical judgment, but I felt I had to break a futile dream. "Performance as an entertainer" is not projected in the vocational profile, in my opinion. We had to get to what was practical for him.

B: (Quietly) OK.

N: I think you have to realize that you have such exquisite leadership dimensions potentially for the "selling" of beautiful "items." "Things."

B: That's what my job is now! I'm an art curator for a Hip-Hop club. I handle artist relations, getting the work of the artists onto the walls and then I interview the artists on the night of their show. In front of the crowd.

N: Of course, I had no way of knowing this. So…or idealistic ideas or both!

B: Uh…

N: That's where you belong, my dear. That's the vocational profile here. This is allowing all your creativity to come out. All your conviction. All your circumspect eclectic knowledge. All of this ends up [to] being an **"aesthetic persuader"**! *Write those two words down.*

B: That sounds pretty much like what I've ended up getting myself into these days!

N: Well, that's who you are. That's who you are. Do you live alone?

B: No. I live with my father.

N: Your stepfather?

B: No. My real father.

N: When did you go back to him?

B: I visited him in 1999 and then, when I got out of recording school, I came back to Tampa, and I'm staying with him.

N: Is he still working with the cocaine?

B: No, sir. He's been done with that for…

N: All right. I hope you're done with it too.

B: Well, crystal meth was my drug of choice.

N: I hope you're done with it too.

B: Oh yes. I've been sober for a long time.

N: You owe God the tribute of being clean and blooming. Because, *now*, people are on the edge of *endorsing you, I think, and taking you seriously.*

B: Yes. It…it seems as if that's starting to happen. I mean, one of my jobs is as a sound-man—and I'm not sure if that is really my…my uh…real vocation or not. I always feel like I'm kind of clutching at not knowing what the parameters are supposed to be and not feeling sure about my decisions on which knob to twist, in a lot of ways.

> *I couldn't quite follow this reply.*

N: Right now you are in a supportive situation; that's "learning the ropes." That's what you would call that.

> *I was beginning to build to the continuing education theme I thought was tenable for the immediate time ahead (tr Jupiter conjunct Moon, ruler of the 9th).*

B: (Strongly) Yeah. Yeah. Definitely.

N: And I think, you know, we have some time here, several years, before you find that niche of leadership. And we just have to realize that, and we have to prepare for that.— So, do you have anything planned for May, May–June? Is there any trip or *plans for further technical study?*

B: No, not yet. It seems like on the first of February, I'm pretty sure I will be moving in with three kids that I know, who are pretty stable and won't be bad roommates at all. One of their roommates is moving out, and it's a good situation for me, because it's not expensive at…

N: Are they in the field that you're thinking about?

B: Well, two of them are; they were interns at a music magazine, so they're like rock critics.

> *Brett's reply to the education probe got us off the track.*

N: The point is to associate yourself with people in the aesthetic persuasion industry. And that can be anything between selling perfume to producing shows!

B: Yeah. Right.

N: Now, where is the spiritual idea *now* in your development?

> *I was trying another approach into the 9th House.*

B: (Very carefully) Uh…awaiting…the physical opportunities…to manifest…

N: Well, let me put it better than that, I think. I think you're waiting for HOW TO INTE-GRATE IT!

B: (Very excitedly) Yes! Yes! Exactly!!

N: Isn't that the key word!? All right. Now, where are you getting your income?

He would have to have the funds for continued education. Where could they come from?

B: From doing my sound job; I work four nights a week…

N: Don't you think you can get a better level of job, now, with the skills you have learned and know?

B: Well, uh, this is the best thing that's come my way so far.

N: All right. Let's look forward to some job mobility here. Late spring, early summer. I think you're probably going to meet somebody in that time period and have it reaffirmed early in July, and I think this can lead you up a notch.

At the same time with tr Jupiter conjunct the Moon, I saw tr Jupiter square the Node and the Midheaven in May with transiting Saturn echoing the same contacts in July. The meeting, the hook-up with someone helpful could happen through the extended education; certainly in parallel with it; or independently, should the education not work out.

B: Do you see a long move? Or will it still be in Memphis?

N: Well, that's up for grabs: there's a lot of angular contact here, but it's not classical "moves," but it is very tenable that you would move. The point is you've got to look at it, not as geography, but as getting nearer to your most reliable supportive resources.

B: Yeah.

N: Got it?

B: Yeah.

N: All right. Now, how are you on the romance side? Are you having any fun? Or are you just swinging around?

Now, I was getting off the track. I guess I wanted to make him feel good and was heading for the Mercury=Asc arc in May 2007 (Mercury ruling the 11th, love received), with an eye as well at the MC=Venus/Uranus "precursor" arc in July 2006.

B: (Sadly) It's been completely dead. I…I…I haven't had a real relationship…ever.

N: I think you're going to, and I think it's going to be just a little bit of a wait, and I think from about December of this year to May of next year, there could be significant developments in this dimension, even to the point of living in with someone.

The build-up period of the romance arc.

B: Oh, cool.

N: Cool. I think so. Now, what that suggests is that *you change* and add stuff to who you are, give off a different vibe, and attract a different kind of person for a different kind of reason. We're talking about *transformation* here.

This was big-time encouragement here. I wondered if anyone had ever talked to Brett so supportively.

B: (Engrossed) Yeah.

N: It is focused around…in May of 2007, around the Arc of Mercury=Asc. Now these things are all formative; they are rushing for evaluation because they have been deprived for so long. You are twenty-four years old, and in the next three to five years, you're mapping your course. And you and I have discussed strongly that you are so special, you have such skills and talents, you've got to put that into your vision, be able to look at the world and the people you meet in it and that…that…gaze has got to say: **I know what I am about…**and I have ideas that can be helpful. And I am in the business of supporting beautiful things and I am an aesthetic persuader. That's were I belong; I'm learning the ropes, and soon I'm going to be on top of it.

This was the major review of our talk. I delivered it with much emphasis.

B: I have considered going back to school…for arts administration or something like that.

Suddenly, Brett brought us back onto the right track! The education point was trying to be born!

N: That's a TERRIFIC idea! That's why I asked you, "What are you planning in the spring?" I would have died with happiness if you had said, "I'm going back to school."

B: Well, financially I have to figure out how I would get it done. Because, like, I can't ask my mother for any more schooling money because she spent money on all my years of school and I think she would be rather pissed off to think that she had wasted her money….

N: She hasn't. She hasn't. She has not wasted it. But she might think that you are just looking to be a perpetual student as a defense position against relating to the world. You can follow that.

B: Yeah. Well, I've already been accused of that!

N: All right, Brett. I think it is important to understand that you're coming to a very big decision. Indeed, with transiting Jupiter coming to your Moon, ruler of your 9th in May and in September, what happens is…this would suggest, with other measurements behind it, that you would return to school. The idea of studying further in Arts management and what have you is absolutely, exquisitely correct. Now if you do that, you're going to have a big fellow like me applauding you! If you don't do it, I'm still going to applaud you, but I'm going to say, "Hey man, you're going to have to learn all these ropes, and you're going to have to do it in the next two, three or four years." And you'll find your place in this world if you stay on this track. Credentialization…through the college experience can be an extremely vital bit of ammunition.

> *It was so clear that the extra, specialized education would fortify Brett most importantly. Not having it would leave him perpetually vulnerable to being pushed around, exploited, overlooked. It would be back to the schoolyard again!*

B: Yeah. It's always…it's always been a very upsetting, guilty thought for me that I stopped my education before I was even eighteen.

N: All right. Let's not go over it all again. But you know we've talked about it and we understand it very well. This has been an extremely good conversation. I feel strong about [it]. I really do. And we can follow it up more. Now: have you ever had a venereal disease? I'm not a medical doctor but I need to ask you that.

B: No…are you seeing…

N: No. No. I'm just saying there's a vulnerability there. There's a vulnerability also in your lower back.

> *The tensions in Libra and with Venus.*

B: Should I or should I not pursue yoga? (jocularly)

N: I think you should. The stretching of yoga is what's important.

B: Yeah. Definitely.

N: All right. You're healthy; you're strong; you've come out of a difficult time unscathed, *and I think you have an enormous amount to look forward to, Brett*...I really feel so very good about this. You're going to be a directorial entrepreneur, and that selling of beautiful ideas, seasoned with the spiritual awareness, and becoming an aesthetic persuader *is your métier.*

B: Well, thank you very much, Mr. Tyl. I appreciate your faith in me.

N: Don't let yourself say anymore, "The world doesn't understand me." Make it your job to show them *how* to understand *you.*

B: Yeah. Yeah. I definitely can relate to that.

N: Thank you, Brett. This is about all we can assimilate today.

B: (Very warmly) Thank you for shedding light on some of my concerns. Thank you so very much, Mr. Tyl.

N: I've really enjoyed this. ***It's been nice to shake your hand....***Bye.

B: Bye.

(Forty-two minutes.)

OVERVIEW: STRUCTURE AND TECHNIQUE

Therapy Flow Planning

I think it is extremely helpful for the astrologer to feel a "therapy flow" from the outset of a consultation; *what overall service will the consultation provide?* Certainly, there are cases that are highly specific in their needs, expectations, and results, like when should I list my home, when will it probably sell; employment issues; relocations. But the general astrological consultation is wrapped in a sense of the client's *persona,* that projected image of the person meeting the outside world throughout his or her development time.

We can see that image easily *ahead of time* through *hemisphere emphasis* (page 20). It is extremely helpful to understand that a therapeutic orientation, an attitudinal adjustment, to each horoscope can be reliably and productively focused within **understanding of the opposite hemisphere**.

In the "Alice" case (page 65), the hemisphere emphasis is to the west, toward giving herself away to others, being assumed, taken advantage of, undervalued. The western orientation of behavioral faculties and concerns calls out for *an eastern balance*, a return to Self. Recall that I worked attentively to get Alice in touch with her re-developing personal values, the shifts she was encountering with them; I worked to show her how to establish resolute anchor in the present and future, not carrying echoes forward from the past. The consultation was a campaign *to confirm Alice*: her brother relationship was the pivotal reference point; the "new" diamond was the reward for the "new" stance.

In Brett's case, the hemisphere emphasis is decidedly to the east, toward arch-defensiveness, withdrawal from others. So clearly, this works against easy acceptance by others, against growth through interaction and the reciprocal exchange of resources with others, against progress. This orientation calls out for therapeutic attention *to breaking defensive habits*, those behaviors routinized over years to protect and isolate him from the harm others easily put upon him. The consultation was a campaign to make him proud of his developing specialness at best; at least, to open the door on this potential, this necessity. He was approaching experiences and fresh frames of assessment that would prove him to himself, and to others around him in the process.

We can note the last words of the consultation with Brett, "It was nice to shake your hand!" This is a strategically unconventional closing statement; it introduces personal endorsement from an authority figure outside himself and suggests what is yet to come from many others. He can remember the "handshake" as symbolic of our fine talk together.

With a northern hemisphere emphasis natally, strongly suggesting unfinished business in the early home that usually delays confident experience and status development in the world, the therapy must be molded to create distance, to establish objectification from the prevailing family inhibitions. We need to elevate the client's status through recognition and commendation.

Carol's case, which will appear here later (page 183), is a clear-cut case: her idealistic mother and raucous father did nothing to recognize Carol's true core identity...her need to be an artist. Astrology discovered that for her, and this became identity corroboration of enormous impact, affecting her entire life to come, finally at age 58! We need to lift up and support. We need to help the client with self-recognition and confidence.

Franz Kafka, with the dramatic hemisphere emphasis to the south, above the horizon, was constantly victimized by his society, his family, and his own mind. The outcry for help could be answered by re-anchoring this intellect to *reliable* emotions, to love and respect (note the Sun in Cancer, the Moon in Gemini). Hypothetically, in our consultation, we would pursue northern hemisphere values, the secure emotional base normally fulfilled

Therapy Flow
Natal Hemisphere Emphasis needs Therapy Flow to **Opposite** Hemisphere
1. *To the east natally* suggests defensiveness, self-withdrawal. *Therapy flow to the west*: break defensive habits, create acceptance for the client.
2. *To the west natally* suggests giving the Self away to others, being assumed, undervalued. *Therapy flow to the east*: a return to Self, adjusting personal values, personal reward recognition, art of selfishness.
3. *To the north natally* suggests unfinished business in the early home, insecurity, not being anchored securely. *Therapy flow to the south*: create distance from the early home experience, objectification, elevate status and image through commendation, recognition, confidence.
4. *To the south natally* suggests victimization, being pushed around, taken advantage of. *Therapy flow to the north*: establish a secure home "feel"; discover who would/does offer credible emotional safety.

in the early home. We would work to discover who *would* give him emotional safety in which he could believe; what state of mind would help that to materialize?

Very often that person or those "support" persons already exist in the client's circle and *are* trying to help; but the victimized client can be blind to this or can simply refuse to believe it; the pattern of victimization or abandonment has persisted for so long.

A recent client with the Moon in Cancer and a pronounced southwest orientation had no support at all throughout her first forty-five years for her heightened sensitivities, her idealism and professional spiritual services to others, neither in her early home nor in her marriage. I worked to rebuild the situation, to confirm her successes and gain a fresh security through them. Early on, she said, "I don't remember my successes, and, you're right, I don't see the support around me." This is a kind of denial that takes some tough talk to vivify and evaluate the obvious.

Howard Stern's hemisphere orientation is much like that of Alice: to the west, the southwest particularly. Stern needs to have his personal values clarified and calmed in reliable emotional security (the balancing eastern and northern orientations). He needs to know he is wanted. The structural reigning need of his Moon in Taurus may be a lone but powerful voice calling from the fearground of his 12th House.

Communication Style

Communication style changes from client to client. How we talk says much about us (using contractions, for example; the tempo of our sentences; word choice; vocal sound and pitch). We should be accessible to the client but also preserve some distance of specialized authority.

Everyone knows the "feel" of a southern accent, for example. It might be too soft in some consultations. How can more authority be added to it? Perhaps by defining diction more; in other words, giving words of importance more bite than usual (emphasizing final consonants is very helpful). The warmth of the accent's lilt will preserve the feel of courtesy and humanity.

What about a tough, fast, so-called New York sound? How can that be warmed up? Perhaps by lowering the volume, slowing the speed, and purposefully picking "softer" vocabulary.

What if your speech normally is ultra-casual, filled with interjections that carry little meaning, like "ya know?", "uh, uh, uh," or dropping the "g" in participles, "We're gettin' to the point." These turns of speech can turn off authority and undermine the poise of the astrologer's study.[2]

And very important throughout the consultation is how we listen. While the client needs to be heard, especially about emotional issues, we must be careful not to allow the client a marathon of time to vent those emotions, to present two sides of an issue in hopes of defining who's right or who's wrong. Of course, that is *not* the issue in the consultation.

We should hear just enough of the situation to judge the situation's value in the client's development, and go on. A very helpful phrase is, "I appreciate what you are saying, but let's take it another step forward...perhaps two years later, when..." Or, "While this was certainly a most difficult and hurtful situation, we can learn a lot if you share just what you have brought forward into your adult life from that event." *We are listening to make creative connections among behavioral traits and values over time.*

---

2. It's a very good idea to record one of your consultations and then study it for what your voice and words do. Or read something aloud two or three different ways. Listen carefully.

6 CASE STUDY: "JOAN"

HOROSCOPE ORIENTATION

For our preparation of Joan's case, the first impression of her horoscope speaks of unfinished business in the early home that leads to defensiveness, and probably some hidden anger that lasts a long time into her development [*Mars in the 12th, near the Ascendant, in a fixed sign, ruling the 12th*]. The therapeutic approach would be orientated to the western hemisphere, toward helping others.

The vocational profile [M.♅. ☿$_{5,A}$ ★ ①; ☉.☿★; ♅♂♀. ☿★;☽ ⑤.☿$_{5,A}$ ★ etc.][1] emphasizes Mercury, the 1st and 5th Houses, a signature of "teaching" in the Aquarian mode; teaching for self-improvement, serving the social condition. This thrust should be present in her life and work to overcompensate for the defensive posture. The profession will be very important to define her self-worth awareness [Uranus ruling the Midheaven placed in the 2nd, disposited by the very important Mercury, ruler of the 2nd and the Ascendant].

Another initial impression may be quite important: *the aspect grid shows a minimal number of tension aspects*. The Sun-Moon square will be absorbed in the earliest parental situation; the Uranus-Venus conjunction does not immediately suggest pivotal importance; and

---

1. Please see Tyl, *Vocations* for full development and presentation of the Midheaven Extension Process for vocational profiling. The "code line" for the vocational deduction is included here as part of the complete preparation of the horoscope consultation. The specialization of the technique cannot be included in this text.

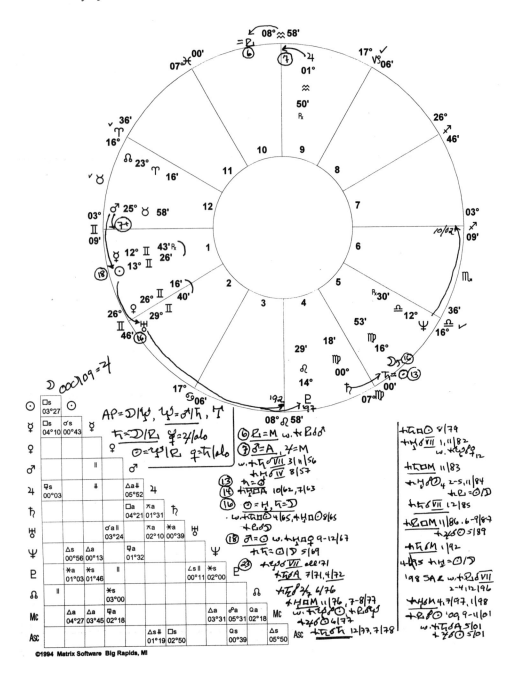

Jun 04, 1949 04:45:00 AM CDT 087W20'47" 41N35'36"

Midpoint Sort: 90° Dial

♂/Mc	002°28'	♄/Asc	016°44'	♂/♆	034°14'	♀/♆	049°23'	☿/Asc	067°56'	☿/♀	079°30'
♃/Asc	002°29'	♀/Mc	017°37'	♃/Mc	035°24'	♄/Mc	049°38'	☉/Asc	068°17'	☉/♀	079°51'
☽/☊	005°04'	♆/☊	017°53'	☽/♀	036°34'	♅/♆	051°05'	☽/♄	068°36'	☿/♅	081°11'
♂/♇	005°13'	♅/Mc	019°19'	♆/Asc	037°49'	♄/♇	052°24'	♆/Mc	070°44'	♄/♆	081°24'
Mc/Asc	006°04'	♀/♇	020°23'	♃/♇	038°09'	☽/♃	054°21'	♀/♂	071°07'	☉/♅	081°33'
☿/♃	007°16'	☽/♂	021°25'	☽/♅	038°16'	♀/☊	054°46'	♃/☊	072°33'	♀	086°16'
☉/♃	007°38'	☿/♄	021°31'	Mc	038°58'	♂	055°58'	☿	072°43'	♄/☊	086°47'
♇/Asc	008°49'	☉/♄	021°52'	♂/☊	039°37'	♅/☊	056°28'	♂/♅	072°49'	♀/♅	087°58'
☿/Mc	010°51'	♅/♇	022°04'	♇/Mc	041°44'	☽/Mc	057°56'	☉/☿	073°04'	♂/♃	088°54'
☉/Mc	011°12'	☊	023°16'	☿/♆	042°36'	♂/Asc	059°33'	☉	073°26'	♅	089°40'
♆	012°30'	☽/Asc	025°01'	☉/♆	042°58'	♄	060°18'	♆/♇	073°29'	☽/♆	089°41'
♂/♄	013°08'	♀/♄	028°17'	☊/Asc	043°12'	☽/♇	060°41'	♀/Asc	074°42'		
☿/♇	013°36'	☽/☿	029°48'	♇	044°29'	Asc	063°09'	☊/Mc	076°07'		
☉/♇	013°58'	♄/♅	029°59'	♃/♄	046°04'	☿/♂	064°20'	♅/Asc	076°24'		
♀/♃	014°03'	☽/☉	030°09'	☿/☊	047°59'	☉/♂	064°42'	☽	076°53'		
♃/♅	015°45'	♃	031°50'	☉/☊	048°21'	♃/♆	067°10'	♇/☊	078°53'		

the very strong Saturn-Mars square suggests an indomitable self-application once one gets going, and possibly a self-defeatism until that freedom is gained.

There is normally more tension in the developmental profile. The house rulers here do not point up any particularly jarred house experience-fields.

When this occurs, we learn to look to midpoint pictures for powerful, guiding statements. Here we see two in particular: Neptune=Mars/Saturn, "confusion, self-torment about identity"; and Saturn=Moon/Pluto, "possible depression." The Sun=Neptune/Pluto picture suggests illuminated interest and experience in the extrasensory, the occult, the spiritual.

So we know that the probability is high that, in her development, Joan experiences a lot of self-torment, and we have to find out why. Additionally suggesting this, we see the Saturn-Mars square keying 12th House anxiety about self-undoing: the two rulers of the 12th are under tension.

The cerebral Sun-Moon blend carries with it the potential for feeling unappreciated.

Looking ahead in the Combo-Search presentation, we see some strong statements: the SA Uranus quindecile with the Midheaven in Spring 2006 (the consultation period) definitely speaks about job adjustment, and the final touch of transiting Saturn upon the fourth cusp in June echoes that. As well, the continuing Uranus transit square the Sun leads us to SA Sun=IC-MC in June 2007, just before the SP Moon square with the Midheaven and the second transiting Saturn return in September! This will surely be retirement time. Quick synthesis of these measurements translates to stirring up much success and fulfillment now at the end of one's career and retiring with *panache*!

Inner Chart

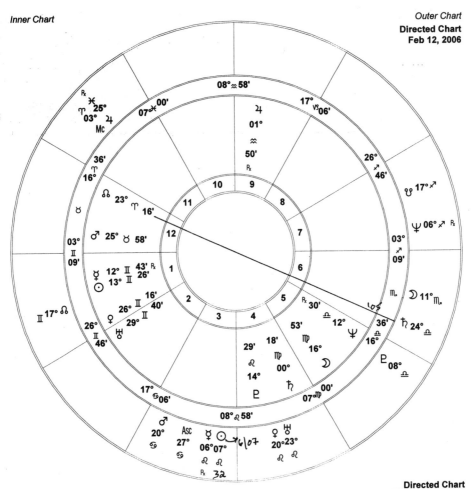

Pl	Geo Lon	Rx	Decl.
☽	16°♍52' 46"		+08° 05'
☉	13°♊25' 50"		+22° 25'
☿	12°♊43' 01"	Rx	+19° 41'
♀	26°♊16' 14"		+24° 05'
♂	25°♉57' 43"		+19° 09'
♃	01°♒49' 42"	Rx	- 20° 06'
♄	00°♍18' 29"		+12° 56'
♅	29°♊39' 45"		+23° 40'
♆	12°♎29' 43"	Rx	- 03° 28'
♇	14°♌29' 14"		+23° 49'

©1994 Matrix Software Big Rapids, MI

Directed Chart

Pl	Geo Lon	Rx	Decl.
☽	10°♏59' 48"		+08° 05'
☉	07°♌32' 52"		+22° 25'
☿	06°♌50' 03"	Rx	+19° 41'
♀	20°♌23' 16"		+24° 05'
♂	20°♋04' 46"		+19° 09'
♃	25°♓56' 44"	Rx	- 20° 06'
♄	24°♎25' 31"		+12° 56'
♅	23°♌46' 48"		+23° 40'
♆	06°♐36' 46"	Rx	- 03° 28'
♇	08°♎36' 16"		+23° 49'

Search From Nov 30, 2005 to Sep 27, 2007 GMT   Page: 1

Aspect	Date	Time	Event	Type	P1 Pos.	P2 Pos	E/X/L
♆ ---- ⚼ ☽/♂	12-01-2005	12:10 pm	♆ ⚼ ☽/♂	Ar-Na	06°♐25'	21°♋25'	Exact
♃ -- □ Mc	12-07-2005	08:58 pm	♃ □ Mc	Tr-Na	08°♏58'	08°♒58'	Exact
♂ -- SD	12-10-2005	04:06 am	♂ SD	Tr-Na	08°♉14'		
♀ - ∠ ♂/♇	12-12-2005	11:43 am	♀ ∠ ♂/♇	Ar-Na	20°♌13'	05°♋13'	Exact
♂ -- □ Mc	12-20-2005	11:02 pm	♂ □ Mc	Tr-Na	08°♉58'	08°♒58'	Exact
♆ ---- ⚼ ☿/♄	01-05-2006	01:01 pm	♆ ⚼ ☿/♄	Ar-Na	06°♐31'	21°♋31'	Exact
Mc --- ∠ ☿/☊	01-05-2006	10:55 pm	Mc ∠ ☿/☊	Ar-Na	02°♈59'	17°♉59'	Exact
♃ -- □ ♇	01-08-2006	04:19 pm	♃ □ ♇	Tr-Na	14°♏29'	14°♌29'	Exact
♂ -- □ ♇	01-12-2006	03:54 pm	♂ □ ♇	Tr-Na	14°♉29'	14°♌29'	Exact
♄ -- ☍ Mc	01-14-2006	04:25 am	♄ ☍ Mc	Tr-Na	08°♌58'Rx	08°♒58'	Exact
♆ --- q ☉/♅	01-18-2006	01:09 pm	♆ q ☉/♅	Ar-Na	06°♐33'	21°♊33'	Exact
☽ q ♂	01-30-2006	02:12 pm	☽ q ♂	Ar-Na	10°♏58'	25°♉58'	Exact
♂ -- ☌ ♂	02-09-2006	02:09 pm	♂ ☌ ♂	Tr-Na	25°♉58'	25°♉58'	Exact
♇ ---- ☍ ♀	02-15-2006	07:20 am	♇ ☍ ♀	Tr-Na	26°♐16'	26°♊16'	Exact
♀ - q ♃/Mc	02-17-2006	03:22 pm	♀ q ♃/Mc	Ar-Na	20°♌24'	05°♒24'	Exact
♂ -- □ ♄	02-18-2006	01:39 pm	♂ □ ♄	Tr-Na	00°♊18'	00°♍18'	Exact
♂ -- ☌ Asc	02-24-2006	04:48 am	♂ ☌ Asc	Tr-Na	03°♊09'	03°♊09'	Exact
♅ ---- ∠ ♇/Asc	02-26-2006	12:49 pm	♅ ∠ ♇/Asc	Ar-Na	23°♌49'	08°♋49'	Exact
♃ -- SRx	03-04-2006	05:38 pm	♃ SRx	Tr-Na	18°♏52'Rx		
♂ -- ☌ ☿	03-14-2006	07:19 am	♂ ☌ ☿	Tr-Na	12°♊43'	12°♊43'Rx	Exact
♂ -- ☌ ☉	03-15-2006	02:44 pm	♂ ☌ ☉	Tr-Na	13°♊26'	13°♊26'	Exact
♂ -- □ ☽	03-21-2006	09:11 pm	♂ □ ☽	Tr-Na	16°♊53'	16°♍53'	Exact
♇ ---- SRx	03-29-2006	10:30 am	♇ SRx	Tr-Na	26°♐45'Rx		
♄ -- SD	04-05-2006	12:09 pm	♄ SD	Tr-Na	04°♌23'		
♅ ---- □ ☿	04-06-2006	09:19 pm	♅ □ ☿	Tr-Na	12°♓43'	12°♊43'Rx	Exact
♂ -- ☌ ♀	04-07-2006	01:07 pm	♂ ☌ ♀	Tr-Na	26°♊16'	26°♊16'	Exact
♂ -- ☌ ♅	04-13-2006	10:56 am	♂ ☌ ♅	Tr-Na	29°♊40'	29°♊40'	Exact
♅ ---- □ ☉	04-22-2006	07:59 am	♅ □ ☉	Tr-Na	13°♓26'	13°♊26'	Exact
♄ -- q ♂/☊	04-25-2006	01:37 pm	♄ q ♂/☊	Ar-Na	24°♎37'	09°♉37'	Exact
♅ ---- q Mc	04-27-2006	08:35 am	♅ q Mc	Ar-Na	23°♌58'	08°♒58'	Exact
♃ -- □ ♇	04-30-2006	05:50 pm	♃ □ ♇	Tr-Na	14°♏29'Rx	14°♌29'	Exact
♇ ---- □ ♇/Asc	05-04-2006	12:39 pm	♇ □ ♇/Asc	Ar-Na	08°♎49'	08°♋49'	Exact
♂ -- □ ♆	05-05-2006	10:41 am	♂ □ ♆	Tr-Na	12°♋30'	12°♎30'Rx	Exact
♇ ---- ☍ ♀	05-12-2006	04:12 pm	♇ ☍ ♀	Tr-Na	26°♐16'Rx	26°♊16'	Exact
♆ ---- ⚼ ☉/♄	05-21-2006	06:18 pm	♆ ⚼ ☉/♄	Ar-Na	06°♐52'	21°♋52'	Exact
Mc --- ∠ ☉/☊	05-22-2006	04:11 am	Mc ∠ ☉/☊	Ar-Na	03°♈21'	18°♉21'	Exact
♆ ---- SRx	05-22-2006	09:23 am	♆ SRx	Tr-Na	19°♒49'Rx		
♂ -- □ ☊	05-23-2006	01:37 pm	♂ □ ☊	Tr-Na	23°♋16'	23°♈16'Rx	Exact
☉ - ☌ ♆/Asc	05-27-2006	05:33 pm	☉ ☌ ♆/Asc	Ar-Na	07°♌49'	07°♌49'	Exact
☽ ⚼ ♀	05-28-2006	08:27 am	☽ ⚼ ♀	Ar-Na	11°♏16'	26°♊16'	Exact
Asc --- ⚼ ♃/☊	06-01-2006	10:48 am	Asc ⚼ ♃/☊	Ar-Na	27°♋33'	12°♓33'	Exact
♂ -- ☍ ♃	06-06-2006	07:26 pm	♂ ☍ ♃	Tr-Na	01°♌50'	01°♒50'Rx	Exact
♂ -- ☌ ♀/♇	06-07-2006	03:07 am	♂ ☌ ♀/♇	Ar-Na	20°♋23'	20°♋23'	Exact
☽ ☍ ☊	06-12-2006	11:03 pm	☽ ☍ ☊	Pr-Na	23°♎16'	23°♈16'Rx	Exact
♂ -- q ♃/Mc	06-15-2006	09:35 am	♂ q ♃/Mc	Ar-Na	20°♋24'	05°♒24'	Exact
♃ -- □ ♀	06-16-2006	07:26 pm	♃ □ ♀	Ar-Na	26°♓16'	26°♊16'	Exact
♂ -- ☍ Mc	06-18-2006	02:19 pm	♂ ☍ Mc	Tr-Na	08°♌58'	08°♒58'	Exact
♅ ---- SRx	06-19-2006	04:32 am	♅ SRx	Tr-Na	14°♓44'Rx		
♄ -- ☍ Mc	06-20-2006	04:45 am	♄ ☍ Mc	Tr-Na	08°♌58'	08°♒58'	Exact
☊ --- □ ♅	06-26-2006	05:43 am	☊ □ ♅	Tr-Na	29°♓40'Rx	29°♊40'	Exact
♂ -- ☌ ♇	06-27-2006	03:13 pm	♂ ☌ ♇	Tr-Na	14°♌29'	14°♌29'	Exact
♃ -- SD	07-06-2006	07:40 am	♃ SD	Tr-Na	08°♏59'		
♂ -- □ ♂	07-16-2006	06:42 am	♂ □ ♂	Tr-Na	25°♌58'	25°♉58'	Exact
♂ -- ☌ ♄	07-23-2006	06:46 am	♂ ☌ ♄	Tr-Na	00°♍18'	00°♍18'	Exact
♂ -- □ Asc	07-27-2006	08:00 pm	♂ □ Asc	Tr-Na	03°♍09'	03°♊09'	Exact
♄ -- ☌ ♇	08-04-2006	04:12 pm	♄ ☌ ♇	Tr-Na	14°♌29'	14°♌29'	Exact
Asc --- ∠ ☿	08-05-2006	12:24 pm	Asc ∠ ☿	Ar-Na	27°♋43'	12°♊43'Rx	Exact
♆ ---- ⚼ ♅/♇	08-08-2006	06:11 am	♆ ⚼ ♅/♇	Ar-Na	07°♐05'	22°♋05'	Exact
☽ q ♅/☊	08-10-2006	01:32 am	☽ q ♅/☊	Ar-Na	11°♏28'	26°♉28'	Exact
♂ -- □ ☿	08-12-2006	02:07 am	♂ □ ☿	Tr-Na	12°♍43'	12°♊43'Rx	Exact
♂ -- □ ☉	08-13-2006	05:15 am	♂ □ ☉	Tr-Na	13°♍26'	13°♊26'	Exact
♂ -- ☌ ☽	08-18-2006	04:03 pm	♂ ☌ ☽	Tr-Na	16°♍53'	16°♍53'	Exact
♅ ---- □ ☉	08-18-2006	11:53 pm	♅ □ ☉	Tr-Na	13°♓26'Rx	13°♊26'	Exact
☊ --- □ ♀	08-29-2006	07:06 am	☊ □ ♀	Tr-Na	26°♓16'Rx	26°♊16'	Exact
♂ -- □ ♀	09-02-2006	09:13 am	♂ □ ♀	Tr-Na	26°♍16'	26°♊16'	Exact
♇ ---- SD	09-04-2006	08:08 pm	♇ SD	Tr-Na	24°♐05'		
♅ ---- □ ☿	09-06-2006	05:19 am	♅ □ ☿	Tr-Na	12°♓43'Rx	12°♊43'Rx	Exact
♂ -- □ ♅	09-07-2006	03:45 pm	♂ □ ♅	Tr-Na	29°♍40'	29°♊40'	Exact
♃ -- □ ♇	09-08-2006	03:47 am	♃ □ ♇	Tr-Na	14°♏29'	14°♌29'	Exact
♆ ---- ☌ ♃/♆	09-10-2006	11:33 am	♆ ☌ ♃/♆	Ar-Na	07°♐10'	07°♐10'	Exact
Asc --- ∠ ♂/♅	09-10-2006	10:44 pm	Asc ∠ ♂/♅	Ar-Na	27°♋49'	12°♊49'	Exact
♅ ---- □ ☽/♃	09-19-2006	10:32 pm	♅ □ ☽/♃	Ar-Na	24°♌21'	24°♏21'	Exact
♄ -- □ ☽/Asc	09-24-2006	06:31 pm	♄ □ ☽/Asc	Ar-Na	25°♎01'	25°♋01'	Exact

tr♄☌IV 2nd "hit"

tr♅□☉
tr♅q=M

tr♄☌IV final

tr♅□☉ 2nd "hit"

Search From Nov 30, 2005 to Sep 27, 2007 GMT Page: 2

Aspect	Date	Time	Event	Type	P1 Pos.	P2 Pos	E/X/L
♂ -- ☌ ♆	09-27-2006	09:04 am	♂ ☌ ♆	Tr-Na	12°♎30'	12°♎30'℞	Exact
☉ - □ ♃/♇	10-03-2006	04:25 pm	☉ □ ♃/♇	Ar-Na	08°♌09'	08°♏09'	Exact
♂ -- ☍ ☊	10-13-2006	03:35 pm	♂ ☍ ☊	Tr-Na	23°♎16'	23°♈16'℞	Exact
♂ -- □ ♃	10-26-2006	09:38 am	♂ □ ♃	Tr-Na	01°♏50'	01°♒50'℞	Exact
♀ - ⚻ Mc/Asc	10-26-2006	09:23 pm	♀ ⚻ Mc/Asc	Ar-Na	21°♌04'	06°♈04'	Exact
♆ ---- SD	10-29-2006	04:57 am	♆ SD	Tr-Na	17°♒02'		
♀ - ☌ ♅/♆	11-03-2006	04:23 pm	♀ ☌ ♅/♆	Ar-Na	21°♌05'	21°♌05'	Exact
♂ -- □ Mc	11-05-2006	09:58 pm	♂ □ Mc	Tr-Na	08°♏58'	08°♒58'	Exact
♃ -- ☍ ♂	11-05-2006	11:01 pm	♃ ☍ ♂	Tr-Na	25°♏58'	25°♉58'	Exact
♂ -- □ ♇	11-13-2006	10:53 pm	♂ □ ♇	Tr-Na	14°♏29'	14°♌29'	Exact
☉ - ☌ ☽/♅	11-15-2006	09:44 pm	☉ ☌ ☽/♅	Ar-Na	08°♌16'	08°♌16'	Exact
☽ ☌ ♇/Mc	11-19-2006	05:08 pm	☽ ☌ ♇/Mc	Ar-Na	11°♏44'	11°♏44'	Exact
♅ ---- SD	11-20-2006	03:57 am	♅ SD	Tr-Na	10°♓49'		
♃ -- □ ♄	11-25-2006	01:58 pm	♃ □ ♄	Tr-Na	00°♐18'	00°♍18'	Exact
♇ ---- ∠ ☽/♃	11-25-2006	10:13 pm	♇ ∠ ☽/♃	Ar-Na	09°♎21'	24°♏21'	Exact
♂ -- ☍ ♂	11-30-2006	11:07 am	♂ ☍ ♂	Tr-Na	25°♏58'	25°♉58'	Exact
♄ -- SR	12-06-2006	01:51 am	♄ SR	Tr-Na	25°♌04'℞		
♂ -- □ ♄	12-06-2006	03:27 pm	♂ □ ♄	Tr-Na	00°♐18'	00°♍18'	Exact
♃ -- ☍ Asc	12-08-2006	09:15 am	♃ ☍ Asc	Tr-Na	03°♐09'	03°♊09'	Exact
♃ -- ⚻ ♇/Mc	12-09-2006	04:05 am	♃ ⚻ ♇/Mc	Ar-Na	26°♓44'	11°♏44'	Exact
♂ -- ☍ Asc	12-10-2006	03:46 pm	♂ ☍ Asc	Tr-Na	03°♐09'	03°♊09'	Exact
☽ ⚻ ♄/☊	12-11-2006	06:24 am	☽ ⚻ ♄/☊	Ar-Na	11°♏47'	26°♊47'	Exact
♇ ---- ☍ ♀	12-11-2006	02:44 pm	♇ ☍ ♀	Tr-Na	26°♐16'	26°♊16'	Exact
Asc --- ∠ ☉/☿	12-19-2006	05:21 pm	Asc ∠ ☉/☿	Ar-Na	28°♋04'	13°♊04'	Exact
♂ -- ☍ ☿	12-24-2006	01:49 am	♂ ☍ ☿	Tr-Na	12°♐43'	12°♊43'℞	Exact
♂ -- ☍ ☉	12-25-2006	01:39 am	♂ ☍ ☉	Tr-Na	13°♐26'	13°♊26'	Exact
♂ -- □ ☽	12-29-2006	08:33 pm	♂ □ ☽	Tr-Na	16°♐53'	16°♍53'	Exact
♃ -- □ ♄/☊	12-30-2006	05:20 pm	♃ □ ♄/☊	Ar-Na	26°♓47'	26°♊47'	Exact
♂ -- ☍ ♀	01-11-2007	06:46 pm	♂ ☍ ♀	Tr-Na	26°♐16'	26°♊16'	Exact
♂ -- ☍ ♅	01-16-2007	09:53 am	♂ ☍ ♅	Tr-Na	29°♐40'	29°♊40'	Exact
☽ □ ♃	01-20-2007	00:03 am	☽ □ ♃	Pr-Na	01°♏50'	01°♒50'℞	Exact
♃ -- ☍ ☿	01-24-2007	12:06 pm	♃ ☍ ☿	Tr-Na	12°♐43'	12°♊43'℞	Exact
♃ -- ☍ ☉	01-28-2007	02:43 pm	♃ ☍ ☉	Tr-Na	13°♐26'	13°♊26'	Exact
♅ ---- □ ☿	01-28-2007	07:14 pm	♅ □ ☿	Tr-Na	12°♓43'	12°♊43'℞	Exact
♂ -- □ ♆	02-02-2007	06:19 pm	♂ □ ♆	Tr-Na	12°♑30'	12°♎30'℞	Exact
♅ ---- □ ☉	02-11-2007	11:12 am	♅ □ ☉	Tr-Na	13°♓26'	13°♊26'	Exact
♂ -- □ ☊	02-17-2007	03:24 am	♂ □ ☊	Tr-Na	23°♑16'	23°♈16'℞	Exact
♃ -- □ ☽	02-20-2007	06:57 pm	♃ □ ☽	Tr-Na	16°♐53'	16°♍53'	Exact
☊ --- ☍ ☽	02-22-2007	03:24 pm	☊ ☍ ☽	Tr-Na	16°♓53'℞	16°♍53'	Exact
☿ - ☌ ♆/Asc	02-24-2007	03:28 am	☿ ☌ ♆/Asc	Ar-Na	07°♌49'	07°♌49'	Exact
♅ ---- □ ♀/☊	02-24-2007	08:24 pm	♅ □ ♀/☊	Ar-Na	24°♌46'	24°♉46'	Exact
♂ -- ☌ ♃	02-28-2007	11:29 am	♂ ☌ ♃	Tr-Na	01°♒50'	01°♒50'℞	Exact
♂ -- ☌ Mc	03-09-2007	09:10 pm	♂ ☌ Mc	Tr-Na	08°♒58'	08°♒58'	Exact
Asc --- ☌ ♀/♄	03-12-2007	00:28 am	Asc ☌ ♀/♄	Ar-Na	28°♋17'	28°♋17'	Exact
♂ -- ☍ ♇	03-17-2007	02:40 am	♂ ☍ ♇	Tr-Na	14°♒29'	14°♌29'	Exact
♇ ---- SR	03-31-2007	08:06 pm	♇ SR	Tr-Na	28°♐58'℞		
♂ -- □ ♂	04-01-2007	02:28 am	♂ □ ♂	Tr-Na	25°♒58'	25°♉58'	Exact
♃ -- SR	04-06-2007	00:22 am	♃ SR	Tr-Na	19°♐47'℞		
♂ -- ☍ ♄	04-06-2007	06:28 pm	♂ ☍ ♄	Tr-Na	00°♓18'	00°♍18'	Exact
♂ -- □ Asc	04-10-2007	11:10 am	♂ □ Asc	Tr-Na	03°♓09'	03°♊09'	Exact
♅ ---- ☍ ☽	04-15-2007	05:38 am	♅ ☍ ☽	Tr-Na	16°♓53'	16°♍53'	Exact
♄ -- SD	04-19-2007	08:44 pm	♄ SD	Tr-Na	18°♌09'		
♂ -- □ ☿	04-22-2007	10:39 pm	♂ □ ☿	Tr-Na	12°♓43'	12°♊43'℞	Exact
♂ -- □ ☉	04-23-2007	09:00 pm	♂ □ ☉	Tr-Na	13°♓26'	13°♊26'	Exact
♂ -- ☍ ☽	04-28-2007	09:07 am	♂ ☍ ☽	Tr-Na	16°♓53'	16°♍53'	Exact
☊ --- □ ☉	04-28-2007	06:32 pm	☊ □ ☉	Tr-Na	13°♓26'℞	13°♊26'	Exact
♇ ---- ⚻ ♀/☊	05-02-2007	07:58 pm	♇ ⚻ ♀/☊	Ar-Na	09°♎46'	24°♉46'	Exact
Asc --- ∠ ☉	05-04-2007	10:06 pm	Asc ∠ ☉	Ar-Na	28°♋26'	13°♊26'	Exact
♂ -- □ ♀	05-10-2007	04:23 pm	♂ □ ♀	Tr-Na	26°♓16'	26°♊16'	Exact
☊ --- □ ☿	05-12-2007	05:56 am	☊ □ ☿	Tr-Na	12°♓43'℞	12°♊43'℞	Exact
♂ -- □ ♅	05-15-2007	03:27 am	♂ □ ♅	Tr-Na	29°♓40'	29°♊40'	Exact
♃ -- □ ☽	05-21-2007	00:38 am	♃ □ ☽	Tr-Na	16°♐53'℞	16°♍53'	Exact
♆ ---- SR	05-24-2007	10:27 pm	♆ SR	Tr-Na	22°♒02'℞		
Asc --- ∠ ♆/♇	05-28-2007	02:55 am	Asc ∠ ♆/♇	Ar-Na	28°♋29'	13°♍29'	Exact
♂ -- ☍ ♆	06-01-2007	03:52 am	♂ ☍ ♆	Tr-Na	12°♈30'	12°♎30'℞	Exact
♂ -- ☌ ☊	06-15-2007	04:04 pm	♂ ☌ ☊	Tr-Na	23°♈16'	23°♈16'℞	Exact
♃ -- ☍ ☉	06-17-2007	06:03 pm	♃ ☍ ☉	Tr-Na	13°♐26'℞	13°♊26'	Exact
Mc --- ⚻ ♀/♆	06-21-2007	10:47 am	Mc ⚻ ♀/♆	Ar-Na	04°♈23'	19°♌23'	Exact
♅ ---- SR	06-23-2007	01:08 pm	♅ SR	Tr-Na	18°♓42'℞		
♃ -- ☍ ☿	06-23-2007	07:00 pm	♃ ☍ ☿	Tr-Na	12°♐43'℞	12°♊43'℞	Exact
♄ -- ∠ ♆/Mc	06-27-2007	09:09 am	♄ ∠ ♆/Mc	Ar-Na	25°♎44'	10°♐44'	Exact
♂ -- □ ♃	06-27-2007	10:07 am	♂ □ ♃	Tr-Na	01°♉50'	01°♒50'℞	Exact
☿ - □ ♃/♇	07-03-2007	01:56 am	☿ □ ♃/♇	Ar-Na	08°♌09'	08°♏09'	Exact

♃♅□☉ final

Search From Nov 30, 2005 to Sep 27, 2007 GMT Page: 3

Aspect	Date	Time	Event	Type	P1 Pos.	P2 Pos	E/X/L
♂ -- □ Mc	07-07-2007	09:51 am	♂ □ Mc	Tr-Na	08°♉58'	08°♒58'	Exact
♂ -- ☌ ☽/♂	07-09-2007	08:56 pm	♂ ☌ ☽/♂	Ar-Na	21°♋25'	21°♋25'	Exact
♂ -- □ ♇	07-15-2007	06:15 am	♂ □ ♇	Tr-Na	14°♉29'	14°♌29'	Exact
☽ □ Mc	07-24-2007	03:46 pm	☽ □ Mc	Pr-Na	08°♏58'	08°♒58'	Exact
♂ -- ☌ ♂	08-01-2007	02:46 am	♂ ☌ ♂	Tr-Na	25°♉58'	25°♉58'	Exact
♄ -- □ ♂	08-01-2007	02:57 pm	♄ □ ♂	Tr-Na	25°♌58'	25°♉58'	Exact
♃ -- SD	08-07-2007	00:45 am	♃ SD	Tr-Na	09°♐56'		
♂ -- □ ♄	08-07-2007	05:23 pm	♂ □ ♄	Tr-Na	00°♊18'	00°♍18'	Exact
♄ -- q ☿/Mc	08-08-2007	03:52 pm	♄ q ☿/Mc	Ar-Na	25°♎51'	10°♈51'	Exact
♂ -- ☌ Asc	08-12-2007	02:55 am	♂ ☌ Asc	Tr-Na	03°♊09'	03°♊09'	Exact
♂ -- ☌ ☿/♄	08-13-2007	09:33 pm	♂ ☌ ☿/♄	Ar-Na	21°♋31'	21°♋31'	Exact
☿ - ☌ ☽/♅	08-15-2007	07:07 am	☿ ☌ ☽/♅	Ar-Na	08°♌16'	08°♌16'	Exact
♂ -- ☌ ☿	08-27-2007	02:22 pm	♂ ☌ ☿	Tr-Na	12°♊43'	12°♊43'℞	Exact
♂ -- ☌ ☉	08-28-2007	07:11 pm	♂ ☌ ☉	Tr-Na	13°♊26'	13°♊26'	Exact
♂ -- □ ☽	09-03-2007	05:18 pm	♂ □ ☽	Tr-Na	16°♊53'	16°♍53'	Exact
♄ -- ☌ ♄	09-05-2007	00:32 am	♄ ☌ ♄	Tr-Na	00°♍18'	00°♍18'	Exact
♅ ---- ☍ ☽	09-05-2007	01:17 pm	♅ ☍ ☽	Tr-Na	16°♓53'℞	16°♍53'	Exact
☊ --- ☌ ♇/☊	09-06-2007	03:14 am	☊ ☌ ♇/☊	Ar-Na	18°♊53'	18°♊53'	Exact
♇ ---- SD	09-07-2007	10:33 am	♇ SD	Tr-Na	26°♐18'		
♃ -- ☍ ☿	09-19-2007	05:43 pm	♃ ☍ ☿	Tr-Na	12°♐43'	12°♊43'℞	Exact
♂ -- ☌ ♀	09-21-2007	04:45 am	♂ ☌ ♀	Tr-Na	26°♊16'	26°♊16'	Exact
♃ -- ☍ ☉	09-25-2007	07:25 am	♃ ☍ ☉	Tr-Na	13°♐26'	13°♊26'	Exact
♃ -- q ♆	09-27-2007	09:27 am	♃ q ♆	Ar-Na	27°♓30'	12°♎30'℞	Exact
Mc --- ⚼ ♄/Mc	09-27-2007	04:25 pm	Mc ⚼ ♄/Mc	Ar-Na	04°♈38'	19°♏38'	Exact

SP□M

THE CONSULTATION

N: Hello, Joan! Thank you very much for being on time!

J: Yeah.

N: What's the weather like up there?

J: Oh, it's nice! It's gonna be nice; it's gonna be, like, 52.

N: We're getting 80s already!

J: Oh my gosh!

N: Early 80s; I'm so happy: the birds are getting a tan…you know, the whole thing! (Laughter) I really appreciate your calling me. We have a little bit of concern, as I explained to you [during the appointment call], about the birth time.

J: Uh-huh.

N: But certain measurements that guide our conversation are not necessarily so tightly dependent upon the birth time, but some are. And so I'm going to make that decision as we go along. OK?

J: OK.

N: Basically the horoscope is suggesting, developmentally, some unfinished business in the early home life, and that is the basis of a lot of defensiveness in your behaviors, in the patterns…

The northern and eastern hemisphere emphasis.

J: Uh-huh.

N: (Cordially) Don't go "Hmm" and "uh-huh." Please respond. We have to have a dialogue.

J: Uh, in early home life; like how…you mean now?…

N: No, at home, when you were seven years old, for example!

Keying immediately on the powerful Pluto=MH arc, followed up by Mars=Ascendant. This was age six–seven, surely the event situation that formed her "hidden anger."

J: Oh, yeah. Big problem!

N: All right. Thank you.

Courteously rewarding her compliance with dialogue.

J: *Huge* problem.

N: There's a lot of hidden anger about this…and self-torment.

J: Yeah.

N: And confusion…

J: Yeah.

N: Leading even to depression!

Here, I successively introduced the anger focus and the midpoint pictures issuing out of whatever the event was.

J: Yeah. Very much so.

N: Have you ever been treated clinically for depression?

J: Uh…Well, now, not really…not diagnosed, but I know…uh…I have chemical imbalances…that it was mostly hormonal, but, uh, certainly could be true for depression. I have a HUGE family history of it.

N: All right. This is what I'm seeing. And you and I have to talk about it, Joan.

J: Uh huh.

N: Now, I need to know…the focus of this, and I see it at ages six and seven especially. How was the family completely turned around, restructured, at that time?

J: Uh, well. At six, my brother was born, my little brother…

N: And what did that mean?

J: Uh, well, *that Mom's focus was all on him.* And, um, for me it was starting school and that was horrendous; I *hated* school.

N: And nobody was helping you! And that's why you hated it.

> *Clearly the baby brother's birth isolated Joan; the school experience, taking her out of the home, added onto the sense of being neglected, fearing abandonment perhaps? Support was needed; she didn't get it.*

J: Well, one thing that happened was just typical, though. It was: Mom went to the hospital, and nobody told me that she was going to have a baby. I didn't even know! I was devastated. Because I thought she was really sick! I didn't understand.

N: My goodness!

J: This is pretty normal. At age two, it was pretty traumatic as well: I had my tonsils out at two. And, still, you know…it still comes up: the ether over my face; not being able to talk and waking up and not knowing where I was.

N: Hmm.

J: So…then after that, I distinctly remember sitting on my mother's lap and her trying to feed me…and just *hating her.*

N: Hating her.

J: *Hating her.* Despising her for putting me through that.

N: Well, it's interesting, isn't it? Really, you're rejecting the attention you wanted.

J: (With surprise) Yeah!

N: And thereafter, when the baby boy is born…

J: Who I adore, by the way…I loved him…

N: In retrospect.

J: Yeah.

N: But we get into a pattern of steaming, buried anger.

J: Uh-huh (in agreement).

N: I think that's fair to say, in those strong terms.

J: Yeah. That's true.

N: You know what I'm talking about.

J: Yes. And plus my parents were pretty critical, *both* of them.

N: Of you?

J: Oh yeah!

N: And that didn't make you feel very lovable!

J: Oh no.

N: And there's an over-compensatory development potential here of *idealization*, and per-fectionism, and getting things *right*. So that you *can't* be criticized. You know what I'm talking about.

> When the Sun conjoins Mercury and/or Venus or both, we have a conspicuous statement of idealization, usually used defensively.[2] The reference to "getting things right" issues from the Moon in Virgo, the reigning need to be correct.

J: Oh yeah; *absolutely*.

N: Tell me a little bit about that; how that fits in.

J: Well, I think I'm very hard on myself about *everything*, and one comment, you know, and…I tended to pick a husband that's pretty critical, so one comment of just…as other people would say, you know, "Not a big deal," I…I just can't let go of it. Still. You know, any comment, I…I remember it and hold out, as opposed to remembering the good stuff, I sometimes can focus only on the negative…

N: All right; you know that's a pattern you've brought forward from those early years. They [the years] were terrible. Please tell me, uh, I want to know if your parents were at each other's throats when you were born?

> This is usually a reliable deduction when the natal Sun and Moon are in tight square, within 3 degrees. The Sun and the Moon are symbols of the father and mother in the client's birth moment.

---

2. Please see *Synthesis & Counseling in Astrology*, pages 105–112, "Idealization."

J: I don't know.

N: They never told you?

J: Uh-uh.

N: Did they ever at any time tell you…that they didn't…

J: Oh! (strong surprise; discovery) NOW you're hitting a nerve; now I remember! Boy! Talk about holding things down [in]! I still remember my mom packing her suitcase… at age four or five…and crying, and being really scared because they had one of their usual fights, that they had every week. And she was going to leave. She never did, but I was terrified that she would. This happened quite frequently…

> *Again a statement about being left alone, fearing abandonment, not getting support.*

N: That's an explicit threat of abandonment…

J: Yeah. Big time!

N: Which is an echo of when your brother was born a year later…

J: Yeah!

N: But they were probably doing this for some time [having at each other], even before you were born.

J: Yeah, you're probably right.

N: And when you said *"usual"* fights…

J: Well, I meant, it happened all the time.

N: It happened all the time, so it happened when you were born.

J: Uh-huh.

N: Now, was there ever any reference that they didn't want you?

> *Very often, with this situation, especially keyed by the tight Sun-Moon square, there is argument about having the baby, attempts to abort it, etc. Then, the child is told these things punitively by the mother or an older sibling or by the father, projecting upon the child their upset with/among themselves.*

J: (Pause) Only when I was ten: my dad was really upset with me because I was really sick…really, really sick, like death/life thing, and they couldn't figure out what was wrong with me, and I'll never forget: he said, *"I just wish she was never born!"*

N: Wow.

J: Because it was so difficult.

N: Isn't it amazing how astrology can get at it?

J: Yeah! I trust that.

N: Well, we've got to be very sharp here, checking the [birth] time; I'm confident now of it, but I am going to make a few more tests. But thank you for corroborating things here.

J: Yeah.

N: Was there a move in 1957?

J: Yes, in 1957.

N: In the summer? In August?

J: Well, I don't know, I don't really know that, but I know I started school in a different school district.—Either '57 or '56; I guess when I was eight. So, I was eight years old.

N: Yes, it was August '57

J: And it was very, very difficult.

N: All right.

J: There were good things about it, because I liked school finally, and I had a *wonderful* teacher, but, uh…a *huge* move. We moved away from the city out to the country on a lake…

N: OK. Well that's a very important series of tests that you've just passed with your birth time of 4:45!

J: Really?

N: I mean, how can I sit here and say these things to you if…

J: You couldn't. So that's accurate? Is that what you're saying?

N: I think it is. I'm continuing to test.

J: OK.

N: Now, when we get to age fourteen…

The transit of Uranus square the Ascendant with the background arc of Saturn=Sun.

J: Oh! Big, big change.

N: All right. Again.

J: Well, that's when my brother almost died and my mom, my brother and I moved from our home and went to New Mexico and lived in Albuquerque for six months, and everything changed for me. I stopped being sick. Uh, I mean, nobody knows what was wrong with me, but I started getting my period, I was doin' well with boys. I mean my whole life changed.

N: It's perfectly clear, but you understand in retrospect from that time, why you got so terribly sick...*because of your victim-like reaction to the terrible stuff around you.*

J: Yeah. Actually I wrote a paper on it in graduate school!

> *This statement about graduate school offsets the expectation that her education was interrupted: Saturn, ruler of the 9th, squared by Mars. This could have been the time when she really "got going" on her own.*

N: All right. But you hear what I'm talking about?

J: Yeah.

N: Now the most important thing, starting to emerge in your life, if I may suggest, is *the need to get out of yourself and start working with other people.*

> *This is the antidote to the defensive withdrawal, the fears of being alone, abandoned; the western hemisphere.*

J: OK.

N: Well, you know, you're fifty-seven years old...

J: Hm mn...fifty-six! (laughing)

N: (Laughing) Now, I just want to keep that thought in your mind because there is talent in you to teach, lead, inform, help people, and it'll make you feel a hell of a lot better...

J: Well, I've been a social worker for twenty-two years...

N: Well, there you are!

> *This corroborates the vocational profile perfectly.*

J: And I've been working with abused children...

N: All right.

J: And what I do now is I'm an adoption and foster care specialist, and I do training, and I love it.

N: Well, this is what I'm seeing, not seeing that specifically...

J: Yeah.

N: But I'm seeing the...*the teaching and helping*...leading people to a better life...

J: (In confirmation) Hm mn.

N: And it's based upon what you know and how you communicate it. Are you with me?
     The Mercury component.

J: Yes. Exactly.

N: All right. Thanks.

J: Yeah, I love, I love, uh, I love *teaching*; I'm passionate about it. You know, not necessarily children—I've done that too...

N: Would you ever have wanted to be a science teacher?
     Checking the Midheaven ruler Uranus involvement with Mercury by dispositorship.

J: (Giggling) No...No, I was terrible at science...I would love to teach astrology...I mean, I'd love to go into astrology!

N: Teaching is very, very clear here. [Mercury ruling the 5th; the Moon in Virgo in the 5th.]

J: OK.

N: Now, when we get into age sixteen, there are all kinds of developments *again*, and your mother is having a hard time at that time.
     The strong Sun=Uranus and Saturn=Moon arcs with, especially, transiting Pluto conjunct the Moon.

J: Yeah.

N: Tell me about that, please.

J: Well, uh, I remember sixteen as, uh, she started drinking more; my dad was traveling more; and as I was...You know I was getting my own life and becoming more independent, she just seemed 'on the edge' all the time, like she wasn't doing real well. She seemed very depressed. I just avoided her. I didn't eat dinner with them. I just would leave. I had my own friends, my own life…

N: Well, my next question would be, would you have wanted to run away?

J: Absolutely!

N: Well, that's what I'm seeing…

> *This is the Uranian component of the arc and the transit. A typical manifestation under these conditions of neglect and frustration at this age.*

J: I thought about it all the time!

N: Especially that summer of 1965?

J: Yeah. I did. You know, I didn't have any money. Yeah, I often talked about it. If I could have, I would have left in a heartbeat. But I didn't have the resources to do that.

N: There seems to be a major romance here…

J: (Surprised, smiling) Yeah!

N: Well, then *another* one, in '67….

J: Yes! The love of my life!

N: The love of your life; between September and December.

J: That's right. '67.

N: Did it last longer than two years?

J: For me it did. We broke up when I went to college in, uh, '67. He went to Vietnam and I went to college. And he wanted me to come see him, and I got involved with somebody else then.

N: Right. There's a break-up here in May of '69, something like that

J: Actually, I got married in '69. My first marriage was in April of '69.

> *Transiting Saturn square Sun/Moon, always a severe commentary on relationship.*

N: Well, I don't think that was the best thing to do (with clear understatement in my voice).

J: No. Looking back, *no*. (Light laug.) I rue the day I walked down the aisle. I knew it was wrong.

N: Right. Do you think it was a rebellion against the fact that you had had this love of your life, who had gone away, and then you had another relationship that you faked through…

J: Yeah, I think so. You mean the "fake through" with the husband I married?

N: I guess. Was that the man?

J: Yeah. I met him in '68 and we got married in '69.

N: There you are.

J: And I had a child with him…actually.

N: So, you're agreeing with me.

J: I am agreeing with you.

N: Because all through 1971, gosh…it's just not good.

J: No. I wanted to leave, but I got pregnant. Abortion wasn't legal then. To be honest with you….otherwise I would have.

N: Again, in '76.

J: '76…(thinking)

N: Severe problems.

> *The MH becomes the "point of status" during a problematic marriage; it is waiting for resolution through separation and/or divorce; a change of status.*

J: Yeah. I was out here then; I wanted a divorce. In fact, I separated.

N: It should have happened November '76, summer of '77.

J: Yes. That's right. That was a really hard time of life. Horrible.

N: Of course it was, and that's why you changed professional direction conspicuously at that time too.

> *Here the Midheaven reasonably reverts as well to the job reference. Along with the build-up to the tr Saturn return, it is only reasonable.*

J: Yep!

N: What was that change?

J: Um, well, I was a stay-at-home mom; I didn't really work. And to earn money, I started cleaning houses, and then I started substitute teaching.

N: There you are! That's what I was looking for; something like that. You're a born teacher, by the way, as we've said several times.

J: (Feeling good from the recognition) That's good!

N: At the same time, I have to ask you what may seem like a strange question: that uh, some sort of relationship with the occult?

> *Any contact by arc or transit between Neptune and Pluto, Pluto and Neptune usually registers in terms of interest in the supernatural, the occult, the off-beat. It can play a critical part in development, often rationalizing life-changes, etc.*

J: Which kind?

N: That period.

J: The one when I started a new career?

N: Hm mn…(letting her go on)

J: Uh, actually it was before then: I was involved in something in St. Louis when my son was born in '72. I was involved with people, when someone was killed. But it wasn't a cult. It was more like drugs.

N: Yes, but I'm looking for the study of spiritual things…

J: Uh, OK. Well, that would have happened: I went into a spiritual group, almost like an occult group, when I was thirty-one or thirty-two…

N: Yes. That's what I'm looking at right here.

J: But I don't know what year that was.

N: '81.

> *Her timing recall is a bit off on this. I overlooked it. The involvement did not seem important, it was probably the feel of a family away from home.*

J: Yes. I was pretty involved within it.

N: All right. Now when does that divorce come through actually? At the end of '77?

J: Uh,…I knew that [the date]…Uh…I blocked it out, it was so awful.

N: OK (kindly). Then there's another relationship.

J: Yeah. My son was five, six when I got divorced, so it was '78, November '78. And what do *you* say? The date?

N: December '77.

J: It could have been '77.

N: All righty. Now let's just jump ahead to 1983. At the end of the year '83...

J: Uh-huh.

N: There seems to be a professional break. A new job or direc...

J: Right. I started social work then.

N: Was it November?

J: Actually in '83, in the fall of '83, I started working retail. My second husband and I were going to split up. He wasn't working, and I did retail for about six months. Then in '84, in May of '84, this is when I got into social work.

N: I have February to May or November of '84.

J: That's true. That's when I was doing the retail.

N: And then there is a power struggle in the relationship.

J: Oh yeah!

N: All right. There's another huge change here: at the end of '86 or spring–September of '87 with regard to your profession.

J: When I was thirty-six, I went into family therapy work...

N: I'm just picking up that shift, and it's very rewarding in May of '89. Did you get some special kind of recognition?
The transit of Jupiter conjunct the Sun.

J: Ohhh...in '89, I did!

N: What was that recognition?

J: Uh...Just an "Outstanding Social Work" award. And in...'89—I'm trying to figure out how old I was...

N: Forty.

J: Yeah, at that time, I got recognition for the work I was doing, just working with, you know, kids and social worker acknowledgment by different people.

N: Terrific! Just terrific!

> *Intentionally building her up for strategy and good times ahead; building to the finish of the consultation. I wanted everything I said to be endorsing.*

J: Yeah.

N: Then there's another gainful shift in your job status and responsibilities, very early in '92.

J: Yeah. In '92, I shifted jobs: I went out of child protection into adoption.

N: OK. Good. '96? There are a lot of shifts here: changing gears. I mean, could have gone into some kind of *private practice* or something here!

J: I was doing private work then!

N: All right. '96, the whole year, into '97: there's a, there is a sharpening of your skills...

J: Oh yeah!! I became a supervisor...

N: There you are! (Complimentary!)

J: They made me a supervisor!

N: All right. 2001, there seems to be a terrific reward again, in May especially.
> *A repeat of the Jupiter-Sun transit.*

J: So that was five years ago almost? Five years ago I would have been...fifty-one. That was a really hard time, and that's when I had...and my mom was sick, my sister-in-law was dying, and I cut back on my work, actually, and started to help them take care of my grandsons, but I don't know if that actually...

N: No. That wouldn't figure unless I did a whole lot of extra measurements...

J: Yeah, it was in May.

N: Basically, it's a repeat of a reward cycle that did so well for you in '89. And, you just weren't in the right spot to get that to happen.

J: No.

N: All through 2004, was there any kind of resurrection of spiritual studies or offbeat studies, things like that?
> *Still looking for Neptune-Pluto significance, noting the natal midpoint picture Sun=Neptune/Pluto.*

J: That was two years ago?

N: Yes.

J: I've always been seeking, and always been looking, but I don't recall...

N: How about your astrology study?

J: Oh yeah, but I think that was 2003. I actually studied Vedic astrology.

N: There's a whole lot here in that period that is trying to come out. You know?

J: Oh, OK.

N: Yeah. True. And, uh, last September, was there a kind of new start in your...

J: Yeah! You mean as far as spiritual or career?

N: Work. Career.

J: Yeah, I think so. Uh, I guess, I don't know, maybe it was an attitude thing. I just got of-fered to, you know...*Oh! You know what?* What did you say about two years ago? My God, I'm blanking out! Two years ago I went to culinary school, and I totally changed my job in 2003 and 2004: I went to Europe, studied in Europe, and I did that for nine months.

She recalls the Jupiter-Sun period in the best light: internationalism, study.

N: I think I have to stay with 4:45 in the morning, and congratulate your mother [her re-call]. We're as close as we can get. Are you pleased with our talk so far?

J: (Exuberantly) I am, I am! Very!!

N: This gives you a 3 Gemini 09 Ascendant.

J: Wow! Well, I don't see myself as a Gemini, but who knows? Maybe. I'm kind of all over the place...

N: Well, that's what Gemini is! (laughing)

J: I know, I know.

N: Now, you're calling me at a time of pressure and change, and a new start. That prob-ably raised its head first in August–September of last year, and has come back now, and isn't really going to work out until this spring.

The transit of Saturn at the fourth cusp, triggering the Uranian transit square the Sun and the Uranus quindecile arc to the Midheaven!

J: OK.

N: I would say, uh, June. Now, this is where I must be extremely careful because *these* measurements are dependent so much on the time...

J: Oh...

N: But I've learned how to talk with you, and we've hit many, many periods of time precisely. The thrust of this is a new start, new independence, even *a change of job*...very strongly. What are you projecting for yourself in the next six months?

J: Well, they just offered me to go full-time.

N: Where?

J: Where I work now, and I would...

N: Where do you work now?

J: Social services.

N: In the social services field.

J: And I was doing half time, and they want me to go full time, you know...

N: Was that offer made to you, just now, in January, the first two weeks of January?
> *The transit of Mars square to Pluto is high-energy; Pluto rules the 6th, employment conditions; simultaneous with transiting Saturn on the 4th cusp opposing the Midheaven.*

J: Yes.

N: I would say it was probably made on the 12th or 14th of January.

J: Wow!

N: Is that right?

J: Yep; that's right.

N: OK. Now, when we get to your decision on that, is there another meeting *that's scheduled in three days?*
> *Looking ahead from the consultation date (February 12) to Venus quindecile Arc to Jupiter/ Midheaven, very positive (on February 17).*

J: I don't know about it, but I haven't been to work for a while. They—you know—I'm going to meet with her this week...

N: That's what I'm saying: in three days.

J: Yeah. Yeah. Because I'm trying to find out when I'm going to start, and no one has been...

N: All right. And you're *going* to go full time. **You are.**

J: I'm doing it for monetary reasons, to tell you the truth.

N: Yes. How tall are you and how much do you weigh?

> *I wanted my studied, strong confirmation to sink in. The switch of subjects allows the meeting and job talk to order itself into the subconscious.*

J: I'm 5'4". I don't normally give my weight, but since you're asking, I'm 162, which is more than I should be.

N: Sure.

J: About forty pounds more than I should.

N: Do you live alone?

J: No, I'm married.

N: OK. Well, you've got to get rid of those thirty or forty pounds.

J: I know.

N: I'm not going to preach to you, but just stop eating the breads, and all that jazz...

J: I've been good for about a month...

N: I want you to know that there's an awful lot more here in your job rather than just going full time. You hear?

> *I was seeking out an opportunity for her to gain stature, not just work further. I wanted to see her retire with a burst of Sun-Midheaven fulfillment, which she will carry with her for the rest of her life.*

J: OK. Is that good or bad?

N: It's good...if you want to work; if you want to get out there and do something innovative.

> *The Uranian measurements in April 2006 and further. Uranus ruling her Midheaven.*

J: OK. Yeah, I do!

N: And I think that will raise its head as soon as you start again.

J: Good!

N: And, uh, There's going to be a project. I think there's going to be project in your work that is going to highlight you individualistically. In other words, you're going to be identified with *some new thing,* or new responsibilities. Is this at all possible?

J: Yeah. She has been talking…that she wants me to do more things, but we haven't specified exactly what that entails.

N: Well, I guess that you might just start to think, "Give me a title that puts me in charge of special innovative things."
   Individual recognition.

J: OK.

N: You know what I'm saying?
   I wanted to hear more enthusiasm.

J: Yeah!

N: In other words, it's not just, "Well, do this, do that, do that, do that, do that." You should say, "I want to be called, uh, Director of Special Operations."

J: OK.

N: Or, Director of…of Creative Logistics.

J: *That* sounds great!

N: That's the kind of stuff that makes you smile! You're smiling right now!
   Finally: confirmation and enthusiasm. She understood.

J: Yeah. Yeah.

N: And those kinds of things are *due, from you now.* They're going to start really to pop in April, then June, then August, and they're going to bloom by next January. I think it's excellent.

J: You know? It's interesting that you're saying this, because I've been thinking about retirement. (Laughing lightly)

N: Now, my next—I just turned the page— and my next statement to you is "retirement."
   Clearly the second Saturn return period with SP Moon square the Midheaven.

J: Uh-huh?

N: It's not really going to kick in until July-September 2007.

J: OK.

N: That makes sense to you?

J: Yes. It does.

N: And what I think you need to do is **establish something wondrous between now and then.**

J: OK.

N: I really do. *I think you need it!*

J: OK.

N: I think you need it to, uh, to combat the echoes of…depression…confusion…and self-doubt…that have haunted you most of your life.

J: Well, you know, I just got off antidepressants…I feel pretty good, and I think I maybe should go on them again…(laughing)

N: No! (lightly) No. I think what you need to go "on" is **helping other people in a special innovative, grand way!**

J: OK.

N: …and making a major statement! And you have every opportunity to do so; don't you think, Joan?
   SA Sun=MH!

J: Yeah. I do.

N: I mean—my goodness alive!—here are the people who are hiring you, wanting to give you all sorts of special things!

J: Yeah. They are!

N: And if you step up to the plate and say, "I want to take them all!" **you gain status**. If you say, "Give me this title," **you gain identity**.

J: That's true.

N: You say, *"I want to do this!"* **You are fulfilled by relating to other people.**

J: That is true! (emphatically)

N: And the weight will drop right off!

J: Really?

N: Yes.

J: Oh! Huge! That's interesting. The weight's been comin' on over years and years. I thought it was my relationship, but…it has to do with a lot of other things.

N: It's, uh, like your getting deathly sick, you know, early on in your life…because of all that stuff around you.

J: It was pretty tough.

N: So, please see these things; and see these things with bright lights and **shine them on the world around you**.

J: OK. Sounds wonderful!

Mission accomplished! This was the peak recognition of the consultation.

N: Thank you. Now, is there any tension in your upper respiratory tract? I'm not a medical doctor, but let me ask you: have you had chronic illnesses there?

The Mercury-Gemini excitations.

J: In my lungs?

N: Yeah.

J: Yeah. I went and saw a—what do you call it—a pulmonary doctor about two years ago, after my mom died, because I kept getting bronchitis every three months, and I have three relatives who've had emphysema, and I had smoked, and my cousin, who's four years older, has emphysema. But he [the specialist] said, "Nope, you're good!"

N: The horoscope suggests a very keen weakness and vulnerability in the upper respiratory tract. I'm not a medical doctor, but I bring this to your attention.

J: Well, I had my tonsils out when I was…

N: Two.

J: …and extreme sore throats. So, when I get sick, it always goes there.

N: Is there anything with the thyroid gland?

The Uranus tension upon Venus; a subsidiary reference to the thyroid is also Mercury.

J: Oh God! Big time. Like big-big-big time! When I was thirty-nine, I had severe depression, and one of the boyfriends I was seeing at the time—I was separated—was killed, and I thought it was just that. My doctor said, "No, no, no." An endocrinologist said, 'You don't have *any* thyroid working!" and I was pretty skinny then. And I've been on thyroid [medicine] for some almost twenty years, and they tweak it…I get tested every three or four months.

N: Wow!

J: To increase it, because they can't ever fix it.

N: Strong stuff! Look what this horoscope has been able to reveal!

J: Yep! Isn't the throat, though, your expression and communication, and "talkin' your truth?" That's what I've been…"Sayin' your truth, your individual truth"?

N: Well, that's….

J: Hocus-pocus?

N: That's…pabulum…There's a lot more to it than that, or I wouldn't be able to grasp this…

J: So you're saying I shouldn't smoke? Right?

N: Well, I'm not going to preach to you. This is not my job. My job is to point…to a mirror.

J: Yeah.

N: How about the lower back, the third-fifth lumbar vertebrae?
  Further investigation into the Venus tensions so far strongly corroborated.

J: No back problems.

N: Good.

J: Feet problems. Where I haven't been able to work out for about nine months.

N: You haven't had that chronically in your life.

J: No. No.

N: All righty. I've "hit" all the hard, hot stuff in your horoscope. We've seen the growth from being totally neglected, if you will, hating school…
  The beginning of the review.

J: I'd say "hating school" is accurate, but I don't feel like I was "totally neglected"…I think my mom was a pretty good mom when I was *really* little…
  She has obviously worked this out, especially with the mother now deceased.

N: But there was a lot of neglect, which caused an awful lot of confusion, self-torment, depression…

J: There's been a lot of depression in the family…

A strange repeat reference to "depression in the family." Perhaps this is her way of explaining things genetically rather than explaining her individual state of depression in personal terms.

N: And wanting to run away, all of those things, you know (Joan is agreeing throughout); then the love of your life goes to Vietnam, then we have a marriage that was pretty poor…

J: Not made in heaven.

N: And now, we've got to really believe in ourselves, and you've got to shine the light, and share it.

J: I want you to tell me if you think I could do astrology, by looking at my chart.

N: Well, yes! You have this absolutely clear teacher's, informer's, perfectionistic helper mental attitude. Certainly you can do astrology.

J: OK. But you know how some things are better…

N: Yes. But you are not a "born astrologer" here. You will have to work and study and all of that, and it's fun!

J: OK.

N: And you have other gifts that most astrologers *don't* have. In working with people.

J: I also have the ability—and I know this is going to sound hokey—I do see things before they're going to happen.

Again, the midpoint picture of Sun=Neptune/Pluto.

N: Fine. All of what a fine astrologer does is concretize [impressions, intuition] in measurement and then artistically extrapolate therefrom to put them into your reality, and you and I have done a hundred-thousand percent here today! Don't you think?

J: Yeah. I do!!

N: Say something nice to your astrologer!

J: I think you're really good; I don't want [this to end]…I want this to go on for a while!

N: All right. Now, we've done our job; we've done our job. Everything is clear; *the future should be absolutely as clear as we see it…*

J: Well, I have one more thing: about the Saturn return in my chart…that's coming up?

N: Yes. That's 2007, and that's what I covered with you about the retirement; that is the trigger for that.

J: When it happened before, it was definitely affected by home, especially home; it was when I pulled up and left...

N: Yes. It was in 1977.

J: Right. So is that going to repeat in the same area?
Was she thinking of dissolving her present marriage? We hadn't discussed any of those tensions. And she is fifty-seven years old.

N: No. No. NO.

J: OK. It was a hard thing in my life.

N: Is your marriage OK?

J: (Laconically) Eh, it's OK.

N: You know, let's face it; this period in your life right now is orientated to *professional shining of your light.* I can't put it better than that!

J: I know. I know!

N: I know people who would *pay* you for this opportunity!

J: OK, well, I'm changing my thoughts instead.

N: You're off the anti-depressants; now don't put it [depression] into your speech!

J: Or my thinking!

N: Use words like "shine, share, shed."

J: "Step up to the plate!"

N: Right!! Those are rallying cries of motivation!

J: Self-realization!

N: Yes. When Tony Robbins uses them, everyone pays him money!!!

J: He's great...

N: All right. Well, I'm giving them to you too! So, thank you, my dear.

J: Thank YOU!

N: You're sounding better now than you did at the start of this call!!

J: Yeah, I'm feeling better too! Thank you!

N: **Shine, share...**

J: ...and uplift!

N: **Uplift.** You can do it, and the meeting will be in two or three days with your employer...and: **step up to the plate!**

J: I will.

N: Thank you, my dear.

J: Thank *you*! Goodbye!

N: Bye!

(Forty-five minutes.)

OVERVIEW: STRUCTURE AND TECHNIQUE

The therapy flow here was certainly to the west. This was necessarily in mind in the preparation of the horoscope for analysis, planned to counteract what was anticipated from the reactionary (emphasis on mutability) confusion, self-torment, and depression to the early home life (led by the strong midpoint pictures).

The therapy flow bloomed as the review of the consultation began. Phrases and word images were used to pep things up and to become mnemonics for the consultation. Toward the end of the discussion, Joan began using the phrases and words herself. I felt that the mission had been accomplished!

Helping with Recall

It is advisable to keep simple notes during the consultation. Quickly write a cryptic key word that describes a major event in development and the client's reaction, the values attached to the event. For Joan, these were very clear: her tonsillitis episode, vividly establishing hate for her mother "for putting her through the ordeal"; her mother's frequent arguments with the father and her frequently packing her suitcase to leave the family; being upstaged by the baby brother; sent off to school apparently unsupported; losing the love of her life, who went off to Vietnam; a disastrous marriage and difficult divorce...all of these occurrences reiterated the fear of abandonment, Joan's being stranded somehow, being victimized.

Joan's defense reactions were quite confused and were negative implosions to self-torment and depression. Only through her profession (as anticipated) was her self-worth confirmed. And now at the end of her career, there is every opportunity for her *to shine* and be fulfilled. When she succeeds in approaching retirement *with personal accomplishment and fanfare,* she will surely lose weight and pay premium attention to refreshed values in her marriage.

Taking short notes during the consultation dialogue supports continuity impact for the summation; creative connections throughout development build the portrait impressively.

7 CASE STUDY: "MARION"

HOROSCOPE ORIENTATION

The orientation to Marion's horoscope is dramatically clear: Marion undoubtedly wrestles with very strong pressures to give herself away to others; to give, give, give. There must be a reason for this, and we can certainly suggest that the lifestyle is linked to Saturn-℞ phenomenology, self-worth anxiety (Saturn ruling the 2nd and under tension from oppositions from the 9th), and the anxiety about being lovable (Venus, ruler of the 11th is *retrograde* and conjoined the nodal axis, focused on the Aries Point!).

It is extraordinary that we can make such a diagnostic profile so quickly. Such is the incisive introspection power of astrology!

Within this initial orientation, we then will have to pursue the involvement with the mother and the passive father syndrome.

The orientation of the therapy flow will be to the eastern hemisphere, helping Marion to re-find herself, to pay attention to her own self-development and confidently focusing on that development to attract appreciation, love, and acclaim from others, all of which she was probably starved for in her developmental years.

This consultation took place in July 2004. We are studying it here—with these pages being written in March–April 2006—because in this consultation a major prediction was made to March–April 2006, and, indeed, Marion has reported in with big change in progress just as projected two years earlier!

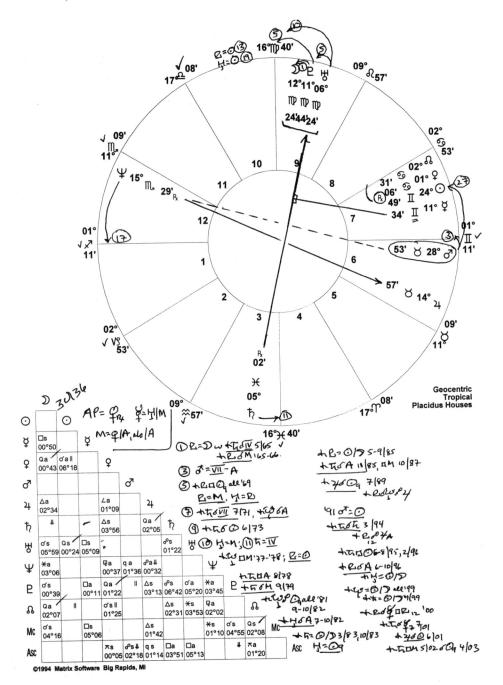

Jun 15, 1964 06:30:00 PM EDT 074W00'00" 40N43'00"

Midpoint Sort: 90° Dial											
♀	001°06'	♅/Asc	018°48'	☽/☉	033°36'	♃/Asc	053°04'	♄/♇	068°23'	♀/♂	075°00'
♀/☊	001°49'	♂/♇	020°19'	♀/♅	033°45'	♆/Asc	053°20'	☽/♄	068°43'	♂/☊	075°42'
☊	002°31'	☽/♂	020°39'	♄/☊	033°47'	☿/♃	058°15'	♃/☊	068°44'	♀/Asc	076°09'
♃/♄	010°00'	♇/Asc	021°28'	♅/☊	034°28'	☿/♆	058°32'	♆/☊	069°00'	Mc	076°40'
♄/♆	010°16'	☽/Asc	021°48'	☉/Mc	035°44'	♂	058°53'	♅/♇	069°04'	☊/Asc	076°51'
♃/♅	010°41'	♂/Mc	022°47'	♀/♇	036°25'	♂/Asc	060°02'	☽/♅	069°24'	☉/☿	078°11'
♅/♆	010°57'	☿/♄	023°18'	☽/♀	036°45'	Asc	061°11'	♄/Mc	070°51'	☿/♀	081°20'
♃/♇	013°21'	Mc/Asc	023°56'	♇/☊	037°08'	☉/♃	064°53'	♅/Mc	071°32'	☿/☊	082°02'
♆/♇	013°37'	☿/♅	023°59'	☽/☊	037°27'	♄	065°02'	☿	071°34'	☉	084°49'
☽/♃	013°40'	☿/♇	026°39'	♀/Mc	038°53'	☉/♆	065°09'	♇	071°44'	☉/♀	087°58'
☽/♆	013°56'	☽/☿	026°59'	☊/Mc	039°35'	☿/♂	065°14'	☉/♂	071°51'	☉/☊	088°40'
♃/Mc	015°48'	☿/Mc	029°07'	♃	044°57'	♄/♅	065°43'	☽/♇	072°04'		
♆/Mc	016°04'	☉/♄	029°56'	♃/♆	045°13'	☿/Asc	066°23'	☽	072°24'		
♂/♄	016°58'	☉/♅	030°37'	♆	045°29'	♅	066°24'	☉/Asc	073°00'		
♂/♅	017°39'	♀/♄	033°04'	♂/♃	051°55'	♀/♃	068°02'	♇/Mc	074°12'		
♄/Asc	018°07'	☉/♇	033°17'	♂/♆	052°11'	♀/♆	068°18'	☽/Mc	074°32'		

We can see the basis of the prediction very quickly from the combo-search January–May 2006. Note how clear the applying Jupiter=Sun arc is in the double-ringed horoscope for the initial consultation in July 2004.

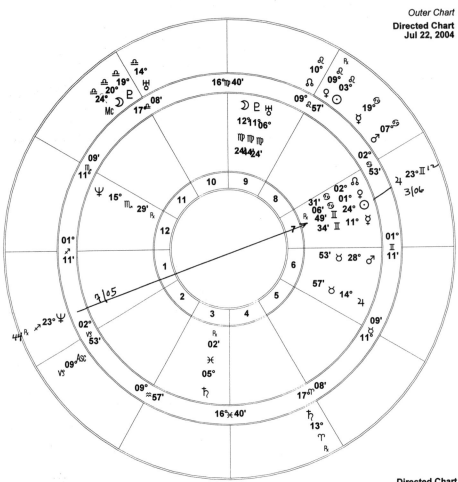

Outer Chart
Directed Chart
Jul 22, 2004

Pl	Geo Lon	Rx	Decl.
☽	12°♍23′ 41″		+11° 31′
☉	24°♊48′ 46″		+23° 21′
☿	11°♊33′ 44″		+21° 29′
♀	01°♋06′ 27″	Rx	+22° 34′
♂	28°♉53′ 27″	Rx	+19° 45′
♃	14°♉57′ 13″		+15° 22′
♄	05°♓02′ 19″		- 11° 05′
♅	06°♍24′ 26″		+09° 52′
♆	15°♏29′ 17″	Rx	- 14° 45′
♇	11°♍44′ 18″		+19° 56′

©1994 Matrix Software Big Rapids, MI

Directed Chart

Pl	Geo Lon	Rx	Decl.
☽	20°♎38′ 51″		+11° 31′
☉	03°♌03′ 56″		+23° 21′
☿	19°♋48′ 54″		+21° 29′
♀	09°♌21′ 36″	Rx	+22° 34′
♂	07°♋08′ 36″		+19° 45′
♃	23°♊12′ 22″		+15° 22′
♄	13°♈17′ 29″	Rx	- 11° 05′
♅	14°♍39′ 35″		+09° 52′
♆	23°♐44′ 26″	Rx	- 14° 45′
♇	19°♎59′ 27″		+19° 56′

Search From May 31, 2004 to Apr 30, 2006 GMT   Page: 1

Aspect	Date	Time	Event	Type	P1 Pos.	P2 Pos	E/X/L
♅ ---- SRx	06-10-2004	12:48 pm	♅ SRx	Tr-Na	06°♓48'Rx		
♇ ---- ⚼ ☉/♃	06-11-2004	11:13 am	♇ ⚼ ☉/♃	Ar-Na	19°♎53'	04°♊53'	Exact
♃ -- □ ☿	06-17-2004	06:04 am	♃ □ ☿	Tr-Na	11°♍34'	11°♊34'	Exact
♃ -- ☌ ♇	06-18-2004	05:53 pm	♃ ☌ ♇	Tr-Na	11°♍44'	11°♍44'	Exact
♃ -- ☌ ☽	06-23-2004	11:54 pm	♃ ☌ ☽	Tr-Na	12°♍24'	12°♍24'	Exact
♆ ---- □ ♃	06-28-2004	06:27 am	♆ □ ♃	Tr-Na	14°♒57'Rx	14°♉57'	Exact
♄ -- ∠ ☿/♃	07-09-2004	09:42 pm	♄ ∠ ☿/♃	Ar-Na	13°♈15'	28°♉15'	Exact
♅ ---- ☍ ♅	07-12-2004	08:38 am	♅ ☍ ♅	Tr-Na	06°♓24'Rx	06°♍24'	Exact
♂ -- □ ♃	07-17-2004	02:34 pm	♂ □ ♃	Tr-Na	14°♌57'	14°♉57'	Exact
♂ -- □ ♆	07-18-2004	10:54 am	♂ □ ♆	Tr-Na	15°♌29'	15°♏29'Rx	Exact
☽ □ ☽/♂	07-20-2004	09:31 pm	☽ □ ☽/♂	Ar-Na	20°♎39'	20°♋39'	Exact
♆ ---- q ♃/☊	07-21-2004	03:33 am	♆ q ♃/☊	Ar-Na	23°♐44'	08°♊44'	Exact
♃ -- ☌ Mc	07-21-2004	01:41 pm	♃ ☌ Mc	Tr-Na	16°♍40'	16°♍40'	Exact
☉ - □ ♀/♄	07-25-2004	01:22 pm	☉ □ ♀/♄	Ar-Na	03°♌04'	03°♉04'	Exact
♂ -- □ ♂	08-08-2004	04:12 pm	♂ □ ♂	Tr-Na	28°♌53'	28°♉53'	Exact
♂ -- ∠ ♂/♆	08-09-2004	06:05 am	♂ ∠ ♂/♆	Ar-Na	07°♋11'	22°♌11'	Exact
♇ ---- ⚼ ♄	08-09-2004	10:20 pm	♇ ⚼ ♄	Ar-Na	20°♎02'	05°♓02'Rx	Exact
☉ - q ♄/Asc	08-10-2004	07:32 am	☉ q ♄/Asc	Ar-Na	03°♌07'	18°♑07'	Exact
♂ -- □ Asc	08-12-2004	07:19 am	♂ □ Asc	Tr-Na	01°♍11'	01°♐11'	Exact
♄ -- □ ♃/♇	08-12-2004	01:11 pm	♄ □ ♃/♇	Ar-Na	13°♈21'	13°♋21'	Exact
☿ - ∠ ☉/♃	08-17-2004	06:10 pm	☿ ∠ ☉/♃	Ar-Na	19°♋53'	04°♊53'	Exact
♂ -- ☍ ♄	08-18-2004	08:55 am	♂ ☍ ♄	Tr-Na	05°♍02'	05°♓02'Rx	Exact
♂ -- ☌ ♅	08-20-2004	12:38 pm	♂ ☌ ♅	Tr-Na	06°♍24'	06°♍24'	Exact
☽ ∠ ♄/♅	08-20-2004	01:02 pm	☽ ∠ ♄/♅	Ar-Na	20°♎43'	05°♐43'	Exact
♅ ---- ☌ ♄	08-22-2004	03:41 am	♅ ☌ ♄	Tr-Na	05°♓02'Rx	05°♓02'Rx	Exact
Mc --- q ♃/♄	08-23-2004	02:28 am	Mc q ♃/♄	Ar-Na	25°♎00'	10°♈00'	Exact
♂ -- □ ☿	08-28-2004	03:07 pm	♂ □ ☿	Tr-Na	11°♍34'	11°♊34'	Exact
♂ -- ☌ ♇	08-28-2004	09:44 pm	♂ ☌ ♇	Tr-Na	11°♍44'	11°♍44'	Exact
♂ -- ☌ ☽	08-29-2004	10:28 pm	♂ ☌ ☽	Tr-Na	12°♍24'	12°♍24'	Exact
♇ ---- SD	08-30-2004	02:12 pm	♇ SD	Tr-Na	19°♐32'		
♃ -- □ ☉	08-31-2004	11:59 pm	♃ □ ☉	Tr-Na	24°♍49'	24°♊49'	Exact
♂ -- ☌ Mc	09-05-2004	02:54 pm	♂ ☌ Mc	Tr-Na	16°♍40'	16°♍40'	Exact
☉ - ∠ ☉/☿	09-07-2004	08:48 am	☉ ∠ ☉/☿	Ar-Na	03°♌11'	18°♊11'	Exact
♆ ---- ⚼ ♀/Mc	09-15-2004	03:18 pm	♆ ⚼ ♀/Mc	Ar-Na	23°♐53'	08°♌53'	Exact
♂ -- □ ☉	09-18-2004	08:03 am	♂ □ ☉	Tr-Na	24°♍49'	24°♊49'	Exact
♇ ---- ∠ ☉/♆	09-21-2004	03:52 pm	♇ ∠ ☉/♆	Ar-Na	20°♎09'	05°♍09'	Exact
♂ -- □ ♀	09-28-2004	02:25 am	♂ □ ♀	Tr-Na	01°♎06'	01°♋06'Rx	Exact
♃ -- □ ♀	09-30-2004	06:29 am	♃ □ ♀	Tr-Na	01°♎06'	01°♋06'Rx	Exact
♂ -- □ ☊	09-30-2004	06:50 am	♂ □ ☊	Tr-Na	02°♎31'	02°♋31'Rx	Exact
♃ -- q ♄/♇	09-30-2004	09:41 am	♃ q ♄/♇	Ar-Na	23°♊23'	08°♐23'	Exact
♃ -- □ ☊	10-06-2004	08:09 pm	♃ □ ☊	Tr-Na	02°♎31'	02°♋31'Rx	Exact
☉ - ☌ ☉/♇	10-11-2004	00:15 am	☉ ☌ ☉/♇	Ar-Na	03°♌17'	03°♌17'	Exact
☿ - ⚼ ♄	10-16-2004	05:14 am	☿ ⚼ ♄	Ar-Na	20°♋02'	05°♓02'Rx	Exact
♀ - ☌ ☊/Mc	10-18-2004	07:16 pm	♀ ☌ ☊/Mc	Ar-Na	09°♌35'	09°♌35'	Exact
♄ -- ⚼ ☿/♆	10-20-2004	02:19 am	♄ ⚼ ☿/♆	Ar-Na	13°♈32'	28°♌32'	Exact
♇ ---- ⚼ ☿/♂	10-20-2004	06:34 pm	♇ ⚼ ☿/♂	Ar-Na	20°♎14'	05°♊14'	Exact
♆ ---- SD	10-24-2004	06:30 am	♆ SD	Tr-Na	12°♒36'		
♅ ---- q ☉/♄	11-01-2004	09:32 am	♅ q ☉/♄	Ar-Na	14°♎56'	29°♈56'	Exact
♄ -- SRx	11-08-2004	06:04 am	♄ SRx	Tr-Na	27°♋21'Rx		
♅ ---- SD	11-11-2004	04:38 pm	♅ SD	Tr-Na	02°♓52'		
♇ ---- □ ♂/♇	11-23-2004	09:59 am	♇ □ ♂/♇	Ar-Na	20°♎19'	20°♋19'	Exact
☿ - ∠ ☉/♆	11-27-2004	10:44 pm	☿ ∠ ☉/♆	Ar-Na	20°♋09'	05°♍09'	Exact
♂ -- ☍ ♃	12-03-2004	01:12 pm	♂ ☍ ♃	Tr-Na	14°♏57'	14°♉57'	Exact
♂ -- ☌ ♆	12-04-2004	08:12 am	♂ ☌ ♆	Tr-Na	15°♏29'	15°♏29'Rx	Exact
Asc --- q ☉	12-11-2004	07:44 am	Asc q ☉	Ar-Na	09°♑49'	24°♊49'	Exact
♅ ---- ⚼ ♂/Asc	12-15-2004	04:27 am	♅ ⚼ ♂/Asc	Ar-Na	15°♎02'	00°♓02'	Exact
♄ -- □ ☽/♃	12-16-2004	01:37 am	♄ □ ☽/♃	Ar-Na	13°♈40'	13°♋40'	Exact
♂ -- ☍ ♂	12-24-2004	01:12 am	♂ ☍ ♂	Tr-Na	28°♏53'	28°♉53'	Exact
☿ - ∠ ☿/♂	12-27-2004	01:24 am	☿ ∠ ☿/♂	Ar-Na	20°♋14'	05°♊14'	Exact
♂ -- ☌ Asc	12-27-2004	09:42 am	♂ ☌ Asc	Tr-Na	01°♐11'	01°♐11'	Exact
♂ -- □ ♄	01-02-2005	00:00 am	♂ □ ♄	Tr-Na	05°♐02'	05°♓02'Rx	Exact
♂ -- □ ♅	01-03-2005	11:37 pm	♂ □ ♅	Tr-Na	06°♐24'	06°♍24'	Exact
♂ -- ☍ ☿	01-11-2005	10:23 am	♂ ☍ ☿	Tr-Na	11°♐34'	11°♊34'	Exact
♂ -- □ ♇	01-11-2005	04:29 pm	♂ □ ♇	Tr-Na	11°♐44'	11°♍44'	Exact
♀ - ∠ ☉	01-11-2005	07:59 pm	♀ ∠ ☉	Ar-Na	09°♌49'	24°♊49'	Exact
♂ -- □ ☽	01-12-2005	03:10 pm	♂ □ ☽	Tr-Na	12°♐24'	12°♍24'	Exact
♂ -- □ Mc	01-18-2005	06:20 pm	♂ □ Mc	Tr-Na	16°♐40'	16°♍40'	Exact
♅ ---- ☌ ♄	01-25-2005	10:01 am	♅ ☌ ♄	Tr-Na	05°♓02'	05°♓02'Rx	Exact
☿ - ☌ ♂/♇	01-29-2005	04:47 pm	☿ ☌ ♂/♇	Ar-Na	20°♋19'	20°♋19'	Exact
♂ -- ☍ ☉	01-30-2005	09:50 am	♂ ☍ ☉	Tr-Na	24°♐49'	24°♊49'	Exact
♆ ---- □ ♃	01-31-2005	02:52 pm	♆ □ ♃	Tr-Na	14°♒57'	14°♉57'	Exact
♃ -- SRx	02-02-2005	01:01 am	♃ SRx	Tr-Na	18°♎52'Rx		
♃ -- q ☽/♄	02-02-2005	10:02 pm	♃ q ☽/♄	Ar-Na	23°♊43'	08°♐43'	Exact

♂♅☍♅ 2nd "hit"

♀∠☉

Search From May 31, 2004 to Apr 30, 2006 GMT Page: 2

Aspect	Date	Time	Event	Type	P1 Pos.	P2 Pos	E/X/L
♂ -- ☍ ♀	02-08-2005	08:09 am	♂ ☍ ♀	Tr-Na	01°♑06'	01°♋06'℞	Exact
♂ -- ☍ ☊	02-10-2005	08:04 am	♂ ☍ ☊	Tr-Na	02°♑31'	02°♋31'℞	Exact
☉ - ☌ ☽/☉	02-13-2005	12:35 pm	☉ ☌ ☽/☉	Ar-Na	03°♌36'	03°♌36'	Exact
♆ ---- □ ♆	02-14-2005	05:30 pm	♆ □ ♆	Tr-Na	15°♒29'	15°♏29'℞	Exact
♅ ---- ☍ ♅	02-19-2005	05:28 am	♅ ☍ ♅	Tr-Na	06°♓24'	06°♍24'	Exact
Asc --- □ ♃/♄	02-19-2005	09:15 am	Asc □ ♃/♄	Ar-Na	10°♑00'	10°♈00'	Exact
♄ -- ∠ ♂	03-08-2005	09:29 pm	♄ ∠ ♂	Ar-Na	13°♈53'	28°♉53'	Exact
♄ -- SD	03-22-2005	02:05 am	♄ SD	Tr-Na	20°♋24'		
♇ ---- SR℞	03-26-2005	11:45 pm	♇ SR℞	Tr-Na	24°♐31'℞		
♇ ---- □ ☽/♂	03-28-2005	10:14 pm	♇ □ ☽/♂	Ar-Na	20°♎39'	20°♋39'	Exact
♃ -- ∠ ♀/Mc	04-08-2005	00:10 am	♃ ∠ ♀/Mc	Ar-Na	23°♊53'	08°♌53'	Exact
♂ -- □ ♃	04-10-2005	09:30 am	♂ □ ♃	Tr-Na	14°♒57'	14°♉57'	Exact
♂ -- □ ♆	04-11-2005	03:10 am	♂ □ ♆	Tr-Na	15°♒29'	15°♏29'℞	Exact
☉ - ☌ ♀/♅	04-13-2005	04:43 am	☉ ☌ ♀/♅	Ar-Na	03°♌45'	03°♌45'	Exact
☉ - □ ♄/☊	04-21-2005	02:03 pm	☉ □ ♄/☊	Ar-Na	03°♌47'	03°♉47'	Exact
☽ ∠ ☿/Asc	04-27-2005	07:22 am	☽ ∠ ☿/Asc	Ar-Na	21°♎23'	06°♍23'	Exact
♇ ---- ∠ ♄/♅	04-28-2005	01:38 pm	♇ ∠ ♄/♅	Ar-Na	20°♎43'	05°♐43'	Exact
♂ -- □ ♂	04-29-2005	02:16 pm	♂ □ ♂	Tr-Na	28°♒53'	28°♉53'	Exact
♂ -- □ Asc	05-02-2005	06:21 pm	♂ □ Asc	Tr-Na	01°♓11'	01°♐11'	Exact
♂ -- ☌ ♄	05-08-2005	01:54 am	♂ ☌ ♄	Tr-Na	05°♓02'	05°♓02'℞	Exact
☽ ∠ ♅	05-09-2005	04:17 am	☽ ∠ ♅	Ar-Na	21°♎24'	06°♍24'	Exact
♂ -- ☍ ♅	05-09-2005	11:20 pm	♂ ☍ ♅	Tr-Na	06°♓24'	06°♍24'	Exact
☽ □ ♂	05-16-2005	09:20 am	☽ □ ♂	Pr-Na	28°♒53'	28°♉53'	Exact
♂ -- □ ☿	05-17-2005	02:58 am	♂ □ ☿	Tr-Na	11°♓34'	11°♊34'	Exact
♂ -- ☍ ♇	05-17-2005	08:50 am	♂ ☍ ♇	Tr-Na	11°♓44'	11°♍44'	Exact
♂ -- ☍ ☽	05-18-2005	06:45 am	♂ ☍ ☽	Tr-Na	12°♓24'	12°♍24'	Exact
♆ ---- SR℞	05-19-2005	08:24 pm	♆ SR℞	Tr-Na	17°♒36'℞		
♂ -- ☍ Mc	05-24-2005	05:37 am	♂ ☍ Mc	Tr-Na	16°♓40'	16°♍40'	Exact
☽ ☌ ♇/Asc	05-30-2005	10:42 pm	☽ ☌ ♇/Asc	Ar-Na	21°♎28'	21°♎28'	Exact
Asc --- ☌ ♄/♆	06-01-2005	01:31 pm	Asc ☌ ♄/♆	Ar-Na	10°♑16'	10°♑16'	Exact
☿ - ☌ ☽/♂	06-04-2005	04:55 am	☿ ☌ ☽/♂	Ar-Na	20°♋39'	20°♋39'	Exact
♂ -- □ ☉	06-04-2005	04:55 pm	♂ □ ☉	Tr-Na	24°♓49'	24°♊49'	Exact
♃ -- SD	06-05-2005	06:50 am	♃ SD	Tr-Na	08°♎56'		
♆ ---- ⚼ ☊/Mc	06-12-2005	03:46 pm	♆ ⚼ ☊/Mc	Ar-Na	24°♐35'	09°♌35'	Exact
♂ -- □ ♀	06-13-2005	04:44 pm	♂ □ ♀	Tr-Na	01°♈06'	01°♋06'℞	Exact
♅ ---- SR℞	06-14-2005	09:02 pm	♅ SR℞	Tr-Na	10°♓46'℞		
♂ -- □ ☊	06-15-2005	05:39 pm	♂ □ ☊	Tr-Na	02°♈31'	02°♋31'℞	Exact
☿ - ⚼ ♄/♅	07-04-2005	08:17 pm	☿ ⚼ ♄/♅	Ar-Na	20°♋43'	05°♐43'	Exact
♂ -- ⚼ ♃/Asc	07-12-2005	02:59 pm	♂ ⚼ ♃/Asc	Ar-Na	08°♋04'	23°♒04'	Exact
Mc --- ∠ ♄/Mc	07-15-2005	02:32 pm	Mc ∠ ♄/Mc	Ar-Na	25°♎51'	10°♐51'	Exact
☽ □ Asc	07-21-2005	07:42 pm	☽ □ Asc	Pr-Na	01°♓11'	01°♐11'	Exact
♂ -- ☌ ♃	08-26-2005	12:59 pm	♂ ☌ ♃	Tr-Na	14°♉57'	14°♉57'	Exact
♂ -- ☍ ♆	08-27-2005	08:05 pm	♂ ☍ ♆	Tr-Na	15°♉29'	15°♏29'℞	Exact
♇ ---- SD	09-02-2005	05:09 am	♇ SD	Tr-Na	21°♐49'		
♆ ---- □ ♆	09-05-2005	05:27 am	♆ □ ♆	Tr-Na	15°♒29'℞	15°♏29'℞	Exact
♂ -- SR℞	10-01-2005	09:59 pm	♂ SR℞	Tr-Na	23°♉22'℞		
☽ ☌ ☽/Asc	10-03-2005	10:35 am	☽ ☌ ☽/Asc	Ar-Na	21°♎48'	21°♎48'	Exact
♅ ---- □ ♃/Mc	10-04-2005	11:46 am	♅ □ ♃/Mc	Ar-Na	15°♎48'	15°♋48'	Exact
♆ ---- □ ♃	10-04-2005	01:42 pm	♆ □ ♃	Tr-Na	14°♒57'℞	14°♉57'	Exact
♂ -- ⚼ ♆/Asc	10-22-2005	07:02 pm	♂ ⚼ ♆/Asc	Ar-Na	08°♋20'	23°♏20'	Exact
♆ ---- SD	10-26-2005	06:34 pm	♆ SD	Tr-Na	14°♒49'		
♂ -- ☍ ♆	11-05-2005	11:44 pm	♂ ☍ ♆	Tr-Na	15°♉29'℞	15°♏29'℞	Exact
♂ -- ☌ ♃	11-07-2005	11:58 am	♂ ☌ ♃	Tr-Na	14°♉57'℞	14°♉57'	Exact
☽ ☌ ♄	11-09-2005	01:54 pm	☽ ☌ ♄	Pr-Na	05°♓02'	05°♓02'℞	Exact
♅ ---- SD	11-15-2005	09:46 pm	♅ SD	Tr-Na	06°♓51'		
♆ ---- □ ♃	11-17-2005	09:19 pm	♆ □ ♃	Tr-Na	14°♒57'	14°♉57'	Exact
♄ -- SR℞	11-22-2005	07:09 am	♄ SR℞	Tr-Na	11°♌19'℞		
♂ -- SD	12-10-2005	04:27 am	♂ SD	Tr-Na	08°♉14'		
♆ ---- □ ♆	12-15-2005	07:02 am	♆ □ ♆	Tr-Na	15°♒29'	15°♏29'℞	Exact
☽ ☍ ♅	12-18-2005	07:43 pm	☽ ☍ ♅	Pr-Na	06°♓24'	06°♍24'	Exact
♇ ---- ☍ ☉	12-29-2005	11:26 pm	♇ ☍ ☉	Tr-Na	24°♐49'	24°♊49'	Exact
♃ -- ∠ ☊/Mc	01-02-2006	11:48 pm	♃ ∠ ☊/Mc	Ar-Na	24°♊35'	09°♌35'	Exact
♇ ---- ∠ ☿/Asc	01-03-2006	07:01 am	♇ ∠ ☿/Asc	Ar-Na	21°♎23'	06°♍23'	Exact
☉ - ☌ ♅/☊	01-08-2006	04:20 am	☉ ☌ ♅/☊	Ar-Na	04°♌28'	04°♌28'	Exact
♃ -- ☍ ♃	01-11-2006	10:07 pm	♃ ☍ ♃	Tr-Na	14°♏57'	14°♉57'	Exact
♂ -- ☌ ♃	01-14-2006	00:47 am	♂ ☌ ♃	Tr-Na	14°♉57'	14°♉57'	Exact
♅ ---- ☌ ♆/Mc	01-14-2006	03:41 pm	♅ ☌ ♆/Mc	Ar-Na	16°♎04'	16°♎04'	Exact
♇ ---- ∠ ♅	01-15-2006	03:53 am	♇ ∠ ♅	Ar-Na	21°♎24'	06°♍24'	Exact
♂ -- ☍ ♆	01-15-2006	01:28 pm	♂ ☍ ♆	Tr-Na	15°♉29'	15°♏29'℞	Exact
♃ -- ☌ ♆	01-15-2006	07:58 pm	♃ ☌ ♆	Tr-Na	15°♏29'	15°♏29'℞	Exact
♇ ---- ☌ ♇/Asc	02-05-2006	10:13 pm	♇ ☌ ♇/Asc	Ar-Na	21°♎28'	21°♎28'	Exact
♂ -- ☌ ♂	02-15-2006	04:37 pm	♂ ☌ ♂	Tr-Na	28°♉53'	28°♉53'	Exact
Asc --- □ ♅/♆	02-18-2006	03:38 am	Asc □ ♅/♆	Ar-Na	10°♑57'	10°♎57'	Exact

tr ♅ ☍ ♅ final

tr ♇ SR ☍ ☉ delay

Search From May 31, 2004 to Apr 30, 2006 GMT Page: 3

Aspect	Date	Time	Event	Type	P1 Pos.	P2 Pos	E/X/L
♂ -- ☍ Asc	02-20-2006	08:04 am	♂ ☍ Asc	Tr-Na	01°♊11'	01°♐11'	Exact
♅ ---- ∠ Asc	02-27-2006	04:32 pm	♅ ∠ Asc	Ar-Na	16°♎11'	01°♐11'	Exact
♂ -- □ ♄	02-27-2006	09:08 pm	♂ □ ♄	Tr-Na	05°♊02'	05°♓02'℞	Exact
♂ -- □ ♅	03-02-2006	12:07 pm	♂ □ ♅	Tr-Na	06°♊24'	06°♍24'	Exact
♃ -- S℞	03-04-2006	05:31 pm	♃ S℞	Tr-Na	18°♏52'℞		
☿ - ∠ ☿/Asc	03-11-2006	01:24 pm	☿ ∠ ☿/Asc	Ar-Na	21°♋23'	06°♍23'	Exact
♂ -- ☌ ☿	03-12-2006	04:14 am	♂ ☌ ☿	Tr-Na	11°♊34'	11°♊34'	Exact
♂ -- □ ♇	03-12-2006	12:02 pm	♂ □ ♇	Tr-Na	11°♊44'	11°♍44'	Exact
♂ -- □ ☽	03-13-2006	05:05 pm	♂ □ ☽	Tr-Na	12°♊24'	12°♍24'	Exact
♅ ---- □ ☿	03-16-2006	06:13 am	♅ □ ☿	Tr-Na	11°♓34'	11°♊34'	Exact
♅ ---- ☍ ♇	03-19-2006	09:51 am	♅ ☍ ♇	Tr-Na	11°♓44'	11°♍44'	Exact
♂ -- □ Mc	03-21-2006	11:44 am	♂ □ Mc	Tr-Na	16°♊40'	16°♍40'	Exact
☿ - ∠ ♅	03-23-2006	10:15 am	☿ ∠ ♅	Ar-Na	21°♋24'	06°♍24'	Exact
♃ -- ☌ ☉	03-28-2006	11:56 pm	♃ ☌ ☉	Ar-Na	24°♊49'	24°♊49'	Exact
♇ ---- S℞	03-29-2006	09:56 am	♇ S℞	Tr-Na	26°♐45'℞		
♅ ---- ☍ ☽	03-31-2006	01:42 pm	♅ ☍ ☽	Tr-Na	12°♓24'	12°♍24'	Exact
Mc --- ∠ ♅/Mc	04-03-2006	04:27 am	Mc ∠ ♅/Mc	Ar-Na	26°♎32'	11°♍32'	Exact
♂ -- ☌ ☉	04-04-2006	11:49 pm	♂ ☌ ☉	Tr-Na	24°♊49'	24°♊49'	Exact
♄ -- SD	04-05-2006	12:08 pm	♄ SD	Tr-Na	04°♌23'		
Mc --- ⚻ ☿	04-13-2006	10:40 pm	Mc ⚻ ☿	Ar-Na	26°♎34'	11°♊34'	Exact
☿ - □ ♇/Asc	04-14-2006	04:33 am	☿ □ ♇/Asc	Ar-Na	21°♋28'	21°♎28'	Exact
♂ -- ☌ ♀	04-15-2006	11:01 pm	♂ ☌ ♀	Tr-Na	01°♋06'	01°♋06'℞	Exact
♂ -- ☌ ☊	04-18-2006	09:35 am	♂ ☌ ☊	Tr-Na	02°♋31'	02°♋31'℞	Exact
♃ -- ☌ ♆	04-22-2006	04:41 pm	♃ ☌ ♆	Tr-Na	15°♏29'℞	15°♏29'℞	Exact
♃ -- ☍ ♃	04-27-2006	00:54 am	♃ ☍ ♃	Tr-Na	14°♏57'℞	14°♉57'	Exact

THE CONSULTATION

M: (Happily) Hi! Noel Tyl!

N: Hi, Marion! Thanks for being on time.

M: You're welcome.

N: Now, Marion, what is your creative outlet? For goodness sakes…

Note that there are six quintiles in the horoscope! Any time there are over three, I suggest ascertaining the creative outlet the individual ideally must have. If there is none, the probability is very high that the creativity was squelched very early on (by the parents), with serious frustration and diversion of energies in development.

M: (Laughing in recognition) Well, I kind of have three different streams going…and, uh…

N: Well, you should have about fifteen! This horoscope screams creative expression!

M: Really?

Marion's remark suggests she has never been singled out for her creativity, not that my remarking on it is a surprise.

N: Yes.

M: I…and that's actually one of my big issues: *how to focus what!*

N: Yeah. What are the three streams?

M: Well, mostly, I interweave mythology with, uh, psychotherapy—I have a degree in psychotherapy, but I'm not licensed—and so, working individually with clients, but also nature-based work where I bring people out onto the land, and…

> *We note that her Sun, ruler of the 9th, is unaspected. Marion marches to a different drummer than most others.*

N: And what is your second thread?

M: Well, the individual work that sort of threads between astrology and psychotherapy and then, uh, Nature-based work. So there are, so there's kind of three different threads…

N: Oh! I see: *all helping people.*

> *Here's the central reference to the western hemisphere orientation.*

M: Yes.

N: I want to point out to you that this horoscope is filled with creative energies—just filled—and they're all basically cerebral rather than gushing…

M: Mm mn (agreeing).

N: …and I say that advisedly, because the emotional dimension of this developmental profile is frustrated [Mm mn]; it's anxious, anxiety-ridden [Mm mn]; it is pulled back, dysfunctional even [Mm mn], and, when I see this I say, "Well, gee whiz! This is not good for the creative side!" All that cerebral stuff: uh, *we've got to get it wet!* [Mm mn] You know what I'm talking about?

> *Here, I'm referring to the very difficult Venus retrograde, always a difficult measurement; frustrated in fulfillment. We have noted that this Venus rules the 11th (loveliness) and the 6th (cooperation with others to build friendships, partnerships) with Mercury, ruler of the 7th under high developmental tension (the squares from Uranus and Pluto).*

M: I *totally* know what you're talking about!

N: And, uh, we've got to look at the cause here. The cause for the emotional traffic jam in the desert…may I put it that way?

M: (Laughing lightly) That's good enough!

N: And that is related to a very, very poor relationship with your father (Mm mn) who was either remote, passive, taken out of the picture early…something like that…

M: Yeah…

N: …and the mother steps in and, uh, dominates or…

M: Engulfs…

N: …intrudes or engulfs…You've got it?

M: Yes.

N: Now…uh…we did that in two minutes and fifteen seconds or something (laughing)!

M: (Laughing in recognition of the fact.)

N: And I know psychotherapists who couldn't even get to that in…

> *Marion had a wonderful sense of laughter in her talk, much humor wanting to be shared; I just wanted to show off a bit for astrology to a psychotherapist.*

M: Yeah!

N: I'm sorry I had to put that dig in there! (Laughing)

M: (Laughing) That's OK.

(Both laughing)

N: So, that…that's the situation. Now, when one sees that, we see then that you become anxious about your self-worth [Mm mn], we see that you don't feel necessarily that you're lovable [she pauses, then: Mm mn]…There was a pause…?

M: No, actually I was going to fill in something. May I fill in…

N: We will in a moment. Just let me get it all out…

M: OK.

N: And then we see the vulnerability to being pushed around by other people [Mm mn], because you want to help them, you want to give, give, give, give. [Mm mn] You know? [Mm mn] And they take advantage of it.

M: Exactly!

N: And what happens is: you say, "But I'm getting what I need; I'm getting confirmation that I *am* important, that I *am* lovable," you see? [Mm mn] And all of this goodness in you adds up to a kind of personal charisma...that has real trouble getting out of the traffic jam in the desert.

The Mars contact with Neptune; always charisma!

M: Yeah! (wistfully) This is exactly where I am.

N: OK. Now, that's not necessarily the most efficient way to use God's gift of creativity in your work for other people. What is missing is...is a kind of *objectification* [Mm mn]...and I hate to bring that up to you, because, you know, you specialize in helping with that with other people, but you've got to sit down, Marion, and you've got to say, "Now, look! I've had problems here in my early home life, and...I've got to put them into a box and send them to Korea" (euphemistically) [Mm mn] You know? "And I've got to get my sex life under control" [Mm mn]. "I've got to get my emotional life tidied up [Mm mn]. So that I can be freer to help others better" [Mm mn].

The assumptive statement about Marion's sex life comes from the Venus-℞ and the Mars peregrine, ruling the 5th House and the strong aspects to the Moon, ruler of the 8th House.

M: (Long pause) Just let me know if you want me to...

N: Uh, I...That was a Cecil B. DeMille moment! (both laughing) I can't say much more than that about those things.

M: Yeah.

N: Now, I'm going to go through your whole life on those points, but I need you to talk to me.

M: OK. Well, um...I...I've been through an enormous amount of my inner journey...so...in therapy [naming many techniques] and, uh, and about four years...well in '98, there was a real...whole...my whole tendency to give away my power over and over during my life was kind of...just...completely, um, exacerbated and, and getting really confused as a spiritual teacher and being totally manipulated...

N: That was '99; I think it was '99.

M: Yeah. It was the end of '98 and all of '99.

N: We're going to get into all of that. [OK] The point is, let me sum up for you [OK]: you have corroborated absolutely every dimension and image I have shared with you. [Mm mn] That's remarkable that we can do that. We can. There it is. Now: I need a couple more details...just respond to me...[OK]...how remote, passive, out of the picture was the father?

The Saturn retrograde profile.

M: Alcoholic. But not, you know, just sort of...I grew up in a really formal, kind of Republican...the image is the most important thing of everything. Like passed down through generations. So he was, we sort of didn't know if he was or wasn't. But he was just *gone*. It was just numb. And no passion in his life, and I actually became like his surrogate wife...When he and Mom were having problems, I was the one that just...I feel like I put on an emotional straight-jacket when I was about nine. And really identified with her, but kind of "left me" for years.

N: That was in June of '73. I have that. I remember (soft humor).

M: You were there!

N: Now, look, look. We've got to go to bottom lines on this stuff in order to get rid of them easily.

M: OK.

N: It's very easy to put the filigree discussions to it. [Mm mn] You don't need it. I don't need it.

M: OK, I'll try to...

N: We need judo chops here, you know?

M: OK.

N: Like *"He had his problems."* [Mm mn] Boom. *"They had their problems."* Boom. [Mm mn] *"He wasn't interested in family stuff."* [No] He never basically said, "Marion, baby, I love you, let me show you the way." [Yeah] Mother comes in and wants to compete, probably...

Pluto in strong aspect with the Moon.

M: I'm just a narcissistic extension of her.

N: Exactly.

M: Bottom line.

N: All right. Thank you. Man, she's [Marion is] good! (Light laugh)

M: (Light laugh) Fine.

N: You understand it, I understand it. [Yeah] Now, this leaves you with a feeling of *self-worth weakness.*

>*Saturn-℞ rules the 2nd House and is strongly aspected by Uranus and Pluto; and Saturn squares the Ascendant.*

M: [Mm mn] A black hole.

N: It leaves you with the vulnerability to emotional unfulfillment that is very pronounced.

>*Venus retrograde, with Venus ruling the 11th.*

M: Mm mn [pause]…I'm, I'm right in the absolute details and nuances of that right now, and a relationship just came in, and I am just so aware of the deep-seated pattern of uh…unrequited love.

>*A fine portrayal of one of the facets of Venus retrograde.*

N: Thank you. [Yeah] You said it perfectly.

M: Yeah.

N: Is there concomitant thereto a sexual dysfunction?

M: In…in a way, that is, um, even in the last two weeks I've gotten more of a pattern of just this way that I'll go…um…It'll just go into sort of a *numb* place of, especially right now, um, with Saturn in the 8th, uh, this numb place of, uh, just, I just see it, it's a protection of [against] diving in and getting completely out of control.

N: Is there an orgasmic dysfunction?

M: Right now [agreeing]. But there wasn't before.

N: OK. Well, you know, the older you get, and 40 is getting older, the more the body has to be resourceful in masking anxieties elsewhere with symptomatic response dysfunctions.

M: Uh-huh.

N: There's no problem when you masturbate.

M: Well, no. But even that has been pretty low desire.

N: Yes, but I'm just pointing out to you that the [sexual] response potential is reliable; you have *relationship-dynamic concerns…*

M: Although, it's...it's more reliable when I can be large and in charge; it's not so much, you know, when I *crave* this being in a receptive mode and being able to orgasm.

N: Yes. There you go [confirming]. You see?

M: Yeah.

N: And that is having it proved to you that you are desirable, lovable, adorable [hmmm, in acknowledgement]. And even your own erotic fantasies revolve around that. [Hmmmm, further acknowledgement] Even an audience—you know—seeing you and desiring you, is what you've never had [completing the metaphor].

M: [Mm mn] That was the "win Daddy over" phase of my life.

N: OK. We need not go further with that.

M: No, no; I've played that out [in my mind] many times.

N: All right. But there are ways: mechanical, technical ways to make this bridge between, uh, physical aloofness or numbness, as you're calling it [Mm mn] and emotional trusting and communication. And that might be another telephone call, should you wish to do it.

M: Can I say one more thing?

N: Yes.

M: And I've seen the way this is related to relationships and sexual...and I've also been equally caught in the "I have to be of service to the point of giving everything away" and there's no nourishment [left]; and I'm totally burned out...
    Further reiteration of the western hemisphere orientation.

N: And there's nothing left for you!

M: Yes.

N: That's what we said earlier. Remember? "Giving, giving, giving to others"?

M: (Light laughing) Yes! (recalling)

N: And I could have added, "leaving yourself behind."

M: Right!

N: All righty: now, when you were born, right in the very first year of...of life, your mother, your parents, were really upset. Did you hear anything about that?

M: Not those early years. But I do know I had a toxic worm in terms of the Rh factor being…I mean…Mom and I had different Rh, so every time I've gone into those memories, it's like the Universe is out to attack me. So it's a big template.

N: Notice how you're phrasing it: "the Universe is out to attack you."

M: Yeah. That was the feeling for a long time.

N: You know…that is all in those very first three years. There are all kinds of…of problems swirling around you. [Mm mn] We don't need to go into them, but I'm just saying you were uh…away in a manger, in a way that wasn't best for you.

M: I don't actually know much about those first couple of years.

N: You know, often in this kind of a situation, the mother, to be punitive, will say to you, "We didn't want you. We wanted to abort you [Mm mn]…You came along and really disrupted us," because the child is to blame for other things. That's what I'm seeing here; that kind of stuff.

M: Right.

N: OK. Now, uh, in 1969 when you're five years old, can you recall a major change, a relocation perhaps? Move? Real re-organization of family status and position.

M: Um…no…nine to ten is the big move of location, but, I just…sort of there's just a big blank before that in my life.

N: OK.

M: The only thing I *do* remember is—it was around six to seven—I discovered masturbation and, you know, just…

N: That wouldn't be it. That's not abnormal or anything. But the point is [would be] if you were *punished for it* or something like that, that might have been something…

M: Yes. That was all there.

N: Oh. OK. What I was seeing was your father had a new job, you had a new home; 90 percent of the time that's what I would hear. I'm trying to corroborate the angles [of the horoscope]. OK. No problem; that happens. The aloneness that follows on that period becomes very important; and even though that period didn't have upheaval and change in '69, as I think it should have (and you'll probably get off the phone and remember it!)…

M: Yeah, I'm going to call Mom…(laughing)

N: (Laughing) In the summer of '71, you are one lonely, alone lady. You're seven years old. Do you remember just going into your room and closing the door?
A vivid image for young aloneness.

M: Yeah. Yeah…I…I…seven–eight–nine is when it all started; I just "left myself," was the feeling.

N: Right. That's very strong.

M: Yeah.

N: And then into '74, we have another one of those big, big times of potential here: we have moves, changes of status…'74 and '75, the *whole* period [Yeah, Yeah]. What happened?

M: That's…that's when we moved houses; we moved into…um…Mom and Dad's parents' house…um…and…um…Dad's drinking got worse; Mom had an affair, but nobody talked about it—I only found out about it about five years ago…My sister and brother were gone, and I just…I just literally remember putting on an emotional straightjacket; like just *don't do anything out of line. Just do 99 percent of what they need for me to be.*

N: Yeah. And you're just feeling worse and worse and worse about yourself as they're feeling more and more and more about *their* problems.

M: Yeah.

N: It's really that succinctly describable.

M: Yeah. Yeah.

N: All right. Now what [graduating] class were you in your high school?

M: UH…'82. Is that what you mean?

N: Yeah. So you're class of '82.

M: Yeah.

N: Now, did you go right on to college?

M: Yeah…A half-year off…

N: Ah…(recognition)

M: (Recognizing that I was after the "interruption") That's amazing…

N: (Laughing) I was going to say, "Now wait a minute here!"

M: Amazing.

N: Why was there a half-year interruption?

M: Middlebury in Vermont has a special freshman program and I was accepted for that, and um, I can't remember if there is any other…

N: OK. All right. Fine. And the relocation [away to college] did you good!

M: Yeah.

N: Then there's a relationship in '83 that was stormy: February-March, October…

M: (Pause) I'm sure there was something, but nothing really…

N: Not that important. Was there a foreign trip or anything like that that summer? '83–'84?

M: Um…I went abroad…I…I think it…was somewhere…in '85. I spent a half-year in Africa.

N: So you had a trip to Africa.

M: Yeah. That opened my world.

N: Now, what were you doing in 1989, in July?

M: I was in the middle of *the* big trip of my life: to India, Nepal, and Thailand. Uh, month to month, just following huge…just huge spiritual happenings. But right before that in '87, um, there were six months when I thought I was HIV positive, and that was kind of, that was the big…

N: Was that October–November?

M: August '87 through to February '88.

N: I'm seeing it August–October of '87.

M: Yeah. So I had this misdiagnosis, and I moved to Denver, going to massage school, and just…

N: I would never have thought of THAT! As a manifestation…But it was a "fear thing" which I was going to overlook because I saw the tremendous rewarding time here in '89. In the summer.

M: It was total terror, but it was a complete gift!

N: OK. Now, when we get into, um, '91—was there a relationship that really just…

M: Yes. August '91 was when I started seeing my ex-husband, and we got married in '92. And he was my "dad," and dear friend, but it ended in that time…

N: Gotcha. Now, in '94, were you ill? In the beginning of the year, in the spring, were you hospitalized?

M: Uh…No, not hospitalized, but just that chronic fatigue thing, but I kinda think I've had chronic fatigue kinds of things my whole life.

N: Yes. I was going to say that's a symptom of resistance to coming to grips with issues that are swirling around you.

M: Yeah. I was buried in them at that point.

N: I'm very glad to hear that you weren't hospitalized, because all the signs were there. Now, by the time we get to '96, this relationship should have broken open, big time.

M: Yes. I had a miscarriage in '96, right when I basically had this feeling like I can't do my life; I just basically need to give into him [Hmm mm] and then that blew me open again, but then it took me a couple years to leave. There was so much guilt and terror…

N: I see it: April of '99. [Yeah] All right. Now, you know, what this is saying to us, dear Marion, is: you were exhibiting the weaknesses that had been inculcated in you by the bad modeling situation in the home, to the lack of testing of your own will, and all this cerebration and stuff did not get exercised for impact!

M: Yeah.

N: You know? Some people come in here and they say, "Well, I've given up *deciding*. I'm waiting for things to happen."

M: (Light laugh) Right. Yeah. I tried that too! I tried that in my Buddhist years!

N: That's what I'm saying. You get into this situation: it's a passive, victimizable, push-me-around syndrome.

The orientation to the southern (western) hemisphere.

M: Yeah. Yeah.

N: And what you need is a father to come over there and kick your butt and tell you how beautiful and strong you are!

M: Mm mn. True.

N: And then the husband couldn't fulfill that role. And that burst open, and you're back to square one.

M: Yes.

M: Lots of depression about that. [Mm mn] Lots of guilt. Waves of stuff. Huge!

N: Whew! Now, in the spring of 2001, is there some kind of rewarding situation for you? Did you take another foreign trip? Did you get some sort of recognition and pride?

M: Yeah, well, I was divorced by then, and I'd met this man Alcott, whom I now teach with, who was like the father who recognized something in me [Good!] and we still work together, and he...yeah!

N: Is he the one you're in this relationship with now?

M: No. I'm not in a romantic relationship with him.

N: OK. In June, specifically, in 2001, did you get a job reward, raise, recognition, publishing, trip idea...something like that?

M: It's hard to say because I'm looking at my month-to-month breakdown. Literally, April, May, June, July, August, there was just constant...I graduated from CIS in September 2001, but before that all these offers just started happening around me!

N: That's a very rewarding time!

M: Yeah! Huge! I basically feel like, is that a tsunami came and picked me up in 2001!

N: All right. I'm just testing all that stuff. All righty, here we are [in the present].

M: OK. I've been on this big wave, and I don't know how to get off!

N: How do you, uh, earn your money now? Are you an independent astrological psychotherapeutic counselor? Or are you in a school or group or clinic or church organization, what?

M: I'm independent, but I...so partly I, I...I work independently; partly I make my money in that, partly I do it through teaching, and partly I still have family backing, supporting me.

N: Oh, gee...All right. First of all, there's...there's a romantic glimmer here that's pretty strong.

The build-up of the January 2005 arc: Venus=Sun.

M: Just happened!

N: And it's building until the end of the year (pause).

M: Then does it go catapulting off?

N: (Thoughtfully) Noooo…What you're hearing in my voice is that it doesn't necessarily look splendid, in the sense that it is fulfilling. But let's come back to that. Let me ask you something: what do you plan for the next six-ten months of your life, professionally?

M: Well, officially I'm on a mini-sabbatical; I just started last week, because I just literally have tried to get myself off this freight train. And I have a craving and a terror to write: I just want to stop everything and stop anyone else's input and put down the ideas, my journey, the pieces that have come from that. So I was going to do that for a month, and then I just keep having a sense that maybe I should take six months to do it. Um. There's a lot of different questions in here; partly, individual work with clients has become so draining. In terms of just astrology, I over-prepare, I…

N: No. We don't want to do that.

M: Yes. Um…

N: If I said to you, "'What would you be writing about?" What would you say to me in one sentence?

M: (Pause) I was afraid you were going to say "one sentence." The transformative journey and the believing of the small-self identity.

N: Are you basically saying that you know what's right for the world?

M: Am I basically saying that? No. I'm saying about basically what's come from my own journey, and…and the truth for me in that. And offering it to other people, I guess.

N: OK. Has there been any encouragement of this writing project or is it just your own need to cathect?

M: No. There's been a lot of encouragement.

N: Who?

M: Alcott, friends, um.

N: Because they know it's good for you or that it's going to be good, when it gets out, for others?

M: Oh. They know I have something to say and that, if, um, really strong when it comes out, I mean I've had so little faith around my own writing and…

N: So little faith around your own writing, [Yeah] About yourself, you mean?

M: Although it's beginning to get really strong now, and for the first time now, I feel like they're actually things that are culminating from within me and not just concepts I've been grabbing from the outside. So I think partly they see that, and partly they see that there's something I really have to say that's, um, my own thing, not just…

N: Is there anything financial that is worrisome for you right now?

> *The Pluto=Saturn arc and tr Uranus conjunct Saturn measurement in August 2004. Saturn rules the 2nd.*

M: Um, it's a little confusing. Because if I look through the lens of my family, through my dad's eyes, then, yeah! I should be saving and making things greater, and I, if I look through my friends that live out here and other eyes, I'm fine, and I have a cushion behind me.

N: That sounds good. Now, the writing things I see. It's going to be very strong…very strong through August. And there doesn't seem to be anybody coming into the picture to…bless the adventure…

> *Guided by tr Uranus opposed Uranus, ruler of the 3rd.*

M: "To bless the adventure"?

N: Yes. You've had enough of that…we always need more…but your answer about this coming from within is something that I…I recognize here. Are you with me? [Mm mn] Now, you say you'd like to continue this through the year for the next six months?

M: Well, I see the way that if I can take time now, it's going to set me up for a lot of my other pieces for my teaching next year.

N: Of your teaching next year. Teaching where?

M: Teaching on my own; I work with a group in Oregon, I work with Alcott here, some partnerships with other people, a lot nature-based…

N: It seems to me that you're *scattered* [Yeah…strong recognition and agreement] And it seems to me that this teaching business is not really going to focus itself until YOU focus it.

> *Here is the build-up to the therapy flow target: accentuation of the eastern hemisphere.*

M: That's right.

N: It's not just going to happen! It's not running around being a very pretty, charismatic person. *Now's the time to be recognized as an expert in a specific location, doing a specific set of things.*

M: Right.

N: And that's important!

M: That's where I feel I am at. If I am going to continue with astrology or nature-based things, or whatever the individual thing is...

N: *It's what you call yourself.* You know? It's not what you're using to fulfill the mission. *Identification of Self. This has been so difficult for her because of the natal square from Saturn-℞ to the Ascendant.*

M: But in a way, it feels like I need to decide that a little bit because I can't go...

N: Not for your own efficiency! I'm talking about your image.

M: OK.

N: I'm talking about the image. I want the...the very powerful 9th House stuff you've got and the very, very sensitive rulership of that 9th House by the Sun to really *blaze itself into a clear perspective.* [Mm mn] Right now, it's scattered. [Mm mn] And I think that you have a transition period that is going to take you until March 2006—nothing wrong with that at all—to get it all together and be a tremendously defined figure in the field of helping others in your specialized way. [Mm mn] There's very little doubt that in the first three months of 2006, a tremendous success is in the offing. This is really and truly a very big, powerful, grand time for your life!
  Pluto=Uranus; Uranus=Ascendant; Jupiter=Sun!

M: Wow! A long time coming!

N: A long time coming? [A lot of work] But you know, Newton had to go into the garden in order for the apple to drop!

M: (Brightly) Yeah, Persephone had to go into the Underworld...

N: There you go! (Light laughter) I like it better upstairs! And I think there is a high probability of a relocation [Aha!] early in 2006 connected with a job focus, a profession focus. [Mm mn] *You have to start thinking now about what you want then!...*"**I want to run this In-sti-tute!** You hear? **Nobody else. Me!**"

Here is the major consolidating, reinforcing idea!

M: Mm mn.

N: "**I want to run it.**" Do you feel that kind of energy?

M: Yeah! That's actually, um, been part of an idea: sort of an institute, mentorship program, that does incorporate a lot of the different threads.

N: That's right!!

M: They all feel very big when I look out.

N: Yes. **It has to be big!** [Mm mn] **And that's who you are!** You understand me? And now is the time to do that. Now the writing: the writing is going ideally to turn into, uh, uh, **a curriculum guide**. You hear?

Here is a coming together of her half-idea for self-projection with a grand idea involving everything she stands for.

M: (Relaxed with recognition) Yes!

N: And then, out of that and the unique, distinctive selling proposition of your institute leadership. THEN, in 2006, there will be an inception of a tome...a book...that could be written for popular consumption and popularity. (Pause) Those are the steps that I see.

M: It feels like...would you say the writing right now is more exploration in a way of kind of pulling in all the various pieces and getting the main current of what's going forward?

N: (Firmly) Yes.

M: What I have a sense of...partly because my body is a Richter scale saying the exhaustion I've been going through...just to step away from clients right now while I do that gathering, and stop getting my energies sucked out?

N: (Firmly) Yes.

M: And the writing will inform at a deeper level, because I've been trying to restructure my individual work, trying to find out what it is, how to make it more efficient...

N: We just said that!

M: Yes.

N: Isn't it nice that you can now reiterate it back? Because that's what you feel. You see: that's the whole point! [laughing in recognition…I need repetition!] I'm just complimenting you! I'm holding up a mirror! [Mm mn. Thank you.] **Congratulations. That's what it is!**

M: Well, I think that saying it all back is the fear: *can I really do all that?* Can I really take that for myself? And the guilt of, uh…

N: Well, you have to handle that. You have to say—excuse my French—"Fuck it! I deserve this!" (Laughter) You know? You hear me? You have to get that kind of reaction. And if anyone is telling you any different information, kick them out of your house.
  Giving as strong a paternal endorsement as I can.

M: OK.

N: I think that's the only way to bring out the strength of all of this. I'm giving you a…a dose of **passionate self-confirmation.** Which you've never had. [Mm mn] You know you need it desperately. [Mm mn] And now start giving it to yourself first [before giving it to others]. And then people will want to say, "Gosh! She's turning into a goddess!" (Both laughing.)

M: Do you have a sense about the astrological thread and…I keep having images…not images…but feelings that, if I were to go further with it, I'd have to leave everything else and just go more deeply into astrology.

N: No. You don't want to do that. You have too many other gifts. How tall are you and how much do you weigh?
  Now, Marion does have a 17-mutable Midheaven accentuation, one of the "hot astrologer degree areas" curiously corresponding to astrology as a profession (not necessarily only at the Midheaven). But I felt she was looking for an easy way out with her professional thrust; the Institute idea, major relocation, would be a new lease on her professional life, consonant with the grand measurements in early 2006. I tried to get her off the subject of intensifying her astrology work; to think big.

M: 5'6", 125.

N: You're in great shape. Probably lovely to look at. You talk beautifully; you have a kindness in your voice. Ah! These are the things that, no matter what you do—you can read entrails of ducks! (laughter) or a Ouija board...anything, as long as you can communicate. And you have a sensitive, empathic being. You do well.

M: So a lot of the creativity you spoke about at the beginning can gather at different points in the chart and be filtered through the Mercury?

> *Marion was referring to her highly charged Mercury ruling the Midheaven, relating strongly with the Moon, Uranus, and Pluto.*

N: Yes. Absolutely. Now, do you have any gastrointestinal concerns with the metabolic management of nutrition?

> *The Uranus-Pluto conjunction in Virgo, opposed by Saturn.*

M: Something that came up a long time ago: I've been constipated since about...I don't know when it started...

N: You were born with it? Are you out of that problem now?

M: No. I have to monitor it all the time. And I've lots of problems...parasites and...

N: The astrology shows that. [Yeah.] That's a *prima fascia* concern; a weakness of the body. Have there been any blood problems?

> *Neptune in the 12th quindecile with Mars.*

M: General blood problems? [Mm mn] Uh, well, lots of, uh, the HIV misdiagnosis, but things like viral malaria...I mean I've picked up lots of things...

N: So you've had a blood weakness in the sense that there have been things in your blood that have been problematic. I'm just showing where things show up here. I'm not a medical doctor.

M: I don't know how to translate "blood problems."

N: Well, you know, it can go from blood pressure to parasites in the system. And it can go all the way to leukemia.

M: And...and...there's always this subtle, depleting, viral...that, that kind of thing.

N: I understand. I'm just clarifying for your knowledge—I'm not a medical doctor: there are two major weak spots in your body. One is the gastrointestinal tract concern that you have said you've lived with all your life [Mm mn] and, number two, there are these things that show up in the blood. So it becomes a very important monitor [for you], and you need to be aware of it.

M: Yes.

N: Now connected with this: have there been liver concerns?
> *Jupiter opposed by Neptune.*

M: Yes (emphatically).

N: One, two, three. This must tell you something! [Yeah. Nervous laugh.] There's nothing going on critically right now.

M: With those three?

N: With anything. Have you had an abortion or two?
> *Moon, ruling the 8th, conjoined with Pluto. The 8th is the fourth of the 5th.*

M: One.

N: Well, that upsets chemistry and tissues and stuff down there; you know that.

M: Yes. All those other things.

N: And the upper respiratory tract?
> *The Mercury involvement with Uranus and Pluto.*

M: Yeah. Lungs.

N: We can't do better than this, Marion. We're going to stop right there. You're not critically ill right now. There's nothing in the offing, or I would have said it right up front. [OK] You hear? [Yeah] You have everything to look forward to; this is one hell of a springtime beginning the year 2006. *You've got to make it happen by planning now,* and you're right on the right track—according to my ears!

M: Thank you (warmly).

N: All right? (gently)

M: One follow-up thing you brought up: because it feels like a very promising relationship that just started, and you left me hanging on the follow-up of it...

N: Well, it's...it just isn't "the bells are ringing," you know? I don't see it classically.

M: Well, I've been in the relationship desert...and this feels like...

N: Yes. Enjoy it! And practice with it...practice getting the sexual response mechanisms under control and reliability. I would. No?

M: Well, I guess I'm just sad to hear that.

N: I haven't said anything negative; I'm just not saying anything hugely grand! First things first: [All right] you have to build *yourself.* [OK] I've told you that what I'm seeing is this relationship building, building, building very nicely into January 2005. Now I can't really take it much further than that, because, all of a sudden, I see you totally caught up with this extraordinary build-up to the springtime of 2006. [Right] And that sounds wonderful. And if he's along with the ride, and you've got things in order by that time, then the whole thing magnifies and you are going to be a happy camper.

The Venus=Sun arc giving way to the tr Pluto opposition with the Sun, the build-up to the final tr Pluto hit in December 2005 and the power arcs of spring 2006!

M: OK. Noel, thank you so much!

N: I thank YOU! What a joy it is to talk with such a sensitive, talented, creative, sensitive-is-the-word lady! Call me any time; I want to keep track of this.

M: I wouldn't do it otherwise.

N: Bless you! Bye.

M: Goodbye.

(Forty-six minutes.)

OVERVIEW: STRUCTURE AND TECHNIQUE

When a person shows a powerful Mercury—here, Marion's Mercury is the final dispositor of her horoscope, it is angular, it squares the Moon and itself is squared by Uranus—we can expect a most loquacious response during consultation. Very often, too much detail is offered in response, is presented within conversation, and, accumulatively, the length of the consultation and its tone of involvement can easily become unruly. Things bog down into cracker-barrel discussion.

This is why I pushed things along with Marion. I wanted to be her peregrine Mars in Taurus! I felt we were restructuring much of her professional life to come, and I wanted to establish the organized, highly energized approach. (See pages 165–166.)

Our therapy flow development to accentuate the eastern hemisphere was clearly fulfilled: Marion understood the tactical plan to pull back from giving, giving, giving in so many directions, and to consolidate / organize her service to others. I felt she welcomed it. A concrete idea of that consolidation was focused on the idea of an institute.

Her idea of writing a book was qualified in our discussion by my probing about who was championing the idea with her. This is important because experience shows that, in transition, so many "Mercurial" people fall back on the secure idea of sitting at home and writing down anything they can think of in order to assuage the tensions of change. They feel that everyone "out there" will be interested in what they have to say. It is a delay mechanism, almost always, protecting against new exposure. And very few people know how specialized and difficult it is to write a book and get it published.

As I tested the idea with Marion, I deflected the idea and put the writing energies into the frame of a curriculum guide for her institute. This is a creative line of thinking that certainly would be engaging for her consideration.

The focus on March 2006 was astrologically dramatic, and the more concrete the considerations became of what could happen to celebrate her teachings and counseling position then, the higher the probability of her making a change with gusto.

On schedule, she contacted me in March 2006 with regard to where she might go to set the plan into action. In our follow-up work together, I was able to suggest a particular city across the country, and it was most gratifying to hear that, in that city, lived a former teaching partner of hers who had long been making suggestions of getting together to make bigger and better things happen in their work![1]

---

1. Geographical determination was accomplished through Astro*Carto*Graphy.

8 CASE STUDY: "CAROL"

HOROSCOPE ORIENTATION

The orientation to Carol's horoscope shows a dramatic emphasis of the northern hemisphere. To the west there is some important unfinished business in the early home and, as she works herself out of this, we will probably see a wholesale giving away of herself to others, to please others, to gain their appreciation and support, to get their applause (Moon in Leo).

The key for discussion will surely involve the mother with Jupiter on the nodal axis and Mercury tightly quindecile the node. The mother's influence on how Carol learns to think about herself and the world around her will be strongly tied to maternal influence. This is reinforced by the conjunction of Mars and the Moon in the 4th, the Moon ruling the 4th.

Mercury is square with the Moon—similar to the Mercury in Marion's case—and we expect quite a talker. This is quite favorable for the consultation, of course, but we have to be alert not to let it go too far. Cases where the client overwhelms the astrologer are not rare. We must think, "How many details do we need to understand the situation and do our job?"

The Jupiter in Scorpio can suggest quite a spectrum of identity structuring: on the one hand, there usually is the need for religiousness, for allying oneself with mysteries; one feels less alone under developmental tension; there is a respect for inner reward. And on the other end of the spectrum, there can be a swampy wandering to find significance, often with drugs and debauchery involved. This complicated position carries with it a

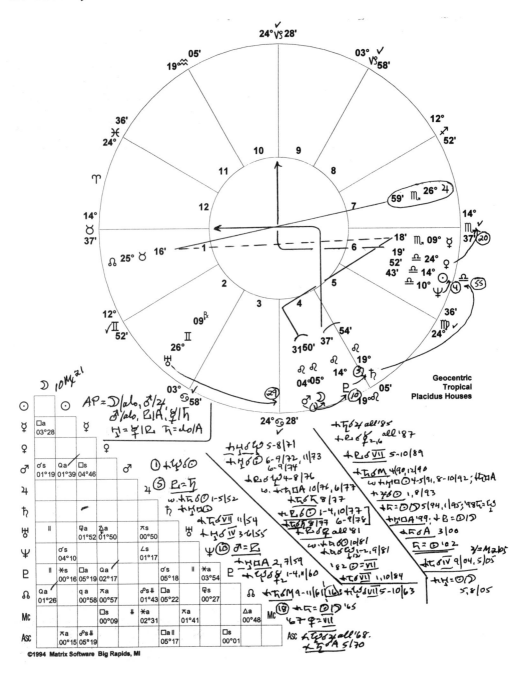

Oct 08, 1947 06:30:00 PM CST 087W54'23" 43N02'20"

Midpoint Sort: 90° Dial

☽/☊	000°33'	♅/♇	020°23'	☉/☊	035°04'	☿/☊	047°17'	☽/♆	068°16'	♀/♄	082°07'
♂/♃	000°45'	♄/♅	023°02'	☽/♂	035°11'	☿/♃	048°09'	♀/Mc	069°24'	☽/☿	082°34'
☽/♃	001°25'	♀	024°19'	☽	035°50'	♅/♆	048°26'	☉/♂	069°42'	♂/Asc	084°34'
♄/Asc	002°16'	Mc	024°28'	☉/♃	035°56'	♄	049°54'	☽/☉	070°21'	☊/Mc	084°52'
♇/☊	004°56'	☿/♆	025°00'	♄/Mc	037°11'	☊/Asc	049°57'	♅/☊	070°43'	☽/Asc	085°14'
♃/♇	005°48'	☉/☿	027°05'	☿	039°18'	☉/♅	050°31'	♃/♅	071°34'	♃/Mc	085°44'
♄/☊	007°35'	♆/Asc	027°40'	♂/♇	039°34'	♃/Asc	050°48'	♆/♇	072°40'	♅	086°09'
♃/♄	008°27'	♂/Mc	029°30'	♀/☊	039°48'	♀/♅	055°14'	♀/♂	074°25'	☿/♇	086°57'
♅/Mc	010°19'	☉/Asc	029°45'	☽/♇	040°13'	☊	055°16'	☉/♇	074°44'	☿/♄	089°36'
♆	010°43'	☽/Mc	030°09'	♀/♃	040°39'	♃/☊	056°08'	☽/♀	075°05'	♇/Asc	089°37'
☉/♆	012°47'	☿/♀	031°49'	☿/Asc	041°58'	♃	056°59'	♄/♆	075°19'	♂/☊	089°54'
☉	014°52'	♆/☊	032°59'	♂/♄	042°13'	♆/Mc	062°35'	☿/Mc	076°53'		
♂/♅	015°20'	♃/♆	033°51'	☽/♄	042°52'	☿/♅	062°44'	☉/♄	077°23'		
☽/♅	016°00'	♀/Asc	034°28'	Asc	044°37'	☉/Mc	064°40'	♀/♇	079°28'		
♀/♆	017°31'	♂	034°31'	♇	044°37'	♅/Asc	065°23'	Mc/Asc	079°33'		
☉/♀	019°36'	♇/Mc	034°32'	♄/♇	047°15'	♂/♆	067°37'	☿/♂	081°55'		

"saint to sinner" spectrum of potential behaviors, all of which work to dramatize the Self (to call attention to the Self), for one set of reasons or another. Jupiter is prominent here above the horizon, angular, and peregrine! We can expect a pronounced religious strain in Carol's development (echoed through the Neptune conjunction with her Sun), or just the opposite: a vociferous rejection of it; and we must be aware of the murky polarity within the spectrum.

The Pluto-Saturn conjunction, with Saturn ruling the 9th and 10th, Pluto ruling the 7th, with the conjunction squaring the Ascendant, suggests that Carol's education was interrupted, that there was a strong father problem, and that similar tensions of nonsupport are experienced in adult one-on-one relationships. The suggestion is strong that Carol would have had a difficult, nonsupportive home life and those dynamics would be repeated in her own married life.

Finally, we see three quintiles that support the creativity focused strongly in her vocational profile: **Mc♑.♄.☉.♀*□Mc**, **♆E**[1] All routings emphasize Venus, the final dispositor. And with Neptune oriental, the vocational profile says "artist." With the Moon in the 4th, the need will ideally be fulfilled by developing and performing art in her home.

1. Please see Tyl, *Vocations* for full development and presentation of the Midheaven Extension Process for vocational profiling. The "code line" for the vocational deduction is included here as part of the complete preparation of the horoscope consultation. The specialization of the technique cannot be included in this text.

Search From Jan 8, 2006 to Dec 13, 2007 GMT Page: 1

Aspect	Date	Time	Event	Type	P1 Pos.	P2 Pos	E/X/L
♃ -- □ ♇	01-09-2006	12:34 pm	♃ □ ♇	Tr-Na	14°♏37'	14°♌37'	Exact
♃ -- ☍ Asc	01-09-2006	02:13 pm	♃ ☍ Asc	Tr-Na	14°♏37'	14°♉37'	Exact
♄ -- □ ☿	01-09-2006	09:40 pm	♄ □ ☿	Tr-Na	09°♌18'℞	09°♏18'	Exact
♂ -- □ ♇	01-13-2006	00:42 am	♂ □ ♇	Tr-Na	14°♉37'	14°♌37'	Exact
♂ -- ☌ Asc	01-13-2006	01:24 am	♂ ☌ Asc	Tr-Na	14°♉37'	14°♉37'	Exact
♂ -- □ ♄	01-26-2006	11:37 pm	♂ □ ♄	Tr-Na	19°♉54'	19°♌54'	Exact
♂ -- ☌ ☊	02-08-2006	02:37 am	♂ ☌ ☊	Tr-Na	25°♉16'	25°♉16'℞	Exact
♇ ---- ☍ ♅	02-10-2006	10:27 am	♇ ☍ ♅	Tr-Na	26°♐09'	26°♊09'℞	Exact
♂ -- ☍ ♃	02-11-2006	06:05 pm	♂ ☍ ♃	Tr-Na	26°♉59'	26°♏59'	Exact
♄ -- ☌ ☽	02-23-2006	10:24 am	♄ ☌ ☽	Tr-Na	05°♌50'℞	05°♌50'	Exact
♃ -- S℞	03-04-2006	06:12 pm	♃ S℞	Tr-Na	18°♏52'℞		
♆ ---- ∠ ♀	03-17-2006	05:33 am	♆ ∠ ♀	Ar-Na	09°♐19'	24°♎19'	Exact
♂ -- ∠ ☿/♃	03-20-2006	04:26 pm	♂ ∠ ☿/♃	Ar-Na	03°♎09'	18°♏09'	Exact
♄ -- ☌ ♂	03-23-2006	07:04 pm	♄ ☌ ♂	Tr-Na	04°♌31'℞	04°♌31'	Exact
♇ ---- S℞	03-29-2006	09:58 am	♇ S℞	Tr-Na	26°♐45'℞		
♄ -- SD	04-05-2006	12:43 pm	♄ SD	Tr-Na	04°♌23'		
♂ -- ☌ ♅	04-07-2006	08:21 am	♂ ☌ ♅	Tr-Na	26°♊09'	26°♊09'℞	Exact
♆ ---- ☌ ♀/Mc	04-13-2006	04:49 am	♆ ☌ ♀/Mc	Ar-Na	09°♐24'	09°♐24'	Exact
♄ -- ☌ ♂	04-18-2006	08:24 am	♄ ☌ ♂	Tr-Na	04°♌31'	04°♌31'	Exact
☽ q Mc/Asc	04-23-2006	01:40 am	☽ q Mc/Asc	Ar-Na	04°♎33'	19°♓33'	Exact
♃ -- ⚼ ♅/☊	04-28-2006	08:56 am	♃ ⚼ ♅/☊	Ar-Na	25°♑43'	10°♊43'	Exact
♃ -- ☍ Asc	04-29-2006	04:28 pm	♃ ☍ Asc	Tr-Na	14°♏37'℞	14°♉37'	Exact
♃ -- □ ♇	04-29-2006	06:22 pm	♃ □ ♇	Tr-Na	14°♏37'℞	14°♌37'	Exact
☿ - q ♄/♅	05-01-2006	05:02 am	☿ q ♄/♅	Ar-Na	08°♑02'	23°♋02'	Exact
♂ -- □ ♆	05-02-2006	10:01 am	♂ □ ♆	Tr-Na	10°♋43'	10°♎43'	Exact
♂ -- □ ☉	05-09-2006	11:10 am	♂ □ ☉	Tr-Na	14°♋52'	14°♎52'	Exact
♆ ---- ∠ Mc	05-10-2006	04:03 am	♆ ∠ Mc	Ar-Na	09°♐28'	24°♑28'	Exact
♄ -- ☌ ☽	05-16-2006	09:16 am	♄ ☌ ☽	Tr-Na	05°♌50'	05°♌50'	Exact
♇ ---- ☍ ♅	05-18-2006	01:20 am	♇ ☍ ♅	Tr-Na	26°♐09'℞	26°♊09'℞	Exact
♆ ---- S℞	05-22-2006	09:40 am	♆ S℞	Tr-Na	19°♒49'℞		
♂ -- □ ♀	05-25-2006	07:54 am	♂ □ ♀	Tr-Na	24°♋19'	24°♎19'	Exact
♂ -- ☍ Mc	05-25-2006	01:55 pm	♂ ☍ Mc	Tr-Na	24°♋28'	24°♑28'	Exact
Mc --- q ☽/♆	05-26-2006	01:37 am	Mc q ☽/♆	Ar-Na	23°♓16'	08°♍16'	Exact
♂ -- ☌ ♂	06-11-2006	06:25 am	♂ ☌ ♂	Tr-Na	04°♌31'	04°♌31'	Exact
♂ -- ☌ ☽	06-13-2006	10:17 am	♂ ☌ ☽	Tr-Na	05°♌50'	05°♌50'	Exact
♆ ---- q ♂/Asc	06-16-2006	04:08 am	♆ q ♂/Asc	Ar-Na	09°♐34'	24°♊34'	Exact
♂ -- □ ☿	06-19-2006	03:09 am	♂ □ ☿	Tr-Na	09°♌18'	09°♏18'	Exact
♅ ---- S℞	06-19-2006	05:24 am	♅ S℞	Tr-Na	14°♓44'℞		
♃ -- ☌ ☿	06-21-2006	06:22 pm	♃ ☌ ☿	Tr-Na	09°♏18'℞	09°♏18'	Exact
♄ -- □ ☿	06-23-2006	04:04 am	♄ □ ☿	Tr-Na	09°♌18'	09°♏18'	Exact
♂ -- ☌ ♇	06-27-2006	08:04 pm	♂ ☌ ♇	Tr-Na	14°♌37'	14°♌37'	Exact
♂ -- □ Asc	06-27-2006	08:27 pm	♂ □ Asc	Tr-Na	14°♌37'	14°♉37'	Exact
♂ -- ∠ ♅/♆	07-03-2006	12:12 pm	♂ ∠ ♅/♆	Ar-Na	03°♎26'	18°♌26'	Exact
♃ -- SD	07-06-2006	07:00 am	♃ SD	Tr-Na	08°♏59'		
♂ -- ☌ ♄	07-06-2006	11:10 am	♂ ☌ ♄	Tr-Na	19°♌54'	19°♌54'	Exact
♂ -- □ ☊	07-15-2006	03:50 am	♂ □ ☊	Tr-Na	25°♌16'	25°♉16'℞	Exact
♂ -- □ ♃	07-17-2006	10:25 pm	♂ □ ♃	Tr-Na	26°♌59'	26°♏59'	Exact
♃ -- ☌ ☿	07-20-2006	10:53 pm	♃ ☌ ☿	Tr-Na	09°♏18'	09°♏18'	Exact
Mc --- q ♃/♄	07-27-2006	05:54 pm	Mc q ♃/♄	Ar-Na	23°♓27'	08°♎27'	Exact
♆ ---- □ ☉/♂	07-31-2006	07:24 am	♆ □ ☉/♂	Ar-Na	09°♐42'	09°♍42'	Exact
♄ -- ☌ ♇	08-05-2006	03:16 pm	♄ ☌ ♇	Tr-Na	14°♌37'	14°♌37'	Exact
♄ -- □ Asc	08-05-2006	05:07 pm	♄ □ Asc	Tr-Na	14°♌37'	14°♉37'	Exact
☊ --- □ ♀	08-23-2006	02:17 am	☊ □ ♀	Ar-Na	24°♋19'	24°♎19'	Exact
☽ ∠ ♄	08-30-2006	09:51 pm	☽ ∠ ♄	Ar-Na	04°♎54'	19°♌54'	Exact
☊ --- □ ♅	08-31-2006	10:32 am	☊ □ ♅	Tr-Na	26°♓09'℞	26°♊09'℞	Exact
♂ -- □ ♅	09-02-2006	04:59 am	♂ □ ♅	Tr-Na	26°♍09'	26°♊09'℞	Exact
♅ ---- ☌ ♀/♅	09-03-2006	04:26 am	♅ ☌ ♀/♅	Ar-Na	25°♌14'	25°♌14'	Exact
♇ ---- SD	09-04-2006	07:52 pm	♇ SD	Tr-Na	24°♐05'		
♃ -- □ ♇	09-08-2006	10:22 pm	♃ □ ♇	Tr-Na	14°♏37'	14°♌37'	Exact
♃ -- ☍ Asc	09-08-2006	11:52 pm	♃ ☍ Asc	Tr-Na	14°♏37'	14°♉37'	Exact
☽ □ ♇/☊	09-12-2006	01:55 am	☽ □ ♇/☊	Ar-Na	04°♎56'	04°♋56'	Exact
☽ ⚼ ☊/Asc	09-13-2006	08:54 pm	☽ ⚼ ☊/Asc	Ar-Na	04°♎57'	19°♉57'	Exact
♅ ---- □ ☊	09-14-2006	06:35 am	♅ □ ☊	Ar-Na	25°♌16'	25°♉16'℞	Exact
♄ -- ☌ ♄	09-17-2006	11:02 am	♄ ☌ ♄	Tr-Na	19°♌54'	19°♌54'	Exact
☊ --- ⚼ ♀/Mc	09-19-2006	01:27 am	☊ ⚼ ♀/Mc	Ar-Na	24°♋24'	09°♐24'	Exact
♂ -- ☌ ♆	09-24-2006	03:46 pm	♂ ☌ ♆	Tr-Na	10°♎43'	10°♎43'	Exact
☿ - □ ♃/♄	09-27-2006	11:58 am	☿ □ ♃/♄	Ar-Na	08°♑27'	08°♎27'	Exact
♅ ---- ⚼ ♅/Mc	09-30-2006	03:35 am	♅ ⚼ ♅/Mc	Ar-Na	25°♌19'	10°♈19'	Exact
♂ -- ☌ ☉	09-30-2006	11:45 pm	♂ ☌ ☉	Tr-Na	14°♎52'	14°♎52'	Exact
♃ -- □ ♄	10-08-2006	04:55 am	♃ □ ♄	Tr-Na	19°♏54'	19°♌54'	Exact
♂ -- ☌ ♀	10-15-2006	05:31 am	♂ ☌ ♀	Tr-Na	24°♎19'	24°♎19'	Exact
♂ -- □ Mc	10-15-2006	10:54 am	♂ □ Mc	Tr-Na	24°♎28'	24°♑28'	Exact
♆ ---- SD	10-29-2006	05:29 am	♆ SD	Tr-Na	17°♒02'		

tr ♇ ☍ ♅ 2nd "hit"

♅ = also tr ♄ ☌ ♄

Search From Jan 8, 2006 to Dec 13, 2007 GMT Page: 2

Aspect	Date	Time	Event	Type	P1 Pos.	P2 Pos	E/X/L
♂ -- □ ♂	10-30-2006	09:10 am	♂ □ ♂	Tr-Na	04°♏31'	04°♌31'	Exact
♂ -- □ ☽	11-01-2006	07:27 am	♂ □ ☽	Tr-Na	05°♏50'	05°♌50'	Exact
♃ -- ☍ ☊	11-02-2006	06:56 pm	♃ ☍ ☊	Tr-Na	25°♏16'	25°♉16'℞	Exact
♂ -- ☌ ☿	11-06-2006	09:24 am	♂ ☌ ☿	Tr-Na	09°♏18'	09°♏18'	Exact
♃ -- ☌ ♃	11-10-2006	02:54 pm	♃ ☌ ♃	Tr-Na	26°♏59'	26°♏59'	Exact
♂ -- □ ♇	11-14-2006	03:11 am	♂ □ ♇	Tr-Na	14°♏37'	14°♌37'	Exact
♂ -- ☍ Asc	11-14-2006	03:32 am	♂ ☍ Asc	Tr-Na	14°♏37'	14°♉37'	Exact
Ψ ---- ∠ ☿/Ψ	11-18-2006	12:21 pm	Ψ ∠ ☿/Ψ	Ar-Na	10°♐00'	25°♎00'	Exact
☽ ☌ Ψ	11-19-2006	11:08 pm	☽ ☌ Ψ	Pr-Na	10°♎43'	10°♎43'	Exact
♅ ---- SD	11-20-2006	03:17 am	♅ SD	Tr-Na	10°♓49'		
♂ -- □ ♄	11-21-2006	06:50 pm	♂ □ ♄	Tr-Na	19°♏54'	19°♌54'	Exact
♂ -- ☍ ☊	11-29-2006	11:22 am	♂ ☍ ☊	Tr-Na	25°♏16'	25°♉16'℞	Exact
♂ -- ☌ ♃	12-01-2006	10:11 pm	♂ ☌ ♃	Tr-Na	26°♏59'	26°♏59'	Exact
♄ -- SR℞	12-06-2006	02:07 am	♄ SR℞	Tr-Na	25°♌04'℞		
♇ ---- ☍ ♅	12-08-2006	12:51 pm	♇ ☍ ♅	Tr-Na	26°♐09'	26°♊09'℞	Exact
☊ --- ∠ ☉/♂	01-06-2007	03:38 am	☊ ∠ ☉/♂	Ar-Na	24°♋42'	09°♍42'	Exact
♂ -- ☍ ♅	01-11-2007	03:02 pm	♂ ☍ ♅	Tr-Na	26°♐09'	26°♊09'℞	Exact
♂ -- □ Ψ	01-31-2007	08:45 am	♂ □ Ψ	Tr-Na	10°♑43'	10°♎43'	Exact
♂ -- □ ☉	02-05-2007	10:47 pm	♂ □ ☉	Tr-Na	14°♑52'	14°♎52'	Exact
Ψ ---- q ☽/Asc	02-06-2007	04:10 pm	Ψ q ☽/Asc	Ar-Na	10°♐14'	25°♊14'	Exact
♂ -- □ ♀	02-18-2007	01:01 pm	♂ □ ♀	Tr-Na	24°♑19'	24°♎19'	Exact
♂ -- ☌ Mc	02-18-2007	05:48 pm	♂ ☌ Mc	Tr-Na	24°♑28'	24°♑28'	Exact
☉ - □ ♀/♂	02-18-2007	09:06 pm	☉ □ ♀/♂	Ar-Na	14°♐25'	14°♍25'	Exact
Ψ ---- ☍ ♄	02-19-2007	09:43 am	Ψ ☍ ♄	Tr-Na	19°♒54'	19°♌54'	Exact
♅ ---- ∠ Ψ	02-20-2007	02:39 am	♅ ∠ Ψ	Ar-Na	25°♌43'	10°♎43'	Exact
Ψ ---- q ☊	02-21-2007	05:56 pm	Ψ q ☊	Ar-Na	10°♐16'	25°♉16'℞	Exact
♃ -- ⚼ ♃/♅	03-03-2007	07:32 am	♃ ⚼ ♃/♅	Ar-Na	26°♑34'	11°♍34'	Exact
♂ -- ☍ ♂	03-04-2007	00:47 am	♂ ☍ ♂	Tr-Na	04°♒31'	04°♌31'	Exact
♄ -- ☌ ♄	03-05-2007	03:48 am	♄ ☌ ♄	Tr-Na	19°♌54'℞	19°♌54'	Exact
♂ -- ☍ ☽	03-05-2007	06:10 pm	♂ ☍ ☽	Tr-Na	05°♒50'	05°♌50'	Exact
♂ -- □ ☿	03-10-2007	07:25 am	♂ □ ☿	Tr-Na	09°♒18'	09°♏18'	Exact
☽ ☌ ☉	03-13-2007	11:11 pm	☽ ☌ ☉	Pr-Na	14°♎52'	14°♎52'	Exact
♂ -- ☍ ♇	03-17-2007	06:33 am	♂ ☍ ♇	Tr-Na	14°♒37'	14°♌37'	Exact
♂ -- □ Asc	03-17-2007	06:52 am	♂ □ Asc	Tr-Na	14°♒37'	14°♉37'	Exact
☉ - ∠ ♂/Mc	03-17-2007	08:09 pm	☉ ∠ ♂/Mc	Ar-Na	14°♐30'	29°♎30'	Exact
Ψ ---- □ ☽/☉	03-23-2007	07:12 pm	Ψ □ ☽/☉	Ar-Na	10°♐21'	10°♍21'	Exact
♂ -- ☍ ♄	03-24-2007	04:43 am	♂ ☍ ♄	Tr-Na	19°♒54'	19°♌54'	Exact
♂ -- □ ☊	03-31-2007	04:46 am	♂ □ ☊	Tr-Na	25°♒16'	25°♉16'℞	Exact
♇ ---- SR℞	03-31-2007	08:18 pm	♇ SR℞	Tr-Na	28°♐58'℞		
♂ -- □ ♃	04-02-2007	10:33 am	♂ □ ♃	Tr-Na	26°♒59'	26°♏59'	Exact
♃ -- SR℞	04-05-2007	11:57 pm	♃ SR℞	Tr-Na	19°♐47'℞		
☽ ∠ ☉/♅	04-06-2007	03:38 pm	☽ ∠ ☉/♅	Ar-Na	05°♎31'	20°♌31'	Exact
♄ -- ☌ ☉/♀	04-09-2007	10:12 pm	♄ ☌ ☉/♀	Ar-Na	19°♎36'	19°♎36'	Exact
♄ -- SD	04-19-2007	08:54 pm	♄ SD	Tr-Na	18°♌09'		
☊ --- □ ☿/Ψ	04-26-2007	08:11 am	☊ □ ☿/Ψ	Ar-Na	25°♋00'	25°♎00'	Exact
☉ - q ♇/Asc	04-29-2007	12:37 pm	☉ q ♇/Asc	Ar-Na	14°♐37'	29°♊37'	Exact
♄ -- ∠ ☉/Mc	05-06-2007	09:14 pm	♄ ∠ ☉/Mc	Ar-Na	19°♎40'	04°♐40'	Exact
♂ -- □ ♅	05-10-2007	12:48 pm	♂ □ ♅	Tr-Na	26°♓09'	26°♊09'℞	Exact
Ψ ---- SR℞	05-24-2007	10:19 pm	Ψ SR℞	Tr-Na	22°♒02'℞		
♂ -- ☍ Ψ	05-29-2007	06:42 pm	♂ ☍ Ψ	Tr-Na	10°♈43'	10°♎43'	Exact
Mc --- ⚼ ☿	05-29-2007	07:48 pm	Mc ⚼ ☿	Ar-Na	24°♓18'	09°♏18'	Exact
♄ -- ☌ ♄	06-04-2007	03:50 am	♄ ☌ ♄	Tr-Na	19°♌54'	19°♌54'	Exact
♂ -- ☍ ☉	06-04-2007	08:12 am	♂ ☍ ☉	Tr-Na	14°♈52'	14°♎52'	Exact
☉ - □ ☉/♇	06-13-2007	03:34 pm	☉ □ ☉/♇	Ar-Na	14°♐44'	14°♍44'	Exact
☉ - ⚼ ☉/Asc	06-15-2007	10:32 am	☉ ⚼ ☉/Asc	Ar-Na	14°♐45'	29°♋45'	Exact
♂ -- ☍ ♀	06-17-2007	02:32 am	♂ ☍ ♀	Tr-Na	24°♈19'	24°♎19'	Exact
♂ -- □ Mc	06-17-2007	07:26 am	♂ □ Mc	Tr-Na	24°♈28'	24°♑28'	Exact
♅ ---- SR℞	06-23-2007	12:36 pm	♅ SR℞	Tr-Na	18°♓42'℞		
♂ -- □ ♂	07-01-2007	04:04 am	♂ □ ♂	Tr-Na	04°♉31'	04°♌31'	Exact
♂ -- □ ☽	07-02-2007	11:59 pm	♂ □ ☽	Tr-Na	05°♉50'	05°♌50'	Exact
♂ -- ☍ ☿	07-07-2007	08:52 pm	♂ ☍ ☿	Tr-Na	09°♉18'	09°♏18'	Exact
♂ -- □ ♇	07-15-2007	10:31 am	♂ □ ♇	Tr-Na	14°♉37'	14°♌37'	Exact
♂ -- ☌ Asc	07-15-2007	10:52 am	♂ ☌ Asc	Tr-Na	14°♉37'	14°♉37'	Exact
☽ ☌ ♃/♇	07-17-2007	11:34 pm	☽ ☌ ♃/♇	Ar-Na	05°♎48'	05°♎48'	Exact
☽ ⚼ ♃/Asc	07-19-2007	06:33 pm	☽ ⚼ ♃/Asc	Ar-Na	05°♎48'	20°♒48'	Exact
♃ -- q ☿/Asc	07-20-2007	11:13 am	♃ q ☿/Asc	Ar-Na	26°♑58'	11°♌58'	Exact
♀ - ∠ ☿	07-22-2007	05:46 pm	♀ ∠ ☿	Ar-Na	24°♐18'	09°♏18'	Exact
♂ -- □ ♄	07-23-2007	02:58 am	♂ □ ♄	Tr-Na	19°♉54'	19°♌54'	Exact
♄ -- □ ☊	07-26-2007	11:18 pm	♄ □ ☊	Tr-Na	25°♌16'	25°♉16'℞	Exact
♂ -- ☌ ☊	07-31-2007	01:47 am	♂ ☌ ☊	Tr-Na	25°♉16'	25°♉16'℞	Exact
♂ -- ☍ ♃	08-02-2007	03:53 pm	♂ ☍ ♃	Tr-Na	26°♉59'	26°♏59'	Exact
♂ -- q Mc/Asc	08-07-2007	01:03 am	♂ q Mc/Asc	Ar-Na	04°♎33'	19°♓33'	Exact
♃ -- SD	08-07-2007	01:35 am	♃ SD	Tr-Na	09°♐56'		

tr ♇ ☍ ♅ final

tr ♄ ☌ ♄ 2nd "hit"

tr ♄ ☌ ♄ final

Search From Jan 8, 2006 to Dec 13, 2007 GMT Page: 3

Aspect	Date	Time	Event	Type	P1 Pos.	P2 Pos	E/X/L
☉ - q ♂/☊	08-08-2007	02:18 pm	☉ q ♂/☊	Ar-Na	14°♐54'	29°♊54'	Exact
♄ -- □ ♃	08-09-2007	07:54 pm	♄ □ ♃	Tr-Na	26°♌59'	26°♏59'	Exact
☊ --- ∠ ☽/☉	08-29-2007	02:35 pm	☊ ∠ ☽/☉	Ar-Na	25°♋21'	10°♍21'	Exact
♃ -- □ ☉/☿	09-03-2007	02:05 pm	♃ □ ☉/☿	Ar-Na	27°♑05'	27°♎05'	Exact
Mc --- ⚼ ♂/♇	09-03-2007	06:10 pm	Mc ⚼ ♂/♇	Ar-Na	24°♓34'	09°♌34'	Exact
Mc --- □ ♂/Asc	09-05-2007	01:08 pm	Mc □ ♂/Asc	Ar-Na	24°♓34'	24°♊34'	Exact
♇ ---- SD	09-07-2007	10:41 am	♇ SD	Tr-Na	26°♐18'		
♆ ---- ☍ ♄	09-10-2007	07:15 pm	♆ ☍ ♄	Tr-Na	19°♒54'℞	19°♌54'	Exact
♂ -- ☌ ♅	09-20-2007	11:17 pm	♂ ☌ ♅	Tr-Na	26°♊09'	26°♊09'℞	Exact
☉ - □ ☽/♀	10-12-2007	07:49 am	☉ □ ☽/♀	Ar-Na	15°♐05'	15°♍05'	Exact
♃ -- q ♂/♄	10-20-2007	11:38 am	♃ q ♂/♄	Ar-Na	27°♑13'	12°♌13'	Exact
Mc --- q ☉/♂	10-20-2007	03:57 pm	Mc q ☉/♂	Ar-Na	24°♓42'	09°♍42'	Exact
♀ - ⚼ ♂/♇	10-27-2007	04:00 pm	♀ ⚼ ♂/♇	Ar-Na	24°♐34'	09°♌34'	Exact
Asc --- □ ☉	10-28-2007	07:06 pm	Asc □ ☉	Ar-Na	14°♋52'	14°♎52'	Exact
♂ -- □ ♆	10-30-2007	02:04 am	♂ □ ♆	Tr-Na	10°♋43'	10°♎43'	Exact
♆ ---- SD	10-31-2007	04:18 pm	♆ SD	Tr-Na	19°♒15'		
♇ ---- ☌ ☉	11-01-2007	09:02 am	♇ ☌ ☉	Ar-Na	14°♎52'	14°♎52'	Exact
☿ - q ♂/Asc	11-06-2007	06:38 am	☿ q ♂/Asc	Ar-Na	09°♑34'	24°♊34'	Exact
☉ - ∠ ☽/Mc	11-08-2007	06:43 am	☉ ∠ ☽/Mc	Ar-Na	15°♐09'	00°♏09'	Exact
♂ -- SR	11-15-2007	08:38 am	♂ SR	Tr-Na	12°♋27'℞		
Mc --- ⚼ ♀/☊	11-24-2007	08:17 am	Mc ⚼ ♀/☊	Ar-Na	24°♓48'	09°♌48'	Exact
♅ ---- SD	11-24-2007	09:14 am	♅ SD	Tr-Na	14°♓46'		
☽ ☌ ♀	11-30-2007	09:21 am	☽ ☌ ♀	Pr-Na	24°♎19'	24°♎19'	Exact
♂ -- □ ♆	11-30-2007	11:34 pm	♂ □ ♆	Tr-Na	10°♋43'℞	10°♎43'	Exact
♃ -- ☍ ♅	12-01-2007	09:34 pm	♃ ☍ ♅	Tr-Na	26°♐09'	26°♊09'℞	Exact
☽ □ Mc	12-04-2007	01:36 pm	☽ □ Mc	Pr-Na	24°♎28'	24°♑28'	Exact

A=☉ ♇
R=☉ ♇
SP☽□M

For Carol at age fifty-eight and a half for the consultation, we anticipate a significant change of life pattern and direction: we see August–September 2006 as a time of change and shift, heralded by the tr Saturn return that will work itself out over nine months, and we see the very, very large focus of new perspective in her life established by October 2007 with the arc Pluto=Sun and the SP Moon square the Midheaven, and more!

THE CONSULTATION

(There had been some difficulty establishing telephone connection. Much laughter, finally.)

N: You thought you were jinxed or something!

C: Well, I was thinking, this must be a bad chart; he just doesn't want to talk to me about it! You know, you always go to the negative….

N: Yes. Sure. Just like when you can't sleep at night, the things that go through your mind are just terrible…

C: Isn't that awful?

N: Where do they come from?

C: (Still laughing) They're very dark thoughts.

N: Well, thank you very much, Carol, for accommodating our schedules together here.

C: I was happy to hear that I was getting in [receiving an appointment] in such a short time frame.

N: Well, I owe you that.

C: Thank you.

N: Now this horoscope here with a 14 Taurus Ascendant—that's what you're using, isn't it?

C: Yes. And I have a Leo Moon as far as I know!

N: Well, that ends this call! (Laughing)

C: No?

N: The Leo Moon. I have one too! You have a queen complex and…

C: (Laughing) Oh! OK. Good!

> *It was clear that she felt good in the Leo Moon embrace. Had it been supported in her development?*

N: Now, how did your mother fit into this? I don't know that she would let you shine like that!

> *Pursuing immediately the Nodal axis ties and the Mars-Moon conjunction in the 4th, with the Moon ruling the 4th.*

C: Oh! She was wonderful; she was wonderful. She passed away in August.

N: Well, yes. But when you were growing up.

C: Oh! She was stern.

> *This is not unusual: hearing, first, an idealization of a parent who actually was confining, punitive, intimidating, etc. What happens is that the client's unconscious idealizes the parent focus as it should have been, and then gradually, with trust of the astrologer established, breaks down to free, realistic discussion.*

N: I just have to point out that your horoscope speaks very strongly about a dominating mother.

C: Well, you know, she was *quietly dominating*. She was just such a perfect woman that you were constantly trying…you know…to please her, and, and, and she was never a complaining person or a…or uh, just soft-spoken. A woman of grace. She had a quiet, quiet power over you.

N: So, it entered your mind that *you had to be as perfect as she?*

C: Yes. I certainly gave it the best try, but I certainly blew the last seven years! (Laughing) But we became good friends through it. It took a while. Because, you know, I retired at fifty, and uh, just, you know, I went after my dream, which was always to live in the country, so I got rid of my job, the husband, and I told my parents they couldn't come and stay with me anymore, which they did every summer. And uh, uh, like I said, uh, just went wacko, ended up in jail a couple times…

N: Well, we'll get into that. I want to point out to you that this discussion has been really very revealing so far: here we have this mother with extraordinary praise, but extreme influence.

C: Yes.

N: I mean, you're praising *her,* but the point was [that] perfection was very hard to attain.

C: Yeah! That's why I had to explain to her, you know; I guess I kept; uh, you know, to-wards the end there, when I went through this experience the last few years, *"Are you still gonna love me if I'm not perfect?"* And I almost went out of my way to *not* be perfect!
  This is a key statement of Carol's developmental anxieties.

N: That's why I'm saying it's revealing. Here you say you end up in jail!

C: Yeah! Yeah! Never had been in my life; had a corporate job, the whole thing. And just couldn't seem to stop myself for a while.

N: Well, there are a lot of unfinished threads of concern in that early home life, because of her perfectionism. I've got to point that out to you.

C: OK. Well, I feel resolved; she passed away August 16…

N: I'm not dwelling on it, but I'm trying to clarify the great image of her passing away recently; it doesn't really jibe with the quiet domination and perfectionism set up as an ideal for you to follow, which was very, very inhibiting.

C: Well, you know, she did leave me enough money so that I was able to pay off my house, so that now I've sort of pulled that string from my gut, and I guess I'm trying to be good for her again, even though she's not here.
  So easily, so often, money takes on the guise of love. Only a very thin line separates them.

N: OK. Be aware of the pervasive influence [OK, OK] because it is very clear here. Because *you've got to be your own person*, you know?

> *This is the beginning of the therapy flow in terms of the southern and eastern hemisphere orientation.*

C: That's why I came up north; got rid of my friends—well, I didn't get rid of them—but spaced myself from them, because I felt everybody was directing me but me! And *slowly*, I'm trying to pull back what I liked about me *into* my life, and be gentle. And I know it's a constantly…a constant thing; I mean *every minute of my day!*

N: This process is very deep; you say it occupies your mind every minute of your life…

C: Pretty much, pretty much. I…I…I go for a lot of walks and talk out loud [about it]…

N: And, uh, your husband wasn't very sympathetic with all of these things?

C: Oh no. He was too young to know. I just…I married him to piss my parents off. (Laugh) I was trying to do things to…he was much younger than me, and…and he wanted to try to tell me that I was going to have to do this, and I didn't want any more people trying to control me in my life.

N: All righty. Who, who near you *has* applauded the queen?

C: (A pause) My friends. My girl friends. My girl friends.

N: They all must think you're very, very special.

C: They…they do. Uh. (Then, a torrent of words) That's what came…what sifted out through all of this, because I ended up in the hospital, and, like I said, I had to go to jail; they drove from Milwaukee to where I am, which is about a two and a half hour drive and they were the ones who picked me up and moved me in. They were stern, I mean, they got me to where I needed to be…

> *This was the third reference to "being in jail." This could have well become a sensationalistic way to dramatize her being, to call attention to herself, calling out for recognition and help.*

N: Why, why do they think you're so special?

C: I think because I *do* strike out on my own; if there's something I want to do, I…I…I…I…uh, you know, I attempt it! I may fail, but then, I…uh…sort of get through it…

N: Now, Carol, there's a lot of energy here. You feel it. I hear it. You really do get things done. There's no doubt about that…

C: I *am* a "Do-Person…"

N: And you desperately, desperately need appreciation for that.
   The Moon in Leo, of course.

C: *I do.* But [if] I get negativity around me, and it will knock me to my knees so quick. And that's something that came out in the conversation with my mother. She said she never realized I was so sensitive. And I said to her, for the last three years, after my dad passed away, you mean "I have no coping skills"? I didn't feel I had any coping skills. When things horribly happened to me, I just went to my knees. (Hmm mnn) And contemplated suicide, and I would call her and tell her, which is so hard. She just couldn't see that side of me. She wouldn't let herself. And I think, you know, towards the end there, she started understanding, and I think, once she realized I was back on my feet again, that's when she decided she was ready to go (nervous laugh).
   Again, the cry for recognition can be sensed within the suicide threat.

N: And the father didn't understand any of these things either.

C: He just…I was "his…his girl," and I could just do it. And, you know, when I got into jail, he dropped me one little note and said he stopped drinking, and I could too. And drinking was never the problem! It was just…
   A fourth reference to "jail." And clearly, another process of idealization of the parent, the way things should have been.

N: Now, I want to go back to those early years here. Here you have this highly perfectionistic mother, but I don't think the father was involved (softly).

C: He was wild. He was wild. He would come home…I was really the mediator in the family. Uh…My father would…uh…because of the war…when he was seventeen… when he, uh, had like malaria when I was in third grade, I stayed at home and took care of that, so I learned more about…
   Now more of the real story is emerging. The war is offered as an excusing explanation.

N: Well, talk about his lack of attention and appreciation and support of you.

C: Well, he…I don't want to…he…he *depended* on me. I was the nurturer. He would come home at two or three in the morning and call my mother all sorts of abusive names, and she would just lay in bed and never argue with him or anything. And I was the one that would go to the motel with him, because he decided that he was leavin' her. But then in the morning, when he sobered up, we'd go back home. I probably was in more motels when I was kid than…

N: But it's fascinating [that] in five minutes, we've revealed here through the horoscope this tremendous family drama!

C: Yeah. Oh yeah!

N: It's very strong.

C: Yeah! When I moved up here, I…you know…and then I got myself into trouble, and I couldn't come to their aid anymore. My dad was dying, and having a lot of problems; my mother…

N: All right. I think that might be a little bit off the track right now. We're trying to get the grounding and get to know each other here through this horoscope. And I need to ask you some questions here about the development in your life, and, uh, first of all, I'm not a medical doctor, but there are clear indications of a vulnerability to illness very early on in your life. Serious ones. And I need to know if you were strong enough to ward it off, or whether it hit.

Neptune, ruling the 12th, transited the Sun right after birth; SA Neptune conjoined the Sun at age four, along with tr Saturn conjunct the Sun.

C: Most definitely.

N: What?

C: I've never been in the hospital for anything other than things like tonsils, gallbladder; I went through lots of bone breaks….

N: But in the first four years of your life, were there any special illnesses?

C: No. Healthy as a horse.

N: That tells me a lot.

C: I'm a walker…I'm…

N: What did you do for a living?

C: I was in the telephone company; started out as an operator and worked my way up to an engineer. And I had a thirty-year career there.

N: That's not necessarily the best profession for you…

I knew that her dramatic artistic identity had certainly never been recognized. I had to bring this to her attention so she could finally find herself.

C: (Light sarcasm) Nooooo. And once I got into it, nobody would let me out of it because…and I kept being promoted all along, and uh, boy! It…it…uh…And I was in a men's environment…

N: (Very slowly with measured words) *There's a lot of creativity in this horoscope, a lot of, dare I say, artistic nature?*

C: Um. I'm a weaver, and that was my goal when I moved up here: it was to do my art. And then, uh, when I got myself straight, I'm slowly bringing that back into my life now!

The door was now wide open to the portents of her vocational profile and what it could mean to the rest of her life!

N: All right! I have gooseflesh, because here I sit so far away from you really, and I'm saying to you, **this is the horoscope of an artist**! Now let's go slowly, Carol; this is a very, very important point. And you are talking about "your art," that you are bringing it back into your life. You've also said to me that you're bringing *yourself* back into your life.

Here, I'm equating her art profession with her true (new) identity.

C: Right.

N: That your friends recognize the strength and talents that you have.

C: Right.

N: And I am recognizing it too! This art expression is really indomitable. And you went through a whole career perfunctorily, earning money, getting promotions, toeing the line, and lurking underneath it all was the artist.

C: Right.

N: I can't say that any more firmly and, dare I say, "happily" than I have. That you tell me that you finally see this [Hmm mn], tells me that you're free.

C: (Audibly emotional) Yeah, I'm, uh, hoping to get into spinning, um, um, I do off-the-loom weavings. Uh, and I don't know what to do with it just yet…

N: That will come! But I'm just pointing out that your vocational profile eloquently says "artist," [Right.] working at home, working at home as an artist. To have a studio or an area in your house that is totally devoted to your stuff, your creativity.

C: You know, I have all this art stuff upstairs and out in a very large garage, and that's what the purpose was, coming to where I am, and now I am just at the point of starting to organize my life…[I'm proud of you, Carol.] And…find that spot, but as you're saying this, I'm tearing up because I know…I know that's what I need to do, and yet I have a fear of it because…

N: Now, hold on. I can feel your energy! But now listen to me further. [Yeah.] The fact that I'm sitting here saying these things to you must be enormous corroboration of the deep feelings you are experiencing. [Yes.] How could I possibly say this if it weren't real? [Carol is crying: "Because you have a picture of me there."] I do. And you say you're tearing up and tears are coming down your cheeks right now [Right.]. These are tears of *recognition* [Right]. Please understand that. It's like seeing an old friend after years…

C: And for you to see it so quickly…

N: Thank you.

C: Thank *you*.

N: Now, uh, let's just check a few things here…there seems to be a very keen spiritual, religious dimension possible in this horoscope, in this life, in this development; has that materialized?

C: I go to church every day before I go to work! There are wonderful little churches up here; I mean, really small churches that are, uh, I mean, just neat! And so there's one I go to every day before I go to work—uh, Saint Teresa's—I burn a couple candles and say a decade of the rosary, and then, at lunchtime, I take my lunch and then I go to Saint Aloysius, and then I'm involved at Holy Family…in fact, I have Alma—my best friend; she's eighty-one years old—and she is basically like hangin' out with a saint! She's a virgin, and she's just about the neatest person I've… [Well, that's fine!] And she's my mentor, and she's got me working with kids on Wednesday nights. She just sort of dragged me there. My religion is very private to me, but, yes, I am…it's very important to me. [It's very important to you.] I talk to God non-stop! [Chuckle.]

N: All right, well, you tell God that you're so happy that the art is coming through you now, because God probably put it there for sure.

C: I'm in his hands. [Good] I've stopped controlling my life...

N: When you were five years old, Carol, was there a huge upset in your family structure?
SA Pluto=Saturn. I could easily have asked, "Was there a death in the extended family?" Note that Saturn rules the Midheaven.

C: Yes, my grandfather died.

N: Why was that so important?
This is an artful follow-up question to early-years trauma. It stimulates discussion in terms of values. Very often, uncles or grandfathers who died early on in the child's life are seen as very difficult upsets because that male may have substituted for the father.

C: He was the...you talk about old families...he was a very strong person. My grandfather went into World War II with his boys, because he missed them so much. He had already been in World War I. So, at that time apparently, my father, and uh...got very close with his father, and then when, uh, they got out, he was racing—he was a stock car racer—and as he went around the track, my grandfather died in the stands. It was just the trauma; from what I know of it, we were removed from Texas. My mother decided...

N: Stay on the point.

C: The grandfather dying shook up the whole family.

N: The whole family.

C: The whole family.

N: Now, at age ten, there is a similar type of shake-up. What was that?
The SA Mars=Pluto.

C: That could have been the malaria. I was in the third grade. Bein' home with my dad and...

N: Who had malaria?

C: My father. My mother worked—we lived in veterans' housing—and I had to stay at home and care for him.

N: I see. This is a very tense time, believe me, and, uh, your personal reaction to that tense time in your third grade year seems to be [guided by the horoscope] a lot more energetic and upsetting than you're telling me.

I didn't have a rich enough picture of the father relationship. We needed that.

C: Well…yeah! Because…I…I realized…It gave me so much empathy for my father that he could do no wrong! Everything he did, I excused because of what he went through, because I got a good taste of the war.

Again, parental idealization. How can Carol find her way in this maze of perfection that was contradicted by actual happenings in the home reality?

N: All right. OK. And then, when you were sixteen, there seems to be another period where you get lost, alone.

Tr Neptune conjunction the seventh cusp.

C: Yeah. I uh, I uh…What happened, uh, then…I had met someone, and uh, progressively, my father was totally against it, to the point that—the night I went to see *One Flew Over the Cuckoo's Nest* my father was picked up and taken away in a straitjacket.

N: Oh my!

C: My mother, aunt, and uncle had signed a…

N: This was in 1963, between May and October.

Tr Neptune conjunct the seventh cusp (derivatively, the father's Midheaven).

C: I married in '65 and left the home…

N: Did you hear what I said? That's the next stop in '65; I have that. But this period between May and October '63 is when this severe problem with your father took place. Am I right?

C: It's right around that time.

N: And the point is it makes you feel totally alone and forsaken.

C: We didn't talk for a couple…a year probably; he couldn't stand it longer than that; he needed me.

Always the self-aggrandizement bottom-line.

N: And then, the next year, uh, [when you were] eighteen: there are two things that are happening here: one, somehow the education extension is denied or interrupted. Was there ever any talk about you going on to college?

> *Age eighteen is college time, normally. Natally, Carol's Saturn, the 9th House ruler, is conjoined with Pluto. This suggests an interrupted education as we have discussed in our preparation notes. In 1965, we see tr Saturn=Sun/Moon. Education will be a major issue, as will relationship (probably as an escape) at the same time or building to the 1967 arc of Venus=Asc-Desc.*

C: I was asked...My mother could help out me OR my brother, and I said it was important that my brother go...

N: All right. The horoscope says that the education was interrupted; that a marriage takes place that shouldn't have taken place; and two, that the marriage took place as an escape from this male problematic family life, and the female idealistic family life. And both of these are coercive elements, dimensions, to you, and what basically it is, is that you get lost in the shuffle. Right?

C: Yep!

N: That marriage was difficult from the very beginning.

> *Tr Saturn=Sun/Moon*

C: Yeah. Uh, his parents never approved, and uh, and uh, it was a...you know, I liked him, but you know, like I said, I just did it to do it, I guess. You know.

N: Yes. I appreciate that. How long did it last?

C: It lasted about nine years, until I was about twenty-five, I think. twenty-four. Right in there.

N: Yes. No. Nine years later you're twenty-seven. [OK] But I see it breaking up here at the end of '73 or June–September '74.

> *Tr Uranus conjunct the Sun, with tr Neptune=Sun/Moon: a protracted emphasis on independence, which, on the insecurity of the marriage, would certainly stir things up.*

C: Right. That's when it was final. Yeah. I got papers.

N: Now. Was there an affair when you were twenty?

> *Going back to the early time in the marriage, trying to capture the Venus arc to the seventh cusp.*

C: No. (Laughing) I think I tried; I was looking!! But I was married, and nothing ever happened.

N: I understand that.

C: I was always a good girl; nobody ever approached that way.

N: All right. But the pressure was on, believe me. [Yeah!]—A research question, please: was there any kind of inheritance that came your way in '68 or '69?
    Tr Neptune conjunct Jupiter, peregrine and ruling the 8th House.

C: Not that I'm aware of.

N: All right. Good. 1970: was there a move or change of job? In May?

C: Oh, yes. Because I moved from Washington, Iowa, from the phone company there, and transferred into Bismarck. He was getting out of the service.

N: That was in May, May–June, I believe?

C: 'Round in there. He was getting out of the service and we relocated to Bismarck, and I got in as an operator there, and then started getting promoted after that.

N: We're right on schedule.

C: Yeah.

N: In '72, in June to September: another promotion? Another big deal?

C: You know, it was like an administrative clerk and then…

N: OK. I'm testing the dates…

C: As much as I can remember, you've got the time frames.

N: Then we see the very, very keen upset in the marriage coming to a head and your getting divorced.
    Keyed on Uranus=IC-MC, with tr Saturn significance.

C: Right.

N: I have to ask you again about any kind of illness in '76.

C: Other than just emotional…you know, nerves, no…never anything physical; never hospitalized, never.

N: All righty! Wow! That's un-u-su-al!

C: Yeah…I'm going to say "depression"…

N: Were you medicated for it?

C: Well, artificially, if you want to say, like smoke marijuana, and, uh, do the alternatives everybody else does…

N: All right. Just remember: don't smoke marijuana in church!

C: (Laughing) No! Do they complain about that? I like *Requiem* masses because I love incense (still laughing).

N: There. Now, listen, my dear: your life is changing '76–'77. Here you are divorced, doing very well in your work. Was there a further shift of responsibilities; an alteration in your job?

C: Yep! I think it was…In '79–'80 was when I got my biggest promotion…

N: We're not there yet! There are several before that. Tell me about this period between June and August—that summer—in '77. It must have been very positive for you!

C: Probably just work going OK; I got my own apartment, I think. Because I know my father kept trying to lure me back into the home, you know. You know, because I think I started taking up photography, started taking a lot of art classes on my own. That's how I justified staying at the phone company because I couldn't afford these.

N: The art classes. Now notice how it's [the art] trying to surface. Now, let's just backtrack for a moment. I'd like to make a suggestion for your self-study.

C: OK.

N: If you had gone on to the university, for higher education, you would have *definitely* worked with art.

C: Most definitely! And children. Young children.

N: And just think where that would have taken the rest of your life.

C: Oh, yeah! It would have been someplace totally different! I can't even imagine it, I guess!!

N: So now, that is frustrated and then we come to this period of time in '76–'77, and you say, "I'm earning money so I can start taking art courses."

C: Right. Now that you're mentioning it, you know what I did? I was at a point realizing I was going to have to support myself the rest of my life, and if there was anything I wanted, I had to achieve it. And, and I wanted to own a home; I wanted to own a home. We had always lived in an apartment. So that was a little goal of mine I had set. Well, anyway, I took drafting courses, because, when I looked in the phone company book, that was a high-paying job. [Hmm mnn] And in order to get into drafting, you had to wait for someone to die! You know, it was the old engineer men. And so, I started taking some drafting courses, and while I was taking that course...like I say, and that's when they offered me management and a drafting job at the same time. [Very good!] and I took management because there was more money, and I thought—this is my thinking—I could help, help other women realize they could get the job by doing the job and not on their looks...

N: All through 1981, the art should have been blooming.
  Tr Pluto conjunct Venus, the final dispositor, etc.

C: Yes. Because I bought my home; I did everything in the house...the curtains, I painted...

N: A very rewarding time, especially about October.
  With tr Saturn-Jupiter conjoining the Sun.

C: Yeah! That's when I put the offer in about the house. It got accepted, and it was sort of a birthday gift to myself.

N: Now, was there another man involved shortly thereafter? A relationship?
  SA Sun=Asc-Desc

C: Yeah. He was a musician. And I lived with him for about six years.

N: Until about '87. Then there's yet another man!
  Tr Pluto building to conjunction with the 7th House cusp.

C: Then I met the young man. Because my father told me this was an old house and I couldn't handle it. And how was I going to repair it? This was a stupid idea, and all that kind of stuff; so I found myself a young guy who was, uh, was handy!

N: To marry?

C: Well, I lived with him for ten years and waited until I was in my forties and, well, you know, he doesn't really rub me the wrong way, even though...

N: Wait a minute: we're just a little off here with this dating, and I want to make sure. I'm looking at the period of time May to October of 1989, when you're forty-two years old. Was that when you hooked up with this gentleman?

C: Yeah. Yeah. This young guy.

N: You call him a "young guy."

C: He was nineteen.

N: He was nineteen (she begins laughing) and you were…forty -…

C: Hey, if you want to piss your parents off, that's a good solution!
Interesting antagonism within the blanketing of idealization.

N: (Laughing) You were forty-two.

C: Yeah. Around there.

N: What was the great reward for you in 1993?

C: I got promoted again to a second level.

N: January or August, one of those two.

C: It was in January. That's when they were walking everybody out of the phone company, after divestiture…

N: Then about three years later, we begin to start to change this…

C: I spiraled down. Slowly but surely.

N: You spiraled down. What does that mean?

C: Meaning I got into drugs too heavily. I still could do my job, but I hated my life, just hated it. My parents came to live with me every summer; I had this young guy…
Perhaps the "other" dimension of Jupiter in Scorpio.

N: All right. What kind of drugs were you involved with?

C: Cocaine.

N: Aw, come on, Carol (with sympathy).

C: Well, it was the '80s, you know?

N: I'm talking about…You keep jumping. I'm talking about '95 to '99. And you're telling me you were taking cocaine then?

C: Yep!

N: Why do you think you did that?

C: (Very intensively spoken) Because I couldn't deal with anybody anymore; I couldn't make anybody happy. That...that...that was something I thought I could control, it was all about me, it was all about money, all about money.

> *This attitude of controlling the self (a new power) is found in the psychological literature often related to drug addiction. Obstreperous behavior, using drugs, heading for jail, etc., all suggest being "in action," discovering and learning new things, intensifying emotional experiences, achieving a sense of belonging, having a voice in one's fate, something to look forward to.*[2]

N: (Interrupting strongly) Now, one moment please. One moment please. *You couldn't make anybody happy?*

C: Right.

N: Now, you were *certainly* making *everybody* happy where you worked.

C: Right.

N: You were all that with successful promotions, etc. Right?

C: Wel,I was sort of gettin' bit there too...

N: (Speaking over her response) **You weren't making your mother happy ever in your life.** Wasn't this getting to you?

> *This was a deliberate apparent non sequitur, to shock to the crux of the matter.*

C: (Resignedly) Yeah. It was all getting to me.

N: And that's why you end up with this cocaine, to put it very simplistically.

C: Yeah. Right! Right!

N: I want you to see that. It's hardcore.

C: Oh yeah! I dealt with that when I came up here.

N: Boy, oh boy. We do understand this, don't we?

C: Hm mmn (in thought).

---

2. For example: the social therapy work/techniques of Dr. Fred Newman, presented in *Favorite Counseling and Therapy Techniques*, beginning page 142. See bibliography.

N: So you decided to retire; were you retiring…you said in '97, I think.

I see just before that in '94, around the spring, and early in '95, a break-up in a relationship.

C: Right. That's when I decided to divorce this man. And it took a little while.

N: And then when we get to '99, this is when I see retirement.

C: That is when I retired.

N: But you said '97.

C: Well, you start thinkin' about it, but '99 is right.

N: In March or September. Very good.

C: I started talking to my parents, telling them I wanted to leave the company. And I really had to convince them that this was OK. I had thirty years. I told them, "I *have* to, or I'm gonna die."

N: I gotcha. And then there's a very powerful period of time that is not very good. March 2000; it lasts a good year. What was going wrong there?

This was Carol's "hell time," as far as I could gather: tr Saturn conjunct Ascendant, equally Sun/Moon leading into the powerful arc Saturn=Sun.

C: Well, I moved up here, everything was won…I had my utopia…This was going to be my utopia. And I put so much, um, into this…

N: What went wrong?

C: I don't know. I hooked up with the wrong crowd, and I just could not get out of trouble. I was in jail. That's when it started. And I met somebody; I met somebody in that March, and helped milk cows to the horror of my mother, and made friends…

N: In September of 2004, were you free of all that stuff?

Looking for a "new start" manifestation with tr Saturn conjunct the 4th cusp.

C: Oh No, no. I uh, I uh, ended up in jail…the car accident was in Octo—

N: Whoa. Whoa! Just answer the question, please. I'm trying to find when you finally got rid of this stuff, because that stuff you're involved in—we understand why, but it is like an accident in your life: it wasn't supposed to be! Do you understand that? Now, stay calm about this.

C: Yeah.

N: You are an artist who's trying to find endorsements and you get endorsed through the experience of other people, and it usually starts at home. You didn't get it. It then transfers to marriage support. You didn't get it. And here you are trying to get the wrong peer group's support—all thought to be artists and things like that—and here we are: I'm looking for the time when you got free of this. Was it just last year? In May–August of '05?

This is the beginning of summation.

C: Yeah. Starting to. Yeah.

N: Thank you. I had to clarify that, because it's very complicated…We've got it now. And I am just thrilled the artist-read of your horoscope has been substantiated throughout your whole life. [Oh, yeah!] It's just never been opened up and fulfilled.

C: Right. And still isn't; but we'll get there!

Encouraging statement.

N: Now, what are you projecting for yourself in the next six months?

C: Well, I'm working at a grocery store, and uh, I'm a check-out, and just uh, recently, they uh, put me up in the office—just as I knew they would; they love me—and they, uh, have asked me, uh, would I consider working there…*and* I've asked to work in the greenhouse; I want to learn about plants. Uh, so they said that they will give me hours in the greenhouse and they're going to have me in the office and they got me uh…uh… you know…workin' check-out. So sounds like I'm gonna do the three jobs. So right now, that's what I'm doing. Then, I'm gonna attempt, I want to attempt to try to find someone to teach me spinning. I want to learn how to spin my yarn.

N: All righty. Good. I think you're going to be able to do this; I think you're going to be able to do this very, very soon. And I think that the first step of doing this is in the middle of April. I think…if you look around for the spinning tutelage, you will find it in the second week of April. I urge you to try.

C: All right. I will!

N: And this you'll think will be revolutionary in your life development because you will finally be *taking action* with the art! Then, we have a situation in August. Now, I think by that time, you're going to feel that your identity is definitely the artist—now for everybody to see.

C: See! That's it: I haven't been able to present myself.

N: I think you *will* then; I think there's going to be something like a…a…a show or something that you will be involved with—maybe not your stuff [Right] but on a very good level, reaching out through an artistic project to the community. Are you with me?

C: Yes. Yes.

N: And I think you'll meet somebody in August who is going to be very helpful to the acceleration of your skills and their development. Make sense?

C: Yes. Yes!

N: And then, I'm saying to you that, by the time we get to March 2007, you're going to be showing your stuff! And I think it can build and be quite successful, and you will know all of that in September-October 2007. It looks awfully good, my dear…

C: (Thoughtfully) OK.

N: Did you write a few of those down?

C: Yeah. I'm writing frantically here!

N: Take your time; you can always call me back; I have the notes in front of me. But that is what I'm seeing, and I think that nothing should be allowed to divert you from this course. You will never have any problem where you're working. You're not hurting for money.

C: No. I'm doing fine.

N: And you've got your faith and you've got your freedom. You know what you need now? **Experience and applause**. Experience and applause. Tell me you understand that!

C: (Peacefully) I understand that.

N: All right. Every time I open the refrigerator door myself and that little light goes on, my Moon in Leo starts to perform! (Laughing)

C: (Laughing strongly)

N: And your uproarious laughter now shows me that you do understand that!

C: I understand TOTALLY!

N: So what you need is experience, *activity* in your art, and *applause for it!*

C: OK.

N: And you're going to earn it! (Pause) How's that?

C: That would be the cherry on the top!

N: And I think that when you go to church now, *light an extra candle...That* one's yours, *that* one's for you.

C: (Most peacefully) All right.

N: I really have enjoyed this talk. It really looks keen and clear.

C: It's been a struggle but I...I know, I know, you know, like you say, that art has been laying under there all the time...all the time.

N: All right. And, and you have the blessing of health!

C: Yes.

N: That's wonderful. There's never been a detection of a heart anomaly, a missing beat or...

> *Neptune on the Sun; Mars on the Moon in Leo; Neptune ruling the 12th.*

C: I have a punctured aorta, when I came up here [from an auto accident].

N: I'm just pointing out that the horoscope says to me that there's quite possibly a congenital heart anomaly—an unknown with which you're born—and we have to ask why *that* organ and not others! There's a proclivity here for that vulnerability.

C: Right.

N: As well, there's lower back—third and fifth vertebrae at the beltline—is there any lower back anxiety?

> *The Libra tensions.*

C: No. What I do to...because of this happening, that's why I like bagging groceries, I lift them out of the cart and do as much as I can physically to keep myself very fit.

N: Is there any weakness in the lower back?

C: No.

N: Good for you! And you've got the "gift of gab," my dear!!

> *Mercury square the Moon, ruler of the 3rd, Mars and Pluto square Mercury.*

C: Yes!

N: It's wonderful! Most delightful and entertaining. And one artist says to you, another artist, "Nice to meet you!"

C: (Warmly) Thank you very much. Do you see anything for relationships?

N: Not quite yet. It's a little hard here in your horoscope, because the relationships I think you're going to be making now will be the relationships linked to the art activity and helping to promote that art activity. It's not necessarily an intimate relationship. And we've got to get some of those things squared away first, because that will change you and you will be attracting a different kind of relational traffic.

C: A different kind of person.

N: Bless you, my dear. You've really enriched me this morning with sharing this new life you have.

C: Thank you, thank you! And I'll go to church with lots of thoughts in my head…

N: And light a candle for yourself.

C: I will most certainly do that.

N: And remember you're your own perfectionist now with the art God gave you.

C: Yes. Thank you.

N: Bless you. Bye-bye.

C: Bye.

(Forty-eight minutes.)

OVERVIEW: STRUCTURE AND TECHNIQUE

Astrology was able to re-establish Carol's identity. We cut through the defensive idealizations about her turbulent early times, discovered her vocational truth, and focused her new start in retired life through confidence in herself—recognition of herself—and the security of her faith. Lighting a candle for herself in her daily church experiences was a poignant and strategic statement, a way for her to remember the recognition-feel of her identity every day of her life forward.

We see how it was necessary to choreograph her volubility, cutting off detailed stories after the central significance of the occurrence being described became clear. *We stayed on track*; this is so important for building the momentum of helpful thinking. Objectivity is comprised of a smooth line of deduction, rather than jigs and jags, stops and starts of sporadic reasoning.

It was vivid indeed to see Carol calling attention to herself repeatedly—not through statements of positive accomplishments, but through references to her being put in jail and upsetting her mother. The jail references were about as far away as possible from the super-idealized poise of her mother! And recall her explaining her relationship with the younger man: "I married him to piss my parents off."

The artist in Carol would not do these things, say these things. At least, that thought guided me well in bringing out her best.

The Unexpected/Surprising Question

So much of social conversation is predictable. It develops that way by mutual consent, to make us all secure with personal confrontation. Think how often every day we are asked, "How are you?" How often we ask the same question! How the replies are perfunctory.

Think through discussions and see the patterns, how they repeat; the word choices; we know how the conversation will end before it even develops. Think how we censor what is in between the sentences.

There is much to be gained on occasion, during the consultation, *to go against the pattern*.

Not too long ago, sitting at dinner with six people—certainly not an astrological consultation atmosphere, but a helpful scenario—I found myself feeling a bit uncomfortable with the lady to my left, foreign born, wearing tight rings on each Saturn finger, which suggested much.

The lady seemed emotionally tight, a bit aloof, afraid to open up; perhaps intimidated somehow by the setting and people present. I asked her the polite questions about her husband, about her work, and then I tried something: I asked the unexpected question, *the surprising question*, as if we *were* in a consultation. I asked it calmly, non-dramatically, and waited patiently for the answer without any sign at all that the question had been unexpected from her perspective.

"How many children do you have?"

"Three."

...and here it comes: gently, matter-of-factly, **"Why?"**

There was a fleeting moment of surprise, I think, but the lady kept it in check and proceeded to answer this way: "Well, the third child…we hadn't really planned it, but we felt the soul of that child waiting around us somehow, you know, to be born through us. My husband had some difficulty with that, but we talked about it a lot, and then the child was indeed conceived and born and…"

Out came this richly dimensioned story that opened the lady up beyond her customary privacy and discipline. All of this, just because I had asked "Why?" when no one in the world would ask that! It seemed to me that the woman *enjoyed* telling the story, opening up; *it showed more of who she was.*

Now, look on page 203. Carol is talking strongly, rapidly, emotionally, about her cocaine years:

C: (Very intensively spoken) Because I couldn't deal with anybody anymore; I couldn't make anybody happy. That…that…that was something I thought I could control, it was all about me, it was all about money, all about money.

N: (Interrupting strongly) Now, one moment please. One moment please. *You couldn't make anybody happy?*

C: Right.

N: Now, you were *certainly* making *everybody* happy where you worked.

C: Right.

N: You were all that with successful promotions, et cetera. Right?

C: Well, I was sort of gettin' bit there too…

    And here is the unexpected question/statement, a deliberate apparent non sequitur, to shock to the crux of the matter:

N: (Speaking over her response) **You weren't making your mother happy ever in your life. Wasn't this getting to you?**

C: (Resignedly) Yeah. It was all getting to me.

Much was accomplished as soon as those words passed between us. Totally unexpected; always to be remembered.

Additionally, note with Alice (page 72) the unexpected introduction of her mother and (page 79) the unexpected introduction of brother.

Another example—and I have used this technique-question many times—a man, married with a family, was troubled for many years with very difficult self-worth concepts. Opportunities for professional advancement—a new life chapter—were presenting themselves. Who would go forward? The "old" self-deprecating man or someone refreshed, unloaded of the excess weight that had hung around his neck routinely?

Our conversation slowed down, and there was a moment of stillness. My client was sad. Everything had registered: the depressed way of seeing himself, how that was communicated to others, and more.

I said calmly and quietly, "George, let me ask you a question that might surprise you." George nodded permission.

"All things considered, George [and it is wise to use the client's name at such a poignant moment of identity focus], *why does your wife love you?*"

Well, you could have heard a pin drop across town! George raised his eyes and met mine, his look supported by a faint knowing smile. [Note that my statement *assumed* his wife did love him!] I just waited as his mind—his unconscious and conscious faculties—whirred to answer that surprising question, which he probably had never ever thought of before!

And then, George began to tell me—*and himself*—just why his wife and children loved him and respected him, how different that was from his early home life and upbringing, and more.

We began to discuss how that could be remembered daily and how those feelings and refreshed self-awareness could be brought front and center in his new image for opportunities ahead.

9

THERAPY IDEAS

APHORISMS

Great thoughts become great words. They go together. The words give life and distribution to the thoughts. They are tied together conceptually and also, ideally, stylistically. For example: "We have nothing to fear, but fear itself!" In this famed Franklin D. Roosevelt quote, the repetition of the word "fear" is supported with the rhythmic stroke on "nothing" and (the first) "fear" and then on the second "fear" and then on "-self": we have NOthing to FEAR, but FEAR itSELF! Presidential speech writers search for opportunities to write words like those, destined for remembrance in stone, so to speak. Alliteration, rhythm, and other devices make phrases memorable. We carry them with us easily.

All great teachers, great religious figures, and political leaders use grand key thoughts and memorable word images to stimulate learning and mobilize action. It's impressive how many turns of phrase we use or hear every day that come from some source we've forgotten about, while the core meaning has been captured by the words to live on for a long, long time. The concept will fit perfectly into the conversation and make a point memorably.

Every youngster in the United States learns these words, "Early to bed, early to rise, makes a man, healthy, wealthy, and wise." This is a beauty of parallel structure and rhythm. Benjamin Franklin engineered it that way some 250 years ago!

These ideas of correctness, natural truth, and wisdom appear in all languages. They are how our language cryptically appreciates the human condition. In German, for example,

Franklin's truth is approached with "Morgenstund' hat Gold im Mund": The morning hour (getting up early) has gold in its mouth (promises gold, pays off).

Sometimes, the truths are translated directly: in German, "Kleider machen Leute" becomes in English, "Clothes make the man."

"Aphorisms" is the name given to some of these thought nuggets: concise statements of some truth or sentiment. They can attract an oooh or an ahhh as being "Oh so true"; they can stimulate a wry smile of wise recognition. They are indisputable, basically. They are memorable.

For example, Alexander Pope is quoted, "Blessed is he who expects nothing, for he shall never be disappointed." This aphorism prods the pessimist in a wry way to see the trap of his or her positioning; making an effort is *indeed* what is called for; we *must* expect something in order for something to happen, for life to go on. *Expecting is involvement.*

Oscar Wilde wrote, "To love oneself is the beginning of a lifelong romance." To some, this is a marvelous recommendation, starting off a self-appreciation program with a memorable smile.

Eleanor Roosevelt said: "No one can make you feel inferior without your cooperation." At the beginning of any name-calling argument or within any routinely tense relationship, this reflection comes in handy indeed. Some people need its wisdom daily.

Pascal observed, "The sole cause of man's unhappiness is that he does not know how to stay quietly in his room." There are times indeed when we should be quiet, stay out of trouble, when we should not involve ourselves in uncharted, inappropriate societal traffic.

And Chateaubriand: "Something you consider bad may bring out your child's talents; something you consider good may stifle them." Or, Shakespeare: "Oh what a tangled web do parents weave, when they think that their children are naïve."

The recognition-smile that inexorably responds to these thoughts is the gateway to remembering what they have to say. We walk away with the "feel," the sentiment, the instruction. The great idea is memorable.

In a consultation, an aphorism can do much good to sum things up, to give the client a way to remember what has been discussed. With clients who are really being pressed to leave a marriage that has been battered and bruised and suffering for many years, the discussion in the consultation will surely point up the necessity for change. An effective aphorism to capture that mind-focus is, "It isn't safe, wise, or helpful...to try to stay afloat in troubled waters." To save your life, you leave those waters behind. You could also say,

"It's time to get out of Dodge," but the cowboy flippancy here is not as intellectual as the situation of change probably demands.

Each of the cases we've studied features a memorable turn of phrase, a memorable image that sums up the benefits of the discussion. For Alice, we have the symbolism of the diamond ring finally for herself; with Brett, the closing handshake, a help to break the defensiveness habit, and note the offering of "applause"; for Joan, doing something wondrous for others (quite an unexpected way of wording it; therefore, high impact) in the short time left before her retirement; for Marion, developing passionate self-confirmation, beginning with "And it seems to me that this teaching business is not really going to focus itself *until **you** focus it*"; and for Carol, the reminder every day in church when she lights a candle for her new identity.

Fascinatingly, giving these turns of phrase and classical aphorisms some thought,[1] the astrologer can learn to create them originally, herself or himself.

For example, I experience so many clients who just wait around waiting for things to happen, waiting for a miracle, for something to adjust their lives without their getting involved themselves with the process of change.[2] I wanted to create an aphorism that would work against that passive position and be particularly memorable. I put this together, and, having used it many times, I have seen it do a remarkably good job with the situation (spoken slowly and clearly, with a wry smile): "Newton had to go into the garden...in order for...the apple to drop."

A parallel statement, an aphorism of unknown origin, is very effective as well to encourage getting active in the process of change: "A ship in the harbor is safe, but that's not what ships are made for!" Or, to guide discussion and strategy from a point of understanding: "The art of living free starts where this detail begins."

THE LAST FIVE MINUTES OF THE CONSULTATION

The last five minutes of the consultation are extremely important. This is the bridge over which your client returns to his or her world. Their content is what lingers first and

---

1. See Gross.

2. People want change; they equate it with improvement and advance. But the transient insecurity in the midst of change is threatening to them. Therefore, they adopt a position of inactivity, not involved in the process; they wait for—indeed, expect—a miracle.

foremost in the mind upon conclusion of the consultation. It is probably the first recollection shared by the client reporting on the consultation to a confidant.

I have had consultations punctuated by clients' tears and anguish, recollections of pain, feelings of despair, intrusions of anger and hate. All can dissolve by the end of the consultation time, by virtue of objectification and understanding. Freshness, buoyancy, and determination almost always return in their place. The wrap-up, the review, the abbreviated recapitulation in those last five minutes—keyed to a creative turn of phrase or a memorable aphorism—can condition so much life spirit for the client in the time ahead.

For some helpful reminders for the close of the consultation, think of the "3Rs": Review, Reinforcement, and Raising Spirits.

Review

Try to review memorably the understandings to which you and your client have come, about the client's developmental themes, routines, and structures. Repeat the key images that summed things up at different levels of learning.

I recently worked with a client—a very successful, wealthy gentleman, who constantly worried about how attractive he was—who brought into his conversation over and over and over again "how sick he had been" at this time, another time, yet another time. I finally pointed out to him the suggestion that he was **defining his identity** *in terms of sickness rather than in terms of his considerable accomplishments!*

The man was startled with this understanding when I suggested that *"There was method to his sadness!"* This turn of phrase jarred him (substituting "sadness" for "madness" in the well-known phrase). Indeed, he did start to become free of his lifelong tendency, by *objectifying* it, and, to summarize where we had been and what we had accomplished, I was sure to remind him of the telling epithet at the end of the consultation. This time, there was a knowing, glowing smile about it!

Reinforce

Here we reinforce the strategies about the near future. [Recall Joan on her way to make her pitch for more responsibilities and a customized title on the job.] The client just mentioned above had business plans that really looked active and strong. The key, though, was to see these continuing business onslaughts *as motivated in over-compensation for his deep inferiority feelings from his early home life experiences.* The successes now—with a changed perception—were to define his matured development, to give him the self-aware pride that is so attractive and valuable in his society and business—not the identification with the illnesses, which we agreed had been used to attract female (maternal) sympathy.

Raise Spirits

We must make our clients feel good about themselves. We must raise spirits with applause, with anecdote, with genuine, sincere compliments. Just realize how seldom in our society one receives a compliment from someone else; how seldom we give compliments to others! Believe it or not, some clients have never, ever heard praise, supportive evaluation in their life(!), especially in the early home life development.

I have had many clients tell me at the end of the consultation, "This is the nicest thing anyone's ever done for me!" Imagine that! How starved so many people are for a sincere pat on the back.

Learn the power of certain phrases like "You've got lots to do!...This is an exciting period of time ahead; promise to put on your calendar that you're going to call me early in December...no matter what!!...Now, on top of all that we've accomplished here, go home and hug your wife long and tight; remember, you shared with me all the reasons she has to love you!...I think you're terrific; look at all you've done here, how many difficult spots you've conquered. Congratulations."

Indeed, not all consultations work smoothly within the choreography suggested by this last-five-minutes outline. The insurance salesman doesn't always get the contract; construction workers smash their hand with the hammer; the mailperson is attacked by somebody's pet; astrologers run into resistance from deeply routined behaviors working against development. But the point here is to highlight the five-minute time at the end of the consultation as very important: much can be salvaged there. More often than not, *much can be celebrated.*

And it bears repeating: the client primarily takes away from the consultation and into the future *the content of the last five minutes of your time together.*

TEN HELPFUL INSIGHTS

1. The Structure of the Consultation

Astrological consultations used to be astrological "readings." The session was dramatically one-sided: the astrologer gave a fatalistic decree guided by memorized cookbook epithets.

There was very little interpretative, individualized creativity about it, and the client certainly didn't bring much to the table. There was little dialogue.

Many astrologers—especially in the early stages of their professional development—feel great insecurity in talking with the client. The insecurity gradually disappears when the structure of preparation for the consultation is clearly understood—what it entails and why—and when it is followed in detail every time a horoscope is under study. The first half of this book is devoted to structuring that preparation technique.

A solid grounding takes place when hemisphere emphasis is noted, the Sun-Moon polarity is added, and then ramifications of aspects to the Sun or Moon and key phenomenological measurements are assimilated (like Saturn retrograde, the nodal axis, peregrination, etc.).

The astrologer must know that tension is absolutely necessary for development in life, and that tension is clearly shown in the horoscope through strong aspects between the planets, symbols of needs and the behavioral faculties to fulfill them. The stress we confront builds the muscles we use to go through it; it makes us strong. In the consultation, guided by the measurements, the astrologer learns *how much* tension was taken in during development, where it came from, how it was managed, what defenses were used, and how much of this behavioral routine and value profile became the adult personality. Overall, how strong is the press for reigning need (the Moon) fulfillment? This is what will be brought to focus when change and further developmental potentials are addressed, with the learned behaviors taking over for better or for worse. Grasping this is a strong orientation for the astrologer; it builds skill in perception and security in communication; sharing an objective view of it all is extremely helpful to most clients...

The astrologer must never underestimate the clients' capacity to use their own mind to help themselves.

For example: the client can start to leave problematic situational reactions behind *by noting the defenses that are not needed anymore*; in other words, the client has outgrown the hurtful situation, but the perceptions and behaviors continue as habit, and they can be relaxed, deprogrammed. The client can learn to forgive a parent, for example, one for whom much animosity has been carried for many years.

The client can change value perceptions conditioned long ago, which simply don't hold up in enterprising adult life, e.g., not being able to interact with others' authority, the fear of abandonment, self-deprecation.

The client can learn *finally* to be proud, to feel loved and valued. The astrologer can lead the client to seeing what experiences are important in sustaining those feelings.

In the consultation, the overview of development reveals value judgments (and this was clearly exposed in all the cases we have studied). Behaviors are attached to these value judgments. And those behaviors define personality.

If those behaviors carry dysfunctional habits with them, they need to be changed. The consultation discussion can study this. The client can establish an objective to make such changes.

All these things considered, the consultation can illuminate the efficacy of new goals, new strategies, going onward with development. We bring predictive measurements into a realistic stream.

2. Practicality and Reality Lead Measurements

There are two keys that lead projections best, that qualify the thrust of prediction most strongly: *the reasonability* of what is projected and *the involvement* of the individual in making it happen.

For a schoolteacher client, for example, you see a clear strong Arc of Mercury=Jupiter occurring at the same time as SP Moon squares the Midheaven. Ideally, these signals are *related* to each other: we get the sense of a trip and/or study related to development in the profession, abetting a job advance.

The astrologer needs to uncover this issue, to see if this "sense" is already being experienced or is soon to be in the reality experience of the client. The astrologer can ask "What's the opportunity now for further study that can help with job advancement? This is suggested strongly here; what's happening?"

The client will probably light up with recognition and say, "Yes! I'm applying to teach at the high school level now, and I need to take a special course to qualify. Should I be taking this course now?"

The situation is practical and real for the client. Therefore the astrology of the situation is strategically significant.

But we must remember that this same measurement could be taking place in the horoscope of, say, a farmer in South Dakota. The farmer's reality experiences are different. The measurement might not guide the discussion to anything important in the farmer's life. If the guideline *were* to manifest, the result could well be a trip somewhere to a convention, where learning and contacts could be made for a new harvesting machine technology. Information would be gained, and it could pay off well in his work.

For someone working at *TIME* magazine, the guideline could be suggesting an important foreign assignment (requiring much travel), which can be career significant in the near future.

The measurement we see must be *fitted into the line of experience issuing from the client.* We must listen to the client, inspect the individual reality carefully, in order to fine tune the strategy that will bring the measurements to life.

Having measurements come to focus in the horoscope does not mean events will happen in the life. Not all measurements manifest. Many measurements fly right by a person's reality experience. Change can happen only if the client is *knowingly* involved and if the environment cooperates. *We must be intent on being practical more than on being textbook-exact.*

Many people underachieve, do not stoke their fires, do not reach for brass rings. Many indeed wait for the apple to drop naturally; they are afraid of transient insecurity away from the norm and standards of their life; they wait for a miracle. The miracle rarely happens unless it is prodded into reality.

When it comes to powerhouse measurements (primarily involving the outer planets, the angles, Sun or Moon), we must be similarly perceptive. For example, a Pluto arc of an angle or square to it, or tr Pluto similarly, are going to be background significant for about a year of the client's life (because of the intrinsic slow speed of Pluto in transit and the duration of an arc by definition). The potential for change of life perspective is very high, and such change almost always requires a protracted span of time; there may be drama in the portents of the change, but the development of it may be gradual, slower than we want. Many details must fall into place. For example, relocating to another country: when the decision is made or en route to the decision, so many plans must be made, so many bureaucratic protocols must be met, communication exchanges and compliance with all sorts of regulations must have their time. When a family is involved, the concerns are compounded, of course.

With Saturn involvement (and/or Pluto), there may be a death experience in the extended family. If it occurred/occurs, it must be assimilated in life progress. What does it represent for the strategy of further growth and advancement?

With Uranus, individuality is awakened, ideally; surprising dimensions come to the foreground; relocation, job change, expressions of independence all must be considered. If things are successful, there is much busyness and excitement; if plans are thwarted, temperamental crisis can prevail. What is a realistic evaluation of pending adjustment? Is the client in sync with what's happening?

With Neptune, there can be extended disappointment, bewilderment, and inexplicable delays. Patience and introspection should displace the feelings of suppression, aloneness. Some dream must be coming into the life.

The astrologer must be keenly alert to the spectrum of practicality and reality. Then the astrologer's work is more reliable.

3. Extending Suggestions Creatively

As we follow astrological guidelines within the horoscope, we learn so much about the individual, where he or she has been developmentally and where he or she wants to go.

We learn to listen, to spot trends, repetitions of behaviors, evaluations of experience, reactions to frustrations, overcompensations, fulfillments, etc. When we come to the end of the consultation and are making projections into future development with the client, all of that insight and awareness comes to important focus. It is an opportunity for us to extend the client's potentials creatively.

I was in consultation with a lady in her fifties, who made an intelligent but drab and tired appearance. At the beginning of our discussion, I had inquired about her creativity (pronounced quintile structures, etc.): "What's all this creativity here? What's your outlet for it?" The lady said, "I'm a painter." Throughout the entire consultation the only life theme/experience that came forward was that the woman had given over her life to her family, children, and husband. *Being a painter* was never once mentioned in the course of our talk! Life had become a colorless routine for her.

All the while we were talking, I was aware of her art being overlooked. Had she given up because she was not very talented? Then why would she proclaim she was a painter to establish her identity, except if she wanted for that to be so someday? Did she not get any support for her painting in the early adult years? Was her family repressing that path? The subject simply did not come up in her life story shared with me.

I determined that we had somehow "to recover her birthright for art." I remember thinking this through on a separate level as we talked about other things. And then, finally, I brought up the subject and shared what I thought was the perfect, nonthreatening, alluring statement for her to remember and perhaps follow: "It would be so fresh and exciting for you to resume painting, Renate. To resume painting [the repetition of the words was planned] NOT for galleries or for sale, but simply **to make other people happy!**" This statement had great impact [she would be making herself happy in the process as well, obviously]. We talked at length about how she could do this, painting for children, for school activities, holding painting parties, shows and talks in extended-care facilities for the elderly, for church groups at fund-raising programs, etc.

If her attitude didn't change, if she didn't "get with it" in the right frame of mind, her identity would *stay* lost, and no matter what promising measurements there were for her, signals of times to come, nothing would change, develop, bloom.

Another lady, a yoga teacher quite depressed about the failure of her attempt to establish a studio because of a government technicality: "*Every time* I tried the business, the government got in my way." In reality, this had happened only once. I replied, "What if, *knowing more now*, you did try *again*? How can that be managed?"[3]

Without refreshed determination and some common sense wisdom, no matter what the promising planet measurements were, nothing would change.

A man highly skilled with computers was having a difficult time getting a job. He made a shabby impression: he was foreign born and had some difficulty with English; he was diffident; he disappeared in the conversation. But his keen talents deserved outlet and recognition; his massage was simply not as fine as his message: he defeated *himself* before anyone had a chance to hire him!

I pointed all this out to him, including how people applying for a job so often overlook *actually asking for the job* with enthusiasm, because they are so afraid of rejection. We rehearsed how he could sit forward in his chair when listening, looking attentively at the interviewer, and then lean forward to say [lots of positive body language], "Here's what I feel about this issue, my views on this point are…" [and then, with a smile of confidence in his skill] "Here's why I really want this job; to be involved and produce good work."

Without this extension of the consultation discussion, without a change in demeanor, in mindset, no planetary promises anywhere would reflect success in the marketplace.

The astrologer adapts insight to the individual situation, and all of that fits the reality situation depicted in the projected measurements.

This statement by Norman Vincent Peale is wisely remembered: "Change your thoughts and you change your world."

---

3. Overstatement of distress is a commonly used bid to command attention: "I'm about to commit suicide," for example, is almost invariably transparent to boil down to "I just wanted to know if my life is going to improve."

4. How Many Defenses Do You Need?

We see defense mechanisms most often as concomitant with eastern hemisphere emphasis, Grand Trines, and idealization measures, all prodded into being through 2nd House, 11th House, 4th–10th, and 7th House tensions in the main. The defenses are *necessary* in the early years when young behaviors are not met by a cooperative environment. This frustration begins with the quality and balance of interaction or lack of it with the parents, works further through siblings, and extends to the young community in school. Recall Brett's case in chapter 5.

Once the defensive structures are uncovered and understanding is achieved as to why they were created and deployed, it is a sobering question to ask, "How many do you really still need?" Just think of that question. "How much of you is weighed down by these protections and aggressions now that you're building your own world as an adult? How much has gone wrong in the last few years because of those constructs?" Then stop talking and listen to your client, who is probably discussing this for the first time in his or her life! Defensive behavior easily becomes a habit. It consumes much, much energy.[4]

Very often, in the plan for refreshed development created with your client, it is helpful to link two sets of behavior together; *one part of the program helps the other.* For example, if your client does not feel very presentable because of excess weight and therefore undermines relationships with mistrust, criticisms, or arguments (projection onto others of self-incriminations and effacement), devising a reasonable weight-loss program to improve self-imaging *and* linking it with a daily program to improve trust and relationship dynamics can be very effective.

For example, "This diet and exercise program will probably pay off with your losing two or three pounds a week right off the bat, and, *at the same time,* if you make sure to give three people sincere compliments every single day…truly work at that also…these programs working together are going to make things a lot different! Keep track! You'll see that it *does* work!!"

Another helpful technique for some cases is to ask the client to help you with making a "Five-Star" list. Take out a piece of paper for the list and ask your client {with a smile, as if this will be fun!), "Please tell me *five* things that are just wonderful about you!"

The deep self-worth anxieties can make this a difficult chore, but, with the astrologer's help, a list *can* be started and completed. It is not surprising that this list-making does

---

4. See Blackman for 101 defenses that shield the mind.

become fun; the client has probably never taken an inventory of personal assets like this before! Make it enjoyable; i.e., "Of course, I see that in you!…Terrific!" Sometimes, at the end of the consultation, I take the list and fold it neatly for the client to take home.[5]

5. Indecision

Very often, the client will understand much, but still be in a quandary about what to do. Indecision understandably reigns with many large issues; the single-session procedural frame of mind in the astrological consultation needs a boost for impact with such large decisions.

Sometimes as well, clients are notoriously, habitually indecisive; they have never had their judgment reinforced in their development and feel stranded when someone is not making decisions for them [especially Mars in Sagittarius, Moon in Sagittarius frustrations].

I like to point this out with humor, relaxing the client and softening the issue. I bring up Yogi Berra, the famous New York Yankees pundit, famous for his malapropisms. "Yogi had a great bit of wisdom for us in a situation like this. He said (spreading the words out, somewhat gravely), "When you come to…a fork in the road…**TAKE IT**!" Invariably, there is a broad smile of understanding.

In other words, a decision must be made; now, how are "we" going to make that decision? And, we must remember, no matter how great the measurements are about opportunity, for example, the decision will have to be made or nothing will happen. Perhaps there has been a lifelong stagnation present because of indecision, and for the best of times, that habit must be relinquished.

Here is a technique that you can recommend to your client to do on her/his own. It is called "Ask a Friend" or "Consulting the Friend Within."[6]

Who has not ever talked aloud with himself, with God, with a trusted long-time friend? Getting the stuff of indecision out into the open helps us see where to go. We hear the solution.

Existentially, a case can be made for the fact that the client will indeed *already* know the answer to the situation requiring decision. It just must be brought out. And that is what the "Ask a Friend" technique does.

The client brings two chairs to the middle of a room. He sits in one and imagines a friend, a trusted articulate friend, sitting in the other. That friend has a problem similar to

---

5. Please see expansion of this self-worth anxiety therapy in Tyl, *Synthesis,* pages 729–732.

6. See Smith and Elliott, pages 201–203.

his and, while he is very articulate about the pros and cons, is slow on taking any action about it, just as your client is. This is an opportunity to talk the issue out.

The client should start talking strongly, making his case aloud to the imaginary friend in the second chair, in a persuasive tone; i.e., "Really talk it over with your friend; make your case and his. *Tell it as it is.*" The client should really get into it (and that does take place after a few moments). The mind presses forward with all the arguments, and out pops some illuminated thinking, very often a bottom line to the issue.

The reason this utterly simple technique works well is because the structuring of the two chairs, the privacy, the deep need for resolution establish *objectification that makes understanding and value judgment easier*. Getting free of the emotions in this formalized debate presentation illuminates reasoning.

6. Faithing: To Support Resilience

Somewhere in some dusty ancient text, some Chinese sage is recorded as saying, "If you want to be happy, *be happy!*" This is wise existential therapy; *the mind wills one's state of being.*

In her fine book, *Resilient Adults: Overcoming a Cruel Past*[7] Gina O'Connell Higgins identifies two "overarching themes" for bouncing back in life, affecting change into the future. The first is to have *faith in surmounting*, and the second is to have *faith in human relationships*.

We must be able to formulate, see, and identify with "the logic of conviction": *this is something I can do and this is how I can do it*, to one level or another. And, second, *I recognize that I can't do it alone*. Faith in oneself is tied to a wellspring of support through relationship(s). We can see this as the two hemispheres, the two halves of the horoscope— east and west—joining together; the I and the Thou.

This bears repeating: we've got to be able to see, to visualize, to imagine, to conjure up the changes we want to make; we must be able to have supportive concurrence with someone to keep us clear and strong.

In many places in therapy literature, there are stories of survival, of survivors, living through the blackest of family scenes, living through the Holocaust concentration camps, etc. *They live by faith in what could be—even what once was—and the faith-strengthening love in relationships*. In every case, the Self is accentuated within change and within supportive love, even if it is just the memory of it!

---

7. See Higgins.

In short, this "faithing" is what expedites change—not the movement of planets. It is the communication of this to the client and then the search with the client for the word pictures of feelings that begin to focus change, development, and maturation, guided by the astrological timetable. The planets (Jupiter, Venus, Neptune) can signal a fine time for faithing to be refocused.

When the client finds it difficult at first to visualize change, to see the mind taking a faithing position, *it is usually because anger is in the way.* The client is hurt, upset, silently or overtly wanting revenge; projections have been frustrated, relationships have failed. Anger has been a longtime defense against further deeper hurt. This is a natural reaction; anger *is* a defense.

Recall Carol's marvelous recognition that she is an artist; will she be able to visualize herself day to day (even lighting a candle for herself daily as a reminder!) in this new identity after all the angry frustrations of so many years past? It was very interesting—it *always is* and it happens so frequently—that her final inquiry was about *a new relationship!* This is not perfunctory; it is very real: faithing the change with determination is one thing, but it is dependent upon another, the support of relationship.

Countless times, I have heard clients speak hopelessly about the rut of feelings they were in, the hopelessness of it all, and I have responded, *"I suggest you feel this way because you live alone…you're alone with your feelings and thoughts; there is no respite, no way to talk over the feelings…and to gain support as you change them."* This observation is profound. It sets up the potential for a faithing concept for change, and invites, through a fresh openness and trust, a relationship for supportive communications and sharing.

7. Bypassing Details

People under tension—people carrying long-established fears and pains, love details. Telling their problem over and over again defines their suffering identity, their negative self-image. While it invites sympathy, it anchors the upset, the complex, even further.

The astrologer must choreograph the consultation to keep it on track with the plan organized during the preparation of measurements, the basic orientation for synthesis, and to keep it efficient in progress, in terms of time. Details use up time, reinforce difficult feelings, and so much of value may not make it into the consultation process.

For example, I have discovered that the midpoint picture AP=Saturn/Pluto curiously suggests "skeletons in the family closet" that the client, under the right conditions, wants to bring out into the open (AP). These skeletons can be horrendous, but thanks to the Aries Point dimension they seem to be revealed, talked about easily. [8]

For example, with a bright young mother in her early thirties in consultation, I said very early in our discussion, "There are some skeletons in the family closet here; what were they?" I said this gently and with caring, professional curiosity. Immediately the young lady leaned forward and said, "My father had a sexual relationship with me for four years, from age…" She was perfectly calm about bringing this information forward to me. It was an immediate response to my question.

Two sentences explained it further for us. I have learned to follow up with, "Did your mother know about it?" And she said, "Yes, but she didn't do *anything* about it; I was alone with it all."

Now, there certainly are a lot of details to be discussed here, especially if the lady were still gruesomely troubled by the protracted molestations, but she had talked it through with a therapist some time back, and she sounded poised and clear about the issue. I certainly did not need any details; the entire consultation could be jarred out of balance.

I replied, "And what have you brought forward from that experience, into your adult life, now?"

And just as quickly, she responded with great fervor, "I understand kids."

I replied, *"And that's why you're a teacher."* [Moon oriental, etc.]

And that was that. We learned something. We captured an enormous thread of her development in a minimalist way, even to explaining the long-enduring pained relationship with the mother. And we saw how knowing and strong my client is.

Recall Carol's constant drive to keep talking, especially about her *sub rosa* combat with her parents over so many years, especially about the five references to who she was *in terms of being in jail*! Recall Marion's ability to take any issue into extended format. We listen for and finally hear the patterns, and then we really have to hold off on the details.

---

8. Howard Stern's horoscope has AP=Saturn/Pluto. He talks about everything and anything, no matter how shocking or intimate. It is his public claim to fame. See page 7.

They are not necessary; the understanding we come up with about "what's happening here" will displace the habitual repetition of details.[9]

Holding off on the details can be done by just raising your hand with palm open and vertical, about a foot off your desk. The client will stop, especially if he or she sees your knowing smile and hears that you have something important to say. On the telephone, the astrologer can say, "We don't need all the details, honestly we don't; I've heard much of this many times before. What is important here for us now is…"

Feel the dramatic value of interrupting a barrage of details with the "unexpected question": e.g., "What about the idealisms? How do they complicate this issue?"

Keep the consultation on track.

8. *Love Received and Given*

Of the three Grand Crosses of houses, the succedent Grand Cross is the pivotally crucial grouping of psychodynamic grounding. It deals with how we feel about ourselves and others; the fundamental underpinning of relationships and procreative interaction.

The 2nd House reflects the self-worth profile. It is always under developmental tension (squares between zones of experience) with one's capacity to give love (the 5th House) and to feel lovable, to receive love (the 11th House). If the aspect condition of the ruler of the 2nd House or strong planets within it is under high developmental tension, self-worth anxiety is suggested. Such anxiety makes it very difficult to give love freely, trustingly. If the ruler of the 5th or planets within the house are under high developmental tension, the problematic condition is pronounced.

Clearly, tensions with self-worth and giving love are recognized within the 11th House should its ruler or tenanting planets be under high developmental tension, i.e., *feeling unlovable*. [Why? Where did that haunting debilitating sense come from, etc.?]

The 8th House is the second house of the 7th, other people's self-worth awareness, which, by opposition with the 2nd, captures the tension between people with regard to

---

9. The emerging professional will have to be careful not to fall into the trap of over-listening, *encouraging* details, because he or she has nothing ready to be said in rejoinder. Listening is safe. But the astrologer must be a step ahead in conversation, in a leading position of dialogue flow. This comes with practice and confidence, with special care given to communication skills.

reciprocal resource exchange potentials (what can you do for me and what can I do for you?). Together, the 5th and 8th portray much of the individual sexuality profile. [10]

Everyone wants to be loved by everybody. Receiving love is reward for being who we are. It is support to grow. It encourages the future and keeps each one of us alive.

But the affairs of this Grand Cross of houses are extremely vulnerable to upset throughout development. All the early "get out of my way" experiences, "I don't have time for you," "you were a mistake," off to boarding school, off to live with grandma, father at work all the time, mother fighting her own battles with her husband…all of these things add up to the young person feeling that they are not loved, that they are not lovable. Very easily, these self-worth difficulties infiltrate the emerging sex profile problematically. Relationships suffer terribly.

If one has difficulty giving love, being loving, trusting, one cannot relate. If one cannot give love, one is not going to receive it.

We have to understand the origins of the concerns. Defining them with the client helps objectivity to develop, values to adjust themselves, and behaviors for relationships to develop differently. Sometimes, we must educate with the simplistic: for example, that giving a compliment does not diminish one's own sense of self-worth! Or, criticism is basically unnecessary since nothing can change from criticism except the amount of strain in the relationship.

Criticism, rejection, abandonment—this trio shows dramatically the escalation of self-worth anxiety that eventually tears relationships apart. Criticism initially issues from the insecurity and fear of relating, of feeling that one will not be accepted. We strike out in any number of ways to "hit" someone else before *we* are hurt or ignored.

We must also understand that love changes with age. Hormones all too soon abate in their prominence; the grace of acceptance becomes more important in life than sexual conquest. The comfort of not being alone eventually reigns supreme.

9. Our Vulnerability to the Negative

We want our work with every client to be maximally helpful; we want to see our clients fulfilling themselves and developing in league with their strategies, hopes, and dreams.

---

10. For full development of the three Grand Crosses of houses, please see Tyl, *Synthesis*, pages 225–270. Please see also, Tyl, *The Astrology of Intimacy, Sexuality and Relationship.*.

We want to support, illuminate, and build on that process of positive development. We want to make our clients happy, to send them off to success, development, and change.

Our astrology reveals the personality portrait vividly. This establishes much authority for the horoscope and for the astrologer, and this authority, this impression of certitude extends itself into the prediction process. Astrologer and client work to believe that projections in time *will* come about.

Astrology's timeframes from the client's horoscope are proved in the discussion about the client's developments in the past and those timeframes accumulate high reliability when extended into the future. *But the environment must cooperate.*

How will our client's horoscope projections traffic with the horoscope projections of others…beginning with the spouse and extending to the employer, to the innumerable others on the client's developmental path? Will a frustration, a denial take place on the interactive path of development and thwart our client's progress? Might Alice's employer change her mind within the week ahead before the appointment? Might the employer herself have an accident, be fired, be moved to a different department? Might Brett lose out on the financing to go on to special schooling, even though we know it is essentially the best thing for him to do, and the horoscope attests to that? Might Marion accumulate indecisiveness and anxiety about where to go with her institute ideas, lose confidence, decide to hibernate and write a book instead, extending her developmental process a long time into what we thought is the wrong direction? Will Carol encounter relapse out of her new identity because she is alone with the idea, without support, even though the horoscope has depicted it all so vividly?

How many times in practically everyone's life are there stretches of five, ten, even fifteen years when absolutely nothing noteworthy develops in relation to what one ideally would project for oneself? Day after day, year after year are basically the same. So often we can search the horoscope projection for angular, solar, or lunar arcs or transits of strength and find none in the immediate future. What can we say to the client? There has been no major development in the past three years, and those kinds of fallow conditions seem to prevail in the time ahead? The more we do not recognize this norm, the more we can stretch astrology out of shape in projecting the impossible for the client.

Difficult, when we are determined…and our work is designed to reinforce our clients, raise their spirits, and register light ahead.

Even cursory discussions of well-being may uncover the commonsense need to have a physical check-up, and then that check-up may reveal nothing at all. Yet, while this in itself is a positive occurrence, there is the thought that detecting the disease and having it confirmed would have been the triumph. The negative occurrence easily works to prove astrology rather than the positive occurrence paying tribute to perceptive caution.

Every astrologer knows the thrill and happiness of a client call confirming a projection, a prediction that has happened just as anticipated. Every astrologer knows that myriad clients leave the astrologer behind when they are "out there" on their own, living the projections; they do not share the development victory with the astrologer. Every astrologer knows the occasional client call blaming the astrologer for not seeing frustration and loss, not predicting it, and sending the client off unaware of downfall. "What you said about my getting that job didn't pan out!" The time was right; the intent was genuine; the environment simply did not cooperate...and no astrologer can claim to see this eventuation all the time.

On the other hand, the astrologer learns to communicate the difficult, the "bad news" situation (of a Saturn-Pluto arc contact, for example) in circumspect terms, fitting loss on the one hand with gain on the other. It is not a difficult thing to do strategically, the client can be shown the benefit of strategic realism; it is difficult for the astrologer emotionally.

The astrologer is vulnerable to the negative, to the sense of underachievement. The astrologer is too alone with the work. On the other hand, our support is in our knowledge, our ever-growing grasp of astrological technique, our learning of the machinations of human behavior and interaction, and our communication skills. With dedication and experience we polish those gifts indeed.

10. The Fear of Counseling

It is remarkable to note that nowhere in the astrological literature can we find verbatim transcripts of astrology consultations, except for the one case I have offered in *Solar Arcs* and now the five here in this volume.[11]

A few years ago, I asked several very seasoned senior professionals about this: why had no transcript ever appeared? Their answers suggested that astrologers were, for the most part, probably embarrassed because they had little of substance to say—especially 50 or more years ago; that the camouflage by jargon would be obvious, and the communication

---

11. And *The Astrological Journal* in the United Kingdom —at their request— published a case consultation by me in the January 2000 issue.

with the client would have been notably clumsy. Several added, "We just don't have any training in this final-product part of our work!"

How true. The mid-century precedent of how to write an astrology book prevailed, and no one broke the mold and published transcripts.

In my teaching, I require advanced students to submit tape recordings of consultations for review; not one word of jargon is allowed in those consultations, which forces the astrologer to say things that are substantively important. In my seminars, I play consultation tapes. This is how we can all learn the art of astrological synthesis and client counseling *in action*.

I feel that astrologers are also afraid of the consultation experience because of a lack of preparedness. This volume works specifically to remedy this. When we *are* well prepared—organized with our measurements and creatively at ease with the art of synthesis—we lose our fear rapidly and gain enormous security.

Many astrologers feel that they lack the learning of psychology, that their views are not polished, that those views will appear to be critical opinions rather than helpful insights—"Who am I to discuss these intimate concerns with the client?" Well, who is *any* therapist talking deeply and sensitively with a client. He or she is an educated human being—living the same human condition as the client—who has set out to learn the craft, has become comfortable with the art, and has dug deeply into the literature that addresses how human beings live and grow.

Astrology is no longer a hobby. It is a profession of skill.

As we grow, as we have success in helping others, how full we have become. A new light grows within us. We go forth, we are fruitful, and we multiply.

APPENDIX

Discovering the astrology surrounding the planned sale of a house property is a demanding re-
quirement for astrological service. Here is a highly detailed Astro-Plan for the sale of a house—
my house!—the prediction and the success.

ASTRO-PLAN FOR SELLING A HOME
—FROM LISTING TO THE SALE

To set the scene, we go back twelve years. In 1993, I was determined to move to the Phoenix, Arizona area. The weather there had attracted me for years and during many visits. I
wanted my dream house to be there.

My wife and I decided to build it, but we went through three architects and contractors,
luckily unscathed but with nothing to show for a year of effort. We were disconsolate. We
abandoned our plans to build.

But the astrology was absolutely compelling [See Tyl horoscope, page 234]: I knew that
transiting Saturn in Pisces would come to my Midheaven for its final "hit" during the last
two weeks of December 1994. This had been our goal for two years. My Midheaven at 7
Pisces 02 is ultra-responsive. This Saturn transit had to be *the move*.

My wife went to Phoenix to study the situation for however long it would take. Three
weeks later, she had found the house, by accident, out for a walk one morning, dejected,
hoping against hope to make the relocation happen. She went around a corner and

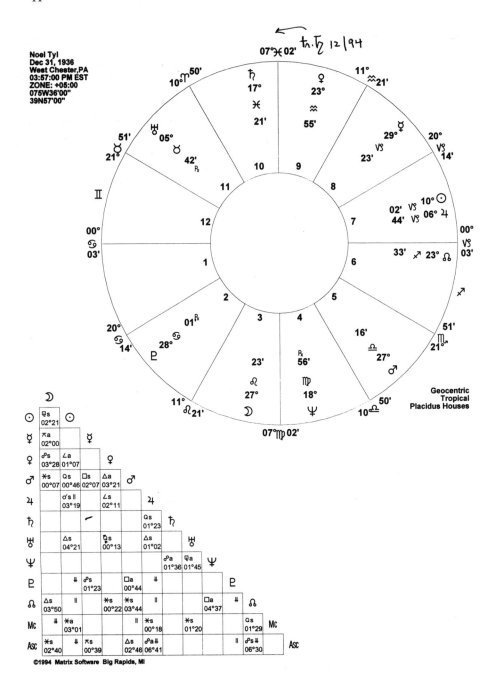

Noel Tyl
Dec 31, 1936
West Chester,PA
03:57:00 PM EST
ZONE: +05:00
075W36'00"
39N57'00"

Geocentric
Tropical
Placidus Houses

©1994 Matrix Software Big Rapids, MI

THERE was the house, with a "for sale" sign outside. She went to the front door, and our lives changed.

We moved into that house on December 22, 1994 as quickly as legalisms and schedules would allow. Tr Saturn was at 7 Pisces 16, precisely as planned, when we walked through the door! The astrology was inexorable.

Now, in March–April 2005, my wife and I had a strategic meeting together about the approaching transit of Uranus in Pisces to conjoin my most sensitive Midheaven. Uranus would touch that Midheaven for the last time in November 2005, eight months into the future.

We decided to leave the dream house—fulfilled after eleven years—and take advantage of the exploding real estate market. We planned to sell the house ourselves, without a realtor.

We needed an astro-plan: when should we announce the house for sale? This moment would have to be an election *that would support a high-probability date of the house being sold shortly thereafter* (guided by much promotion energy and common sense), *all in relation to my natal horoscope.* **The two dates ideally should work dynamically together.** This would increase the strength of the astrology.

I found those dates.

THE ASTROLOGY

I worked backwards specifying the "sell date" in relation to the Uranus transit of my Midheaven, and activation of my Mercury, ruler of my natal 4th, and more.

I found that in October 2005, with the transit "hit" of Uranus to my Midheaven on October 25, tr Jupiter was also in square with my Mercury (October 23), my 4th House ruler, and my Pluto. *That* felt good.

I checked my tertiary progressions for that time period [I am extremely corroboratively responsive to TPs] and found that on October 23, *TP Venus was precisely on my Ascendant!* That felt very, very good as well!

The house would have a high probability of being sold October 22–23.

Now, *when would be the best time to announce the house for sale,* i.e., installing two big signs on the property and scheduling two advertisements in local newspapers? Common sense suggested a time period perhaps two weeks before the projected "sell" date, and even that timing could easily be seen as unrealistic.

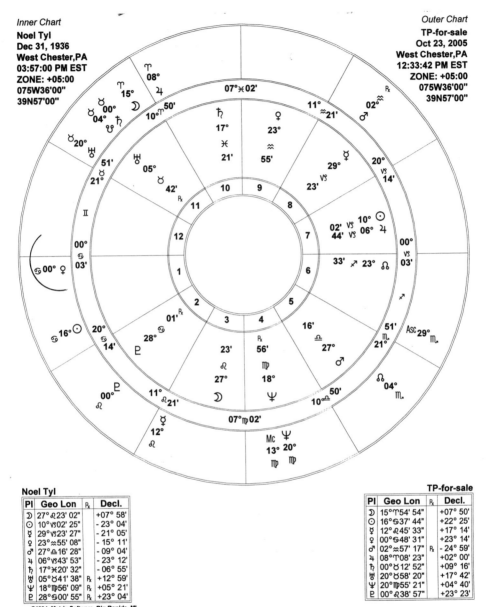

Inner Chart

Noel Tyl
Dec 31, 1936
West Chester,PA
03:57:00 PM EST
ZONE: +05:00
075W36'00"
39N57'00"

Outer Chart

TP-for-sale
Oct 23, 2005
West Chester,PA
12:33:42 PM EST
ZONE: +05:00
075W36'00"
39N57'00"

Noel Tyl

Pl	Geo Lon	Rx	Decl.
☽	27° ♌ 23' 02"		+07° 58'
☉	10° ♑ 02' 25"		- 23° 04'
☿	29° ♑ 23' 27"		- 21° 05'
♀	23° ♒ 55' 08"		- 15° 11'
♂	27° ♎ 16' 28"		- 09° 04'
♃	06° ♑ 43' 53"		- 23° 12'
♄	17° ♓ 20' 32"		- 06° 55'
♅	05° ♉ 41' 38"	Rx	+12° 59'
♆	18° ♍ 56' 09"	Rx	+05° 21'
♇	28° ♋ 00' 55"	Rx	+23° 04'

©1994 Matrix Software Big Rapids, MI

TP-for-sale

Pl	Geo Lon	Rx	Decl.
☽	15° ♈ 54' 54"		+07° 50'
☉	16° ♋ 37' 44"		+22° 25'
☿	12° ♌ 45' 33"		+17° 14'
♀	00° ♋ 48' 31"		+23° 14'
♂	02° ♒ 57' 17"	Rx	- 24° 59'
♃	08° ♈ 08' 23"		+02° 00'
♄	00° ♉ 12' 52"		+09° 16'
♅	20° ♉ 58' 20"		+17° 42'
♆	20° ♍ 55' 21"		+04° 40'
♇	00° ♌ 38' 57"		+23° 23'

But on October 8: tr Uranus was sitting on my Midheaven and *the Moon was exactly on my nodal axis (exposure), conjunct Pluto!*

With a deep, deep breath, I chose October 8 at 6:37 PM MST in Fountain Hills, Arizona to announce the house for sale. This horoscope has a 00 Taurus Ascendant, with the key Mercury (ruler of my critical natal 4th) in 00 Scorpio precisely on the "announcement chart" Descendant! That Mercury in that election ruled the 2nd and the 3rd *and was conjunct Jupiter!* That *had* to be the day and time!

THE WORKING OUT OF THE PLAN

To announce the house, just after sunset on October 8, I drove the stakes into the ground to establish the "For Sale" signs, with info-tubes attached for flyers we had already made up, with color pictures, etc. With stentorian voice I proclaimed to the four compass corners, "far and wide," that this wonderful house was for sale for the happiness of the next family. And then visited the neighbors with the surprise proclamation and with the flyers. It was done. The advertisements would appear the next day.

Six people came to the house by appointment over the period of eight days. There were hopes, but no bids. Everyone "loved" the house, etc.

We worked hard to keep our spirits up. Naturally, with the astrology involved, we thought everything would happen immediately. But I felt and kept believing in the inexorable progress toward the "SELL DATE," October 23.

On October 23, that Sunday, *the* day, a young builder and his wife came to see the house at 10:16 AM. They were pleased clearly, and they left with a cordial "Thank You!"

Sunday afternoon was silent. *This was to be the day!!??*

We were in unspoken despair. The silence was painful. Suddenly the phone rang: it was the young builder. "May we please come back to your house and see it again *at sunset?*" What an odd request, and I started to see the similarity with the For Sale announcement time!

The couple went through the house alone—we had decided to let the house sell itself—and then we all sat together to talk. **At precisely 5:42 PM, the couple said how delighted they were and that they would buy the house.** This was occurring precisely on the date anticipated in relation to the announcement date, some five months before! At full price.

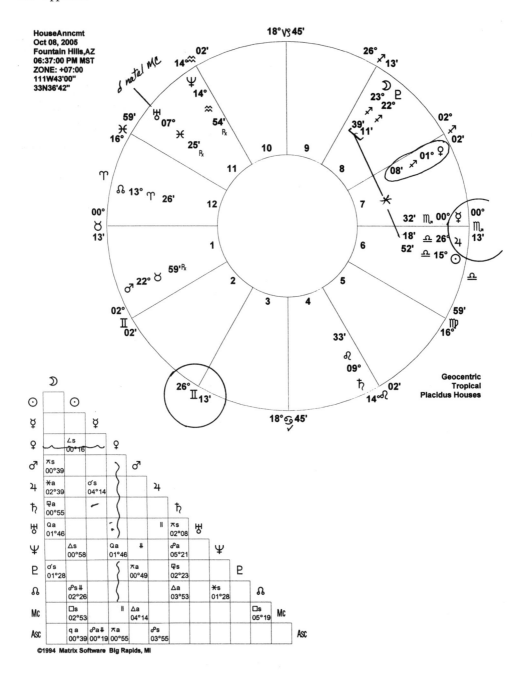

HouseAnncmt
Oct 08, 2005
Fountain Hills,AZ
06:37:00 PM MST
ZONE: +07:00
111W43'00"
33N36'42"

Geocentric
Tropical
Placidus Houses

©1994 Matrix Software Big Rapids, MI

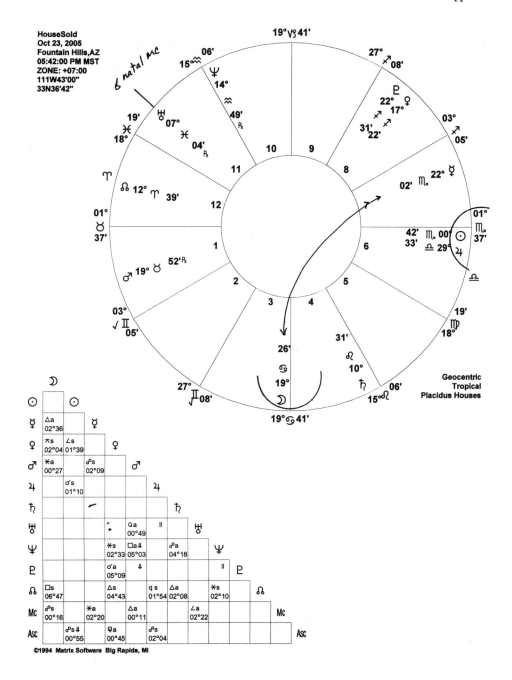

HouseSold
Oct 23, 2005
Fountain Hills, AZ
05:42:00 PM MST
ZONE: +07:00
111W43'00"
33N36'42"

δ natal mc

Geocentric
Tropical
Placidus Houses

©1994 Matrix Software Big Rapids, MI

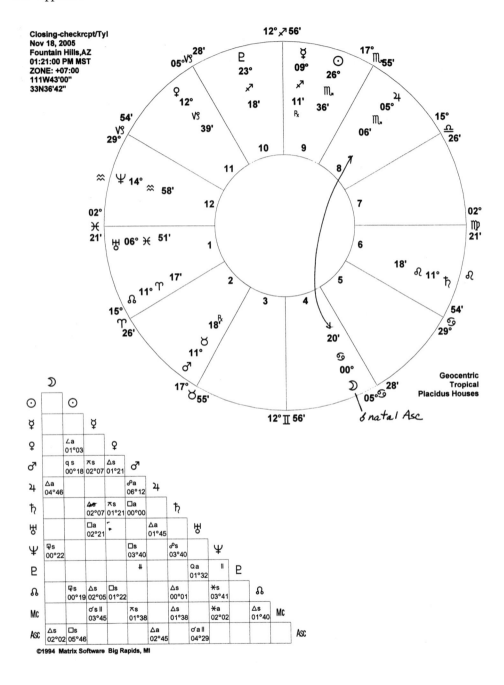

Closing-checkrcpt/Tyl
Nov 18, 2005
Fountain Hills,AZ
01:21:00 PM MST
ZONE: +07:00
111W43'00"
33N36'42"

Geocentric
Tropical
Placidus Houses

δ natal Asc

©1994 Matrix Software Big Rapids, MI

Fascinatingly, the angles of the election chart to announce the house for sale and the SELL horoscope *are practically identical*, with the "sold" Sun in 00 Scorpio on the Descendant conjunct Jupiter!! Absolutely amazing!!

And astoundingly, the closing of the sale took place with the check being given over to us by the buyer's mortgage company, at their appointment timing, at precisely 1:21 PM, on November 18. Incredibly, **the Moon was in the 4th at 00 Cancer 20, precisely upon my natal Ascendant at 00 Cancer 04!!**

From beginning to end, we had seen the art of the miracle we work with.

SUMMARY

1. Find the best time for the house to sell, *keyed with the owner's natal horoscope*, paying great attention to all contacts with the 4th House and/or its ruler. Check key transits, the secondary progressed Moon, salient arc midpoint pictures, and even tertiary progressions to bring things together.

2. With common sense, pick a general announcement date—for self-sell or listing with a realtor—and check the astrology of that time very carefully. Somehow, find how that astrology can be tied in through the owner's horoscope *with the projected SELL-date horoscope*. The three time-references ideally work together.

3. Remember that angles are everything.

BIBLIOGRAPHY

** Entries listed in boldface type are eminently accessible to readers for maximum practical value.

Aronson, Elliot. ***The Social Animal.*** New York: W. H. Freeman and Company, 1995. *This book is an enormously insightful compendium of social psychological tests of behaviors and attitudes, superbly indexed and annotated. Indispensable.*

Blackman, Dr. Jerome S. *101 Defenses: How the Mind Shields Itself.* New York: Brunner-Routledge, 2004.

Gross, John. ***The Oxford Book of Aphorisms.*** Oxford, UK: Oxford University Press, 1987.

Moore, Marcia, and Mark Douglas. ***Astrology, the Divine Science.*** York Harbor, Maine: Arcane Publications, 1971.

Persaud, Dr. Raj. *Staying Sane.* London: Bantam Books, 2001.

Rosenthal, Howard G., Ed.D., Editor. ***Favorite Counseling and Therapy Techniques.*** Philadelphia, PA: Accelerated Development, 1997.

Smith, Laura L., and Charles H. Elliott. *Depression for Dummies.* Hoboken, NJ: Wiley Publishing, Inc., 2003.

Sulloway, Frank J. *Born to Rebel.* New York: Pantheon Books, 1996.

Tyl, Noel. *Synthesis & Counseling in Astrology*. St. Paul, MN: Llewellyn Publications, 1994, 2004.

———. *The Astrology of Intimacy, Sexuality & Relationships*. St. Paul, MN: Llewellyn Publications, 2003.

———. **Vocations: The Midheaven Extension Process**, Woodbury, MN: Llewellyn Publications, 2006.

———. noeltyl.com, MENU, *Counseling Insights:* Scores of essays archived after the essay presently shown on the site; detailed therapy insights.

INDEX

TO WRITE TO THE AUTHOR

If you wish to contact the author or would like more information about this book, please write to the author in care of Llewellyn Worldwide and we will forward your request. Both the author and publisher appreciate hearing from you and learning of your enjoyment of this book and how it has helped you. Llewellyn Worldwide cannot guarantee that every letter written to the author can be answered, but all will be forwarded. Please write to:

Noel Tyl
℅ Llewellyn Worldwide
2143 Wooddale Drive, Dept. 978-0-7387-1049-5
Woodbury, Minnesota 55125-2989, U.S.A.

Please enclose a self-addressed stamped envelope for reply,
or $1.00 to cover costs. If outside U.S.A., enclose
international postal reply coupon.

Many of Llewellyn's authors have websites with additional information and resources.
For more information, please visit our website at http://www.llewellyn.com

LLEWELLYN ORDERING INFORMATION

Order Online:
Visit our website at www.llewellyn.com, select your books, and order them on our secure server.

Order by Phone:
- Call toll-free within the U.S. at 1-877-NEW-WRLD (1-877-639-9753). Call toll-free within Canada at 1-866-NEW-WRLD (1-866-639-9753)
- We accept VISA, MasterCard, and American Express

Order by Mail:
Send the full price of your order (MN residents add 6.5% sales tax) in U.S. funds, plus postage & handling to:

Llewellyn Worldwide
2143 Wooddale Drive, Dept. 978-0-7387-1049-5
Woodbury, MN 55125-2989, U.S.A.

Postage & Handling:

Standard (U.S., Mexico, & Canada). If your order is:
$24.99 and under, add $3.00
$25.00 and over, FREE STANDARD SHIPPING

AK, HI, PR: $15.00 for one book plus $1.00 for each additional book.

International Orders (airmail only):
$16.00 for one book plus $3.00 for each additional book

Orders are processed within 2 business days.
Please allow for normal shipping time. Postage and handling rates subject to change.